Bilderberg People

GW00777398

Bilderberg People explores the hidden mechanisms of influence at work in the private world and personal interactions of the transnational power elite. It is not concerned with conspiracy theories; instead it is about certain fundamental forces that shape the world in which we live. These forces, with their power to bring about transitions in emotion and preference within and beyond the elite community, have potentially profound implications for all of us.

Through exclusive interviews with attendees of the most prestigious of all informal transnational networks – Bilderberg – this book provides a unique insight into the networking habits and motivations of the world's most powerful people. In doing so, it demonstrates that elite consensus is not simply a product of collective common sense among the elite group; rather, it is a consequence of subtle power relationships within the elite circle. These relationships, which are embedded in the very fabric of elite institutions and interactions, result in a particular brand of enlightened thinking within the elite community. This exciting new volume sheds light for the first time on the critical question of who runs the world, and why they run it the way they do.

Ian N. Richardson is an Assistant Professor at Stockholm University Business School and a Visiting Fellow at Cranfield University School of Management, UK.

Andrew P. Kakabadse is Professor of International Management Development, Doughty Centre, Cranfield University School of Management, UK.

Nada K. Kakabadse is Professor in Management and Business Research at the University of Northampton, Business School and Visiting Professor at US, Australian, French, Kazakhstani and Chinese universities.

"*Bilderberg People* shows convincingly how the transnational elite policy making community works and whose interests it serves. This book throws light on many baffling foreign policy issues happening all around us today."

Leslie Sklair, Emeritus Professor of Sociology, London School of Economics and author of The Transnational Capitalist Class

"*Bilderberg People* does a great service to the cause of deepening democracy [...] it is high time that the ways in which a more equitable and transparent global order can be achieved, is placed on the agenda. This book is a solid contribution to that process."

Kees Van Der Pijl, Professor of International Relations, School of Global Studies at the University of Sussex and author of The Making of an Atlantic Ruling Class and Transnational Classes and International Relations

"The mechanisms of consensus building and maintenance apply not only to world affairs but also to the construction an 'ever closer Union' in Europe. It makes this unique book even more fascinating, if not a bit worrying, reading."

Stefan Schepers, Hon. Director General, European Institute of Public Administration

"An illuminating excursion into the intricacies of power and economics and the esotericism that shape global affairs – today and for the future."

Kalu Kalu, Professor of Political Science, Auburn University Montgomery, USA

"At last – a serious study of power elites, with a human touch. Timely and necessary."

Stefan Stern, former FT columnist, director of strategy at Edelman UK and Visiting Professor at Cass Business School, London

"Any modern analysis of the relationships between partnership, collaboration, consensus and legitimacy can only be of benefit to those of us trying to grapple with twenty-first century threats across the national and international policing community. Add elites into the equation and you have an interesting mix!"

Sir Hugh Orde, President of the Association of Chief Police Officers

"The first analysis of the dynamics of consensus building among the world elite – fascinating reading – highly recommended!"

Dr. Celia Romm Livermore, Editor-in-Chief, International Journal of E-Politics, School of Business Administration, Wayne State University, USA

"*Bilderberg People* deftly probes a transnational, elite network; places this intriguing process in theoretical context; and relates it to current policy issues in Europe, the United States and beyond."

James L. Garnett, Professor of Public Policy and Administration, Rutgers University at Camden

"What looks like accidental and dispersed forces that shape world politics, might not be so random after all."

Prof. Baroness Lutgart Van den Berghe, Executive Director, GUBERNA

"The authors of the book *Bilderberg People: Elite Power and Consensus in World Affairs* challenge the fundamental existential problem of the modern world: institutional disharmony between the power relationships at the global scale, from one side, and the ethical imperatives of globalization, from another – the later still to be formed in the environment dominated by the ideology of neo-liberalism. This book – informative, analytical and comprehensive – definitely will be demanded by the community of thinking people."

Niko Melikadze, Director, The Strategic Research Center, Georgia

"This book is an absolute must-read for the globally concerned scholar with an interest in exploring how contemporary politics and the international system of governance seems incapable of creating coherent collective responses to transcendental global problems.

The authors ask the critical question of how change can be brought about without destabilising existing, and advantageous, socio-economic establishments. By providing a first time insight to the powerful Bilderberg eltite network, the authors suggest that transnational elite networks provide dynamics of power and consensuses that serve as a critical mechanism for facilitating change in world politics. Acknowledging the obvious lack of democratic governance, this book attempts to bring understanding to the underlying powers, control and direction of this influential subpolitical activity."

Professor Mette Morsing – Copenhagen Business School

"If privatization can be defined as a situation where private standards are turned into public norms without proof of their representativity, *Bilderberg People* is one of its sources..."

Prof. Yvon PESQUEUX, CNAM (Conservatoire National des Arts et Metiers) Paris, France

"From elite perspectives seeking to control mass behaviour, this exciting study turns the focus back on global elite behaviour itself."

Professor Alex Kouzmin, Southern Cross University, Australia

"An intelligent, informative and level-headed analysis of the real influence of the worlds' leading "élite networks."

Prof. Eric Cornuel, Director General & CEO, EFMD

"So many words are said and written about 'Bilderberg Group'. But the more that is said and written, greater becomes the mystification of this theme and thereafter the savor of society. I dare say that the offered book, the co-author of which is a remarkable academician with singular talent, Mr. Andrew Kakabadse, will clarify this issue and give an answer to those questions."

Mirza Davitai, Minister for Diasporia, Georgia

"A thoughtful and well researched assessment of power elites in the modern age."

Professor Mitchell Koza, Rutgers, The State University of New Jersey, USA

Bilderberg People

Elite power and consensus in world affairs

Ian N. Richardson, Andrew P. Kakabadse, and Nada K. Kakabadse

LONDON AND NEW YORK

First published 2011
by Routledge
2 Park Square, Milton Park, Abingdon, Oxon, OX14 4RN

Simultaneously published in the USA and Canada
by Routledge
711 Third Avenue, New York, NY 10017 (8th Floor)

*Routledge is an imprint of the Taylor & Francis Group, an informa
business*

British Library Cataloguing in Publication Data
A catalogue record for this book is available from the British Library

Library of Congress Cataloging in Publication Data
Richardson, Ian (Ian N.)
Bilderberg people: elite power and consensus in world affairs / Ian
Richardson, Andrew P. Kakabadse, and Nada K. Kakabadse.
p. cm.
Includes bibliographical references and index.
1. Power (Social sciences) 2. Elite (Social sciences) 3. Consensus
(Social sciences) 4. World politics. I. Kakabadse, Andrew.
II. Kakabadse, Nada. III. Title.
JC330.R533 2011
327.1'12--dc22
2011002948

ISBN: 978-0-415-57634-5 (hbk)
ISBN: 978-0-415-57635-2 (pbk)
ISBN: 978-0-203-80784-2 (ebk)

Typeset in Bembo
by Taylor & Francis Books

Printed and bound in Great Britain
by TJ International Ltd, Padstow, Cornwall

For Valerie, Isabelle, and Soren

There is really no reason for supposing that the powerful always threaten, rather than sometimes advance, the interests of others; sometimes, indeed, the use of power can benefit all, albeit usually unequally.

Steven Lukes

Contents

Acknowledgments

As this book owes much to the PhD research that preceded it, we'd like to acknowledge the generous support of people and organizations who have contributed at all stages of its transition from improbable research proposal to published form.

We're grateful for the support of the Economic and Social Research Council, which enabled the research in the first instance. We'd also like to thank our friends at Cranfield University School of Management for their valuable input at various stages in the development of the research – most especially the feedback of Paul Baines, Joe Nellis, and Colin Pilbeam. Thanks must also go to Madeleine Fleure for her fantastic help with the manuscript, Sheena Darby for her support throughout, and the ever-helpful team at the School of Management library.

We'd also like to thank the many people who've helped with guidance, information, and introductions. For obvious reasons we can't detail all of them but, to those we can, our thanks go to Lord Sawyer, whose assistance was invaluable; Orhan Yavuz, for his introductions, support and tremendous hospitality; Bill Hayton, for his ongoing interest and insightful interview material; Kees van der Pijl, for his early, and accurate, reflections on how these things work; and Tatjana Kraljić and Cesar Mascaraque for their very kind help with introductions.

Our thanks also go to the members and attendees of Bilderberg who contributed so frankly to the research – the meetings were invariably thought-provoking and good humoured.

Finally, special thanks to Valerie Watt for her unfaltering support and commitment to this project.

Authors' note

Bilderberg People is based on research conducted by the lead author while pursuing a PhD at Cranfield University School of Management. Andrew and Nada Kakabadse were the supervisors of this project. The PhD, entitled "The dynamics of third dimensional power in determining a pre-orientation to policymaking: an exploratory study of transnational elite interactions in the post-Cold War period," was completed in 2009 and awarded a straight pass by examiners. The thesis contains details of the ontological, epistemological, and methodological considerations that have guided the research throughout its development. It is felt that including information of this kind is unnecessary for the purposes of the book, but we accept that some readers will, no doubt, be interested to understand more of such things. The thesis manuscript has been made available by Cranfield University School of Management and can be readily located online.

We would like to make clear that, for the purposes of preserving the identities of interview participants, some descriptive details, in the book and thesis, have been changed. This doesn't influence the points being made in any material sense, but it will result in inconsistencies for those hoping to identify individual attendees. What we can reveal is that all participants in the original study were male, European, and attended the Bilderberg conference between 1991 and 2008. There were roughly equal numbers of business, political, and media/academic subjects, but there was, and is, no attempt to suggest sampling validity. Thirteen face-to-face interviews were conducted by the lead author, and further interview material from Viscount Davignon, Martin Wolf, and Will Hutton was supplied by a reputable journalistic source. Additionally, the three authors' experience of dealing with governments at the level of policy design in Europe, North America, Australasia, and the Middle East, is woven into the fabric of the book. The combined interview data, most of which has never been seen before, is supported by a wealth of secondary material and represents the most extensive array of Bilderberg commentary available.

Authors' biographies

Ian N. Richardson is an Assistant Professor at Stockholm University Business School and a Visiting Fellow at Cranfield University School of Management, UK. His research interests include global governance, transnational policy networks, business and political elites, transnational corporations, multi-stakeholder collaboration, power and consensus in organizations, and political marketing. As a former business leader and entrepreneur in the European digital information sector, he has an ongoing interest in innovation and regulation related to the internet and continues to advise organizations within the sector.

Andrew P. Kakabadse is Professor of International Management Development, Doughty Centre, Cranfield University's School of Management, UK. Recognized as a world authority on leadership and governance, Andrew has held and also holds visiting appointments at the Copenhagen Business School, Denmark; Université Panthéon Assas, Paris, France; Center for Creative Leadership and Thunderbird, the Garvin School of International Management, United States; University of Ulster; The Windsor Leadership Trust, UK; Institute of Management Economics and Strategic Research, Kazakhstan; and Macquarie Graduate School of Management, Australia. He has consulted and lectured in every region of the world. His bestselling books include *The Politics of Management*, *Working in Organizations*, *The Wealth Creators*, *Leading the Board*, *Rice Wine with the Minister*, and *Leading Smart Transformation: A Roadmap to World Class Government*.

Nada K. Kakabadse is Professor in Management and Business Research at the University of Northampton, Business School and Visiting

Professor at US, Australian, French, Kazakhstani and Chinese universities. She has co-authored seventeen books (with Andrew Kakabadse) and has published over 140 scholarly articles. Her current areas of interest focus on leadership, strategy, boardroom effectiveness, governance, corporate social responsibility and ethics, and the impact of ICT on individuals and societies. Nada is co-editor of the *Journal of Management Development* and the journal *Corporate Governance*.

INTRODUCTION

Iran. Since its revolution in 1979, few countries have been such vociferous critics of western democracy and political consensus. And, with its uranium enrichment program causing undisguised consternation in international diplomatic circles, the western political elite has attempted to forge an international consensus on Iran's intentions and how best to deal with them. In January 2010, US Secretary of State Hillary Clinton stated "we believe that there is a growing understanding in the international community that Iran should face consequences for its defiance of international obligations" and cited the cooperation and support of the Russian and Chinese governments.[1] The implication of her words was clear: an international consensus was emerging and, as it did so, would provide a backdrop to the actions that would surely follow. *International consensus* has thus become a euphemism for legitimacy as a basis for action in world affairs. But such consensus doesn't just emerge accidentally, it is determined. The power to act in world affairs is driven by the power to influence prevailing consensus.

   This is not a book of conspiracies. It is a book about efforts to organize the world at the beginning of the twenty-first century. It concerns the activities of elite networks and, most importantly, their role in forming and disseminating a particular brand of consensus. It argues that to understand the real significance of elites in world affairs today, we need to look beyond crude ideas of power. Instead, we have to come to terms with the more subtle influence of common sense and dominant logic in our societies. After all, nowhere is power more compelling than in our collective imagination.

We live in a time of great uncertainty in world politics. The extent of our problems as a global society easily outstrips the capacity of our governance systems to deal with them. And, despite the successful crafting and relentless advance of economic globalization in recent decades, a lack of collective political will has failed to deliver similarly enthusiastic momentum to global social and political frameworks. This apparent prioritization of the market, ahead of social and political considerations, has led to a significant civil backlash and growing awareness of the obstacles that existing economic arrangements present to the resolution of global problems. Certainly, the faith that many have shown in policies of economic liberalization, designed to facilitate globalization, as a solution to problems of poverty and inequality has been called into question by a growing body of evidence that suggests quite the opposite.[2] And, crucially, globalization and open competition between national economies are affecting the behavior of individual states in ways that make immediate political solutions to global problems seem fairly unlikely. Take, for instance, the cynical horse-trading of developed nations and trade blocs, at the obvious expense of developing countries, in the ill-fated Doha trade talks; the ongoing failure of developed nations to deliver on their promises of Official Development Assistance towards accomplishment of the United Nations Millennium Development Goals; and the dismal spectacle of the Copenhagen Climate Summit in 2009 – touted as the final chance for developed and developing nations to come to a binding agreement on carbon emissions and global warming – failing to reach any kind of meaningful accord.

In essence, the demand for international cooperation has never been greater, yet the forces capable of delivering it have never seemed more incapable of doing so. Even if we were to assume that our world leaders and the constituencies they represent were willing to cooperate for the common good, which is highly debatable, they are stymied by a complex mire of contradictory and irreconcilable policy demands. These demands exist at all levels of the policy process and are set against a backdrop of pervasive, and largely unspoken, forms of consensus. To fundamentally alter the trajectory of our policy responses, first we have to challenge the nature of this consensus. And what the policy lessons of the past fifty years have taught us, if nothing else, is that established policy structures, processes, and ways of thinking are incredibly difficult to shake – even when the case for change seems overwhelming.

An obvious recent example of this is provided by the collective reticence of policymakers to act when called upon to deal with fundamental regulatory gaps exposed by the global financial crisis. The sheer scale, risk, and complexity of the crisis, set against a background of free market consensus and business/government collusion related to deregulation, has seen our political leaders consistently fail to address the "too big to fail" dilemma posed by major financial institutions. Instead of using the crisis as an opportunity to rethink the role of financial institutions in our global society and, importantly, to subjugate them to meaningful oversight and control, a tentative "business as usual" approach was adopted with the promise of political action once the crisis was averted. But the absence of a global regulatory framework, and the inability of global leaders to agree on anything resembling one during this period, has meant that individual governments have once again been left with the prospect of regulating transnational corporations at their own economic expense – something they have consistently demonstrated is beyond them. Amid the turmoil of the crisis, the stability and economic power of major financial institutions has been restored at taxpayers' expense and they have, once again, become too critical to individual governments to control.

But is this outcome more than just an accidental consequence of preexisting arrangements and short-sighted crisis management strategies? Throughout, policymakers have demonstrated that they are guided by the belief that the financial monoliths at the heart of the crisis should, with better oversight, be restored to their primary function of powering economic growth. Within the current policy consensus, very few have seriously questioned the desirability or function, let alone private ownership, of such organizations. Instead, there has been a populist emphasis on excessive profitability and bonuses which, while playing well with the gallery, has fallen short of any meaningful attempt to redefine, in societal terms, the role of banks or the regulatory vacuum that contributed to the crisis in the first place. The Obama administration, for instance, which came to power on a near spiritual chorus of "change we can believe in," in his first year of office conspicuously failed to take the regulatory initiative or challenge the club-like consensus that surrounds discussion of major financial institutions. In the words of Nobel Prize-winning economist Joseph E. Stiglitz, President Obama had failed to grasp a once in a lifetime opportunity and, instead, had "only slightly rearranged the deck chairs on the Titanic".[3]

Responding to such criticism, and a degree of public anger that refused to abate, President Obama subsequently announced the most far-reaching reform plan since the Glass–Steagall Act of the 1930s, with a promise that never again would taxpayers be held hostage by banks that are "too big to fail". It remains to be seen, of course, just how extensive any eventual regulation will be once it emerges from the powerful lobbying practices and inevitable congressional bartering of US politics. What the example demonstrates, however, is a pattern of avoidance among policymakers that is driven, in the United States and beyond, by the acceptance of a powerful underlying consensus concerning the nature and desirability of existing investment activity. Any regulatory changes take place within the context of the parameters of this consensus. It defines the extent of our policy response and effectively limits the capacity for significant change. How, then, given the existence of such a consensus, and the consequent tendency of our systems to do what they have always done, can meaningful change ever be brought about?

In order to think about this question, we need to consider policy-making in the broadest sense and better understand why it is that our policy systems and processes not only lag behind the demand for meaningful change, but are, for the most part, incapable of delivering it. This, in turn, requires that we distinguish between incremental and transformational forms of change. When we look at the systems and logics that have developed around our policy processes – local, national, international, and transnational – it becomes clear that change takes place over time and almost always in tiny, incremental stages.[4] Changing anything, even for those at the very heart of government, is an enormous task involving massive self-sacrifice, diligence, and political compromise. Policy rarely emerges in the way it was envisaged, and invariably fails to deliver what was intended. The idea that our existing policy systems are capable of delivering more transformational forms of change, detached from existing processes or ways of thinking, is clearly nonsense. In essence, the forces that hold policy systems together – the rules, institutions, and ways of thinking – are so entrenched and pervasive that it becomes inconceivable to question their logic. Common sense is defined by the existing policy system, and calls for transformational change are invariably seen as counter-intuitive and potentially destabilizing. As a consequence, emergent ideas that challenge the dominant logic of the policy process are systematically rejected. Put simply, policy systems cling to what they know and represent a forceful opposition to new ideas. Demands for transformational change that garner significant support, and that aren't easily rejected, are assimilated into existing policy processes in ways that nullify the requirement for drastic alterations to the way the overall system works. In this way, familiar patterns of thought and behavior remain intact, for the most part, and the system continues to function in its existing, albeit slightly revised, form. In overall terms, the system evolves gradually, preserving its integrity and ensuring its long-term survival. What this means for policy outputs, of course, is rather unsatisfactory: a diluted and inadequate response that lags well behind the nature and immediacy of the issue at hand.

These characteristics of systems are not peculiar to policymaking. What makes them potentially more interesting where policy is concerned, certainly in liberal democracies, is that the incremental bias is "hardwired" into the system in ways that are far more fundamental than they first appear. Long-term political stability is more than just an accidental consequence of a complex raft of historical policy structures, institutions, habits, and ways of thinking; it is a desirable and intended outcome of policymaking.[5] Conventions such as the need for constitutional "checks and balances" in order to counter the threat of overwhelming power in the hands of one branch of government do more than protect the individual from the tyranny of government. They limit the capacity of policymakers to affect transformational political change. Political stability can be said, therefore, to come at a price, and that price is the ability to change anything too drastically. Indeed, isn't this the very definition of political stability? And, while we may be inclined to think of it as, by its very nature, a good thing, we should at the same time recognize that the arrangement naturally benefits some more than others – in particular, those who stand to lose most through changes to existing arrangements in the allocation of resources throughout society.

The problem with this analysis is that it appears to suggest some kind of hidden design, purpose, or intent when, for many, these outcomes are little more than accidental by-products of the system. Nobody means for these things to happen, they just do, right? At the heart of this thinking, however, lies confusion between an understanding of things that are unconscious and things that are accidental. Liberal democracies do not accidentally produce stability any more than their policy processes accidentally privilege certain interests. Such outcomes are unconscious, perhaps, but they are not accidental.[6] The suggestion that they are accidental implies a degree of randomness when, in fact, such outcomes are clearly the product of established arrangements, relationships, and thinking. There is nothing random about them. Likewise, the extent of the incorporation of private interests into systems of government over the past forty years may have been a largely unconscious, and seemingly natural, development for many of those involved in policymaking, but accidental it was not. The most fundamental cause of the way we are governed today, and the way we tend to think about politics in general, rests in the relationship that exists between politics and markets. Not only have the state's traditional boundaries been called into question by the global market,[7] but the everyday interdependency of politics and markets has become so absolute that it's difficult to know where one ends and the other begins. From the perspective of understanding political change, this lack of delineation between the public and private sectors, between politics and markets, is absolutely critical. After all, the starting point for nearly all market-based activity is political stability.

In macro terms, we don't need to look any further than the experience of countries such as Zimbabwe – with unquantifiable levels of hyperinflation, near full unemployment and considerable civil unrest – to see what happens to market activity when political stability is undermined. But this is only part of the story. Stability may be a precursor to market-based activity, but it is also a product of it. The resilience of the complex, networked policy systems of liberal democracies to demands for change, especially in those policy areas dominated by economic and professional interests,[8] is evidence of such a relationship. In simple terms, the market is deploying its resources to influence government policy in ways that improve the business attractiveness of existing regulatory frameworks. At the same time these forces, largely unconsciously, work to protect existing, and advantageous, social and economic arrangements against calls for more transformational forms of change emerging elsewhere in society. In other words, the market – the cumulative forces of economic growth and accumulation in society – is a major force in protecting existing economic, social, and political arrangements. But this begs an important question: what if transformational change is a necessary requirement for continued economic growth and accumulation?

In a sense, this brings us back to the broader question of how meaningful change can be brought about against a background of entrenched processes and ways of thinking. How can new paths be forged when the thinking that prevents them is still in place? How can change be brought about without destabilizing existing, and advantageous, socio-economic arrangements? And, more specifically, what devices exist to create the latitude for such change in the first place? This book suggests that elite networks, and the consensuses that are formed and disseminated by them, are a critical mechanism for resisting or facilitating change in world politics. After all, the world is given shape and form by our collective understanding of it[9] and, crucially, the shared understandings of our elites. Certainty within this world, such as it is, is a product of how elites think and, moreover, our acceptance of their disseminated logic. It is their collective ability to reinforce or challenge assumptions related to the nature of world problems, in essence to define the terms of reference for the rest of us, which holds the key to unlocking the capacity for political and societal change. While this ability may often be unconscious and lacking obvious control, it is not an accidental consequence of elite interaction. There are underlying forces that play a considerable role in determining the nature, momentum, and general direction of such activity.

The role of consensus in international relations, and the forces that guide its logic, have been the subjects of debate for some time, but this is the first attempt to explore individual mechanisms of consensus formation at the heart of the elite community. It takes issue with the idea that consensus should be seen as naturally emerging from the collaborative interplay of shared beliefs, interests, and resource dependency. If we take resource dependency, for instance, should we really be talking about consensus at all? Was it a shared belief in the "international consensus," for example, that led Pakistan to support the efforts of the United States and Coalition forces in Afghanistan, or was it the fear of not appearing to support the world's biggest economy and military force at a time when, according to its then leader, countries were either "with us or against us"?[10] Similarly, was it an underlying belief in the market-based principles of the Washington Consensus, or just a much more basic requirement for money, that has led so many developing countries to accept the liberalization dictates of the World Bank and International Monetary Fund over the past twenty years? Power clearly has some bearing on our appreciation of consensus, but how is this power wielded, what form does it take, and why bother – if coercive forms of power are so effective – with consensus at all?

The fact of the matter is that consensus bestows legitimacy and, critically, legitimacy as a basis for action in world affairs. In the post-Cold War period, where the structural certainties of old alliances have given way to more fluid forms of international cooperation, it's absolutely critical to our understanding of political action in world affairs. Consider the attempts at legitimacy building made by the United States and Britain before the invasion of Iraq in 2003 and the fractures that existed in the international community at that time. The absence of an international consensus may not have been sufficient to prevent the war, but the subsequent inability of Coalition forces to retrospectively bolster the legitimacy of their actions by providing evidence of Saddam Hussein's weapons of mass destruction has significantly undermined their standing in world politics. At the same time, the standing and legitimacy of those opposed to the war has been significantly enhanced. Consensus and legitimacy, therefore, go hand-in-hand and represent the real power play in world affairs. Owning the consensus, possessing the capacity to legitimize action, bestows considerable control over downstream policy responses. And, moreover, it helps to define what constitutes legitimacy within ongoing consensus-forming activity – a virtuous circle.

This book doesn't seek to overstate the role of elite networks in shaping global outcomes; neither does it conveniently overlook their contribution. In an age of uncertainty, fear, and complexity, the activities of these networks are absolutely critical to our understanding of how – and why – things happen in world affairs. Elite networks, and the power relationships that exist within them, are an integral part of a system of world politics that exists beyond any formal constituency or formal governance framework. And, while the depiction of such networks presented in this book falls short of that of a sinister global elite, gathered in wood-paneled rooms, effortlessly making decisions that affect the lives of millions – like Grand Masters moving pieces across a chess board – there are, nevertheless, important questions concerning the purpose, transparency, accountability, and effects of these networks that demand a response. Why do they exist? What do they do? Why are elite participants engaged in this activity? Is consensus formed? If so, what is driving it? And, crucially, what implications do such networks have for the rest of us?

For the very first time, participants within the most pre-eminent elite network of all, Bilderberg, provide answers to these questions. Noted for its privacy and self-conscious avoidance of publicity, Bilderberg has been an undeniable presence in transatlantic relations since the mid-1950s. Its attendees represent a select network of individuals drawn from the business, financial, and political elites of the United States and Western Europe. Its conference of 120 or so of the most powerful people in the world gathers annually with no public record of its discussions, a conspicuous absence of media coverage, participants who refuse to be drawn into discussing the event, and policymakers who frequently deny attendance – a combination of factors that has led to an almost cult-like interest in the group. Many observers believe it to be intent on the creation of a new world order, and it has been variously described as a modern-day incarnation of the Illuminati, a global socialist conspiracy, a CIA plot, a mechanism for transmitting neoliberal hegemony and, in an extreme case, the vanguard of an alien conspiracy to take over the world.[11] But, leaving aside the rather absurd suggestion of an alien conspiracy, does it resemble any of these things or is it something altogether different? What do its attendees think? How does Bilderberg fit into a global depiction of elite network activity? How does it compare with other elite groups and networks? Is there a pecking order? Do they do different things? Why do people attend? What do they take away? Is power a feature of elite interactions, or is consensus formation a more fitting description of such activity? Is there a function, or is it just, in the words of one attendee, "a gang of high-profile people meeting together and having a chat"? Focused on subtle dynamics of power and consensus in the transnational elite community, *Bilderberg People* provides insights into these questions and many more.

Drawing on interviews with government ministers, heads of international organizations, chairmen of banks and multinational corporations, editors of national newspapers, and heads of media corporations,[12] *Bilderberg People* takes a look at the transnational elite from within. It analyses the highly personal demands of elite membership and the discreet power relationships that exist at the heart of elite networks. More generally, it considers the role of informal networks in contemporary politics and asks whether they are an essential, and desirable, feature of the way the world currently works. And, crucially, it asks where this type of activity may be leading us. The book is comprised of seven chapters.

Chapter 1 considers the challenges of contemporary politics and the shortfalls of an international system of governance that, time and again, seems incapable of generating coherent collective responses to transcendental world problems. It distinguishes between global, international, and transnational forms of political activity, and describes how the latter has emerged as a key collaborative mechanism for the development of consensus in a wide array of policy-related areas. It situates this activity within a universalist tradition that has its intellectual origins in the work of Immanuel Kant and its twentieth-century foundations in the liberal internationalist movement of the United States. The Atlantic relationship, in particular, is explored and the function of elite policy networks such as the Bilderberg group is considered. Various perspectives of this kind of elite activity are presented and a number of well trodden conspiracy theories are challenged.

Chapters 2, 3, and 4 are interconnected and consider the relationship between legitimacy, collaboration, and consensus in world politics. In particular, the chapters emphasize their *mutually constitutive* nature – where each serves to support notions of the other. Policy initiatives, for instance, are made legitimate in the contemporary setting by our sense of the collaboration and consensus that produced them. And, when faced with problems of great complexity, collaboration is, by definition, seen as a legitimate response – the consensus emanating from it being imbued with the same reflective legitimacy. After all, in a world where ideology and zero-sum politics has been replaced with talk of pragmatism, cooperation, and stakeholder responsibility, what could be more legitimate than a consensus stemming from the altruistic and purposeful collaboration of all parties?

Chapter 2 argues that legitimacy should not be viewed as some kind of objective or extant reality; instead, it needs to be seen as a fluid, expedient, and purposeful concept. With this in mind, the role of legitimacy in world politics is explored and the significance of a rhetorical legitimacy based on principles of pragmatism and cooperation is considered – principles, incidentally, so seemingly compelling and obvious that they have the effect of diverting attention away from the lack of formal legitimacy at the heart of many contemporary international and transnational governance initiatives. The reasons for this are explored and the legitimacy of transnational elite networks is discussed in detail – specifically in relation to issues of authority, consent, and accountability. Finally, the challenges of legitimacy in world affairs are described by Bilderberg participants who share their perspectives on its contemporary significance.

Chapter 3 highlights the prevailing logic of collaboration and partnership in transnational elite circles. This logic, which is premised on the need for cooperation in the face of the vast complexity of world affairs, has undoubtedly been fuelled by the forces of globalization and the rise of neoliberal thinking during the past forty years. The chapter focuses on the collaboration between business and political elites and demonstrates how embedded the relationship between public and private has become in matters of policy. What's more, it draws attention to how natural this relationship is for all concerned – the rationale for such collaboration rarely being questioned by members of the transnational elite and generally seen as a desirable state of affairs. Indeed, such pragmatism may be an unintended consequence of bias in the selection procedures of elite networks – since those perceived to be more ideologically minded, or dogmatic, will generally find themselves filtered out at source.

Chapter 4 considers the role of consensus in world affairs and, specifically, the nature of consensus formation in elite policy networks. While most elite participants view elite interactions as producing consensus, shared understanding or, at the very least, narrowed differences, they have differing views on whether this is a purposeful or accidental outcome. The chapter demonstrates that consensus formation is rather misleading as a description of the objective of elite networking, but does tend to describe the overall momentum and consequence of such activity. It also points to discreet forces of bias at work within elite networks – forces that have significant implications for the overall shape and tenor of eventual consensus. In particular, it highlights the highly personal dynamics of selection and membership within such communities, and challenges the contention by Bilderberg organizers that the process is in some way objectively meritocratic. In short, discreet forces at play within elite networks have a considerable bearing on who gets to become an established presence in the network.

Chapter 5 goes one step further in considering how emergent members of the elite community adapt their preferences to the perceived logic of the network in order to ingratiate themselves with more established members. It demonstrates how processes of elite socialization harbor discreet mechanisms of individual compliance and have the capacity to perpetuate bias. Crucially, it suggests that thinking of elite networks as homogeneous clubs of shared purpose and interest is a mistake. Hierarchies of influence within the elite community have profound consequences for the alignment of individual preferences. As a consequence, we shouldn't view consensus as a mystical form of common sense that emerges naturally from enlightened elite engagement. Instead, we should recognize that it is, at least in part, the product of discreet dynamics of power at work within the elite community. Of particular interest are the club-like hubs of the transnational network that, largely unconsciously, influence the perception of common sense within such settings.

Chapter 6, which takes a look at the contemporary significance of elite networks in world affairs, considers some of the more contentious aspects of such activity. First, the coordinating function of transnational elite networks is considered and a global economic imperative, providing grounds for political as well as economic rapprochement within such communities, is identified. Second, the question of how elite transnational networks facilitate the alignment of interests in world affairs is explored. Third, the chapter suggests that we should view transnational elite policy networks as a fundamental, albeit extended, part of the existing national and international policy machinery – a domain in which blurred distinctions between public and private, formal and informal, are of secondary importance to the overarching objectives of the extended policy network, and where the media's relationship with emergent currents of elite thinking begs the question of whether it is any longer distinguishable from the subject of its own analysis. Fourth, the requirement for non-disclosure and privacy is addressed in some detail and its implications for consensus within the network are explored. And, finally, the chapter considers whether transnational elite communities such as Bilderberg are simply an extension of the traditional "old boy" policy network.

Chapter 7 considers the influence of transnational elite consensus. It makes clear that the reality of consensus formation and dissemination in elite transnational networks has far more to do with unconscious processes of preference adaptation than conscious or overt attempts at collective manipulation. Elite participants feel themselves to be part of the process, rather than the subjects of it. They leave network events with their own sense of what has been discussed, and these impressions form the basis of what is communicated externally. The chapter discusses the softness of this process but, at the same time, emphasizes that it should not be confused with a lack of effect. There are, indeed, consequences of such activity – consequences with significant implications for downstream policy discourse and business decision making at the national and regional levels. But, as the chapter explains, these effects are, for the most part, highly idiosyncratic and difficult to interpret – even for those involved.

Bilderberg People is not designed to provide a "silver bullet" to those who view the activity of elite transnational policy networks in highly instrumental terms. The vagaries of contemporary world politics ensure that any such reading would be an overly simplistic interpretation of elite activity. At the same time, it doesn't seek to legitimize the activity of such networks – there remain fundamental questions related to their existence, function, and influence in world affairs. What it does seek to do is demonstrate that networks of this kind are comprised of individuals rather than automons – people whose motivations and interests are more than the product of historical and material dictates. They may share views related to the desirability of certain forms of world governance, and may consciously or unconsciously influence others in pursuit of these ideas; but, ultimately, they have their own reasons for participation. Recognizing the personal dimensions of elite membership enables us to move beyond a crude and inappropriate reading of power within such communities and, instead, allows us to understand better how bias is perpetuated and disseminated within, and beyond, the transnational elite network.

1

TRANSNATIONALISM AND THE TRANSNATIONAL POLICY ELITE

New York, May 3, 2010. The nuclear Non-Proliferation Treaty (NPT) Review Conference, a month-long meeting held every five years, gets underway at the United Nations Headquarters. The treaty, which began in 1970, has 189 signatories of which five – the United States, the former Soviet Union, the UK, France, and China – hold the vast majority of the global stockpile of 23,360 nuclear warheads.[1] Under the terms of the NPT, non-nuclear weapons states commit not to develop nuclear weapons of their own in return for an assurance from nuclear weapon NPT signatories that their arsenals will not be used against them. In addition, nuclear weapon states are committed to a decommissioning of their nuclear stockpiles over time. Three nuclear weapons states are not signatories of the NPT: India, Pakistan, and Israel, which is known to maintain a considerable cache of nuclear weapons but refuses to confirm or deny the existence of its programs. North Korea, which has tested, and announced that it possesses, nuclear weapon capacity, withdrew from the NPT in 2003. Iran, which for the time being at least maintains its seat at the NPT table, is believed to be within a few years of having its own nuclear weapons. Indeed, some believe Iran already possesses them. Increased tension among non-nuclear NPT states at the lack of meaningful disarmament progress demonstrated by the five permanent members of the UN Security Council (its NPT nuclear weapon states) threatens to further destabilize the increasingly fragile nature of the agreement.[2] US officials enter the conference hopeful that a new defense strategy that lessens the centrality of nuclear weapons, and a recent arms reduction accord with Russia, will help to placate non-nuclear NPT signatories. On the opening day of the conference, Iran's President, Mr Ahmadinejad, criticizes NPT nuclear weapon signatories and argues that their "production, stockpiling and qualitative improvement of nuclear armaments […] now serves as a justification for the others to develop their own".[3] As he speaks, representatives of the US, UK and France walk out.

A curious aspect of world politics, if one takes the stated positions of individual governments as a starting point, is the downright implausibility of international consensus. After all, every government seeks to protect its own interests and the interests of its constituents and, unless gaining international consensus is viewed as a means of achieving these ends, they can otherwise be relied upon to pursue protectionist agendas. This, in many ways, is where we find ourselves in international relations today, with efforts at collective action consistently failing to transcend the demands of national interest. There are almost too many cases of this to mention; leaving aside the rather complex dynamics of the NPT, other obvious examples include the consistent wrangling of individual governments over the letter and spirit of EU/US arms embargoes of China; and the failure of the EU to deliver a coherent European energy policy, designed to reduce strategic dependency on external partners, at a time when individual European governments are busy pursuing bilateral deals with the largest existing provider of all, Russia.[4] Is this, then, the reality of world politics? Do these seemingly insurmountable and structural obstacles to international cooperation mean that we're destined to a future of anger, friction, and tension in world politics? Or are other forces at work – forces, largely unseen by us, capable of creating harmony where the visible mechanisms of state interaction cannot?

Despite the protectionist inclinations of states, and somewhat mysteriously perhaps, an enormous consensus in world affairs has emerged during the past fifty years. A consensus so powerful in its scope and persuasion that few in the global policy elite now even choose to question it. This consensus, of course, concerns the desirability and inevitability of economic globalization. It's important to bear in mind, however, that obstacles to free trade and the free flow of global capital were, and are, no less significant than those confronting transcendental policy initiatives in the social and political arenas. It is simply that, in the case of economic interest, powerful motivating forces have succeeded in creating lasting conciliatory paths and binding agreements. So how, given the tendency of governments to be solely concerned with their own interests, could such a consensus have come about? Was it as natural and inevitable as it appears at first sight? Did national governments the world over simply fall into line out of a growing recognition of the benefits of free trade? Or were other forces at work that facilitated, and continue to facilitate, this particular historical arrangement? If so, what are these forces, and how do they fit into our understanding of more formal international relations activity? And, importantly, could they be the stimulus for more successful collective action in the global social and political domains?

In many ways, globalization and its accompanying ideology is a unique development. It provides both the focus and backdrop to many of the processes of consensus formation that take place in international politics. It simultaneously represents the crowning achievement of international consensus-formation activity and the ideological framework within which further forms of international consensus are forged. It is, at once, the product of considerable economic power play within the global political arena and a discreet determinant of power in ongoing forms of international consensus formation. It has become, in a sense, both the means and the end of international political consensus. But, while its role is incredibly important to our understanding of collective action in world affairs today, we should not confuse its overarching presence with the substance or purpose of consensus-formation activity. In order to analyze this, we need to understand the people and organizations at the heart of international consensus formation and, crucially, this means that we look beyond the formal activity of our governments.

International politics and the rise of transnationalism

In recent years, there's been a growing awareness that the traditional view of international relations, where interplay between states is very much the focus of attention, is rather inadequate. The lack of a worldwide regulatory framework, the emergence of multinational entities, the flow of global capital, advances in technology and communications, and the role of multi-stakeholder collaboration have all called into question the relevance of the state model to emerging forms of global governance. The effects of globalization, in particular, have not only increased the number of organizations that exist beyond immediate state sovereignty or regulatory control, but have also created unfathomable degrees of complexity and interdependence between global politics and markets. Consider, for instance, the massive increase in foreign exchange reserves held by individual states as a direct consequence of globalization. Investment of these reserves in foreign assets – via state-owned corporations or through instruments such as sovereign wealth funds – represent stakes taken by one state in the economic activities of another. Over the past twenty years, global cross-border investments have increased at a higher rate than the global trade in goods and services, which itself represented more than twice the growth of global GDP.[5] Between 1999 and 2004 alone, the increase in foreign net investment grew by around 175 percent.[6] Investments of this kind, while representing an obvious consequence of global market activity, have the capacity to fundamentally alter the basis of political negotiations between states. This has led to political tensions in countries as diverse as the United States and Germany, where control of strategic industry sectors has become an increasingly sensitive issue. At the G20's Pittsburgh Summit in September 2009, and very much a comment on China's trade surplus, the UK's Prime Minister Brown noted that there were $7 trillion of global foreign exchange reserves that were "not necessarily being used in a constructive way."[7] An increasingly charged debate within the G20, global trade differences are seen as necessitating a rebalancing of the world's economies by shrinking surpluses in countries such as China while attempting to boost savings in debt-laden nations like the USA.[8]

At a time of great uncertainty and insecurity, therefore, the actions of states remain central to our understanding of world politics, but such activity depends, to a much greater extent than ever before, on activities and participants that exist well beyond any conception of state-based formality or legitimacy. In recognition of this development, the concept of transnationalism has evolved in recent decades to distinguish parallel, collaborative, and often informal forms of global governance activity from that of state-oriented international relations. The description of *transnational*, however, is often used interchangeably with terms such as *international* and *global*, which leads to confusion – a confusion that's particularly evident when one looks into the role of elites in world politics, the key theme of this book. If we're to understand properly the significance of elite networks in world affairs, it's vital that the distinction between the three terms is properly understood. Only then can we identify the specific nature and function of elite interactions and situate them within the context of ongoing, simultaneous, and interrelated forms of world politics. And only then can we hope to get close to understanding the political, and societal, impacts of such activity.

Transnational political activities are distinct from international ones because, while they cross international borders, they do not derive their power and authority from the state.[9] Transnational politics is frequently comprised of non-state and state actors who, together, rely on alternative – and more informal – claims to authority and legitimacy than that of state sovereignty. Both transnational and international political activities differ from global ones, which are concerned with the more focused processes of globalization, specifically, those things that lead to the creation of a global borderless economy.[10] And, while transnational and international political activities have undoubtedly been instrumental in the development of globalization, the scope of international and transnational political activity is broader, in principle certainly, than the purely economic interests of globalization. These forms of activity are nonetheless interrelated, forming an ambiguous web of political enterprise where participants are frequently to be found flitting seamlessly between interconnected and parallel policy domains. This does lead to a blurring of the distinctions between these types of activity, but unpicking them, and viewing them in isolation, is necessary if we're to tackle fundamental issues related to authority, legitimacy, and accountability in world politics. Something that's essential because, as things currently stand, we're presented with a conspicuous absence of each.

Problems of authority, legitimacy, and accountability have sparked a defence of transnationalism in recent years that is rooted in ideas of collaboration and partnership in world politics. Subscribing to the view that complex world problems demand collaborative responses if they're ever to be tackled effectively, the emphasis has shifted away from the need to demonstrate political legitimacy, in a form any of us would recognize, to a rhetorical legitimacy based on principles of maturity, pragmatism, and cooperation. Principles so compelling, and seemingly reasonable, that they divert attention from a critical lack of substance at the heart of transnational governance. And, what's more, principles that have the discreet effect of marginalizing critics who, by definition, are made to appear unprogressive and dangerously isolationist. In short, the question of formal legitimacy in world politics has been successfully, and conveniently, dodged. In its place exists a logic based upon the need for immediate and transcendental cooperation – a logic that, out of necessity, trumps the more parochial niceties of formal political structures, constituencies, and authorities. Indeed, so the thinking goes, to be held back by a respect for state-based structures that continue to fail the collective action test in world politics would be to resign ourselves a future of doomed diplomacy and, in all probability, war.

Given the pervasiveness of this logic in transnational policy circles, it is not entirely surprising that there should be a widely accepted belief, among transnational policy elites, in the need for more discreet channels of policy communication and formation. After all, long-term solutions to complex global problems cannot come from the intransigence of stated positions or the power play of brokered international deals. Neither can new forms of thinking and the capacity for consensus be developed when everyone is being held to account. Instead, logic dictates, what is required is more informal and less transparent arenas in which actors can speak plainly, and communicate freely, without fear of their constituents' wrath. Transparency is limited therefore to those who are "in the room" and, for those who remain outside, it must out of necessity be obscured. The critical challenge is in obscuring what needs to be obscured long enough for those participating to make use of it. Thus, as the informal sphere grows, and a wide range of consensuses form, the role of the policy actor subtly broadens from the negotiation of terms of engagement with other actors to the massaging of respective constituencies into positions of compliance.

To enlightened members of the transnational policy elite, irrespective of whether they subscribe to the concept of one world government or just "thicker" solidarity between international states, the structural legacy of states in international relations must be somehow harmonized with the greater good of emergent transnational consensus before more effective forms of international law and governance can be implemented. Seen through the lens of political transnationalism, the state system – and its protectionist agendas – represents the biggest single hindrance to the resolution of world problems. But it is undoubtedly a legacy that must be managed responsibly if the desirable outcome of greater economic, political, and social alignment – under international law – is to take place. And so it is, at the beginning of the new millennia, that infant structures of global governance, the basis of a *new world order* if you like, are being crafted by transnational policy elites that are largely unknown to us, unaccountable to us and, crucially, unseen by us.

Perpetual peace and liberal interventionism

Back-channel diplomacy is, of course, nothing new to those involved in international policymaking. Without it, it's reasonable to suggest that we'd have lived through a far more insecure and perilous world during the past sixty years than that which we've experienced. Certainly, it's difficult to imagine how the far-reaching multilateral agreements concerning international trade and capital regimes could ever have been brought about without discreet and informal channels of communication. But how much do we really know about these activities? Are they simply smoothing away the brittle edges of an otherwise intransigent, state-based system of international relations, or do they represent something, in governance terms, that has moved beyond this? If, for instance, we look at the impenetrable and surreptitious quality of the club-like[11] policy networks that underpin this activity, we see an entire political ecosystem that is closed to outsiders and increasingly beyond the influence and control of participating governments. The effective functioning of these policy networks may well depend upon the participation of state actors, but the emergence of powerful non-state participants has had the effect of changing the priorities, as well as the composition, of these communities.

The logic that underpins this development is now so pervasive within, and beyond, these policy communities that it is now seen as an aspirational goal, rather than subversion, of democratic principles. Take, for instance, the Global Leadership Fellows program run by the World Economic Forum (WEF), which seeks to identify and groom the "next generation of world leaders".[12] The WEF suggests that this select group of individuals will feel equally at home in the public and private sectors, a skill set it believes becomes increasingly important as the traditional, and well defined, line between the two sectors becomes ever more opaque. In order to be successful, the WEF unapologetically professes, public and private organizations must "align numerous stakeholders so as to most efficiently approach problems, develop strategies and capitalize on opportunities".[13] Similarly, the Council on Foreign Relations, an elite and highly influential foreign policy think tank which, like the WEF, claims to be independent and non-partisan, also takes a rather patrician-like interest in the education of the next generation of foreign policy leaders. And since its members are drawn from the most senior ranks of government officials, business executives, journalists, educators and students, civic and religious leaders, and other interested citizens,[14] it seems apparent that this enlightened next generation is envisaged as extending well beyond the formal foreign policy domains of government. In fact, the largely unchallenged wisdom of multi-stakeholder collaboration is to be found in the rhetoric of practically all transnational policy forums. It informs the rationality of an entire generation of policy thinkers. In order to make sense of this worldview, we need to understand where it comes from and what is driving it today.

The emergence of transnationalism during the twentieth century is the product of a considerable liberal legacy in international relations. And, specifically, a "universalist" strand of thought that can be traced back to the work of the philosopher Immanuel Kant (1724–1804). In his essay *Perpetual Peace* (1795), Kant predicted the emergent, and separate, pacification of relations between republican states, explained reasons for their sustained tendency towards restraint and peace, and identified the propensity for distrust and war that existed between republics and autocracies.[15] He argued that perpetual peace would eventually be brought about as republics replaced autocracies, when respect for the citizens of individual states was enshrined in international law and, crucially, when cosmopolitan ties between states were formed as a consequence of the commerce that would inevitably take hold within, and between, countries. Characterizing the relationship between republics and autocracies in more immediately recognizable contemporary ideas of liberal and non-liberal states, the eminent scholar Michael W. Doyle has continuously highlighted how Kantian theory provides critical insights into the twin tendencies of liberal states towards peace with each other, and suspicion and aggression towards their non-liberal counterparts.[16] From a Kantian perspective, the insecurity and anarchy of world politics is destined to remain as long as the values responsible for peace and cooperation between liberal states serve to create distrust and conflict between liberal and non-liberal states.[17]

It seems remarkable that, over 200 years after *Perpetual Peace* was first published, Kant's thoughts on the nature of this relationship should be as pertinent as they ever were. Consider, for instance, the "axis of evil" characterization of various non-liberal states and the claims that pre-cipitated liberal state attacks on Afghanistan and Iraq. The tendency of liberal states towards interventionism, and the more general distrust that exists between liberal and non-liberal states, remains arguably the single most pressing issue in international relations today. And, despite Kant's prescription for tolerance and understanding between sovereign states under international law, it's clear that such values have been, for the most part, limited in application to those states forming part of the liberal pact.[18] Today, progressives in the liberal foreign policy establishment may present the neoconservative agenda of the George W. Bush administration as one that hijacked a once-proud, anti-war, liberal internationalist tradition,[19] but the historical relationship between the imperialism of coercion and persuasion is not as clear-cut as it first appears. Distrustful of regimes that do not conform to its worldview, a distrust that is no doubt reciprocated, liberal states have consistently sought to export their "enlightened" values by whatever means.

The doctrine of liberal internationalism and the desire to create global structures based upon liberal economic and political values – whether in the form of a "thin" cooperative international community or a "thicker" world government – became a more conscious strategic goal among the elite policy community during, and immediately after, the First World War. Faithful to Kant's vision for a league of nations that would ensure peaceful relations between states, President Woodrow Wilson's "fourteen points" speech to the US Congress in 1918 endorsed the establishment of a "general association of nations [...] for the purpose of affording mutual guarantees of political independence and territorial integrity to great and small States alike".[20] Motivated by a fundamental desire to avoid the horror of further wars, the diffusion of liberal ideals was, and is, seen by members of the western policy elite as the principal mechanism for creating mutual respect and lasting – if not perpetual – peace. And, while the exact nature of liberal interventionism has been the subject of immense debate, and some presidencies are more associated with the doctrine than others, it is clear that the dispersal of liberal values, specifically US liberal values, has been at the heart of US foreign policy throughout the twentieth century.

This emphasis on liberal values is important because, leaving aside US military excursions during the past 100 years, it is the significance of its powerful economic interests that has led to its sustained hegemonic influence in world affairs.[21] Indeed, while it was widely suggested that the USA was losing its clout in international relations terms by the 1980s, others observed that, in fact, its influence was being extended through the transition of global capital from national to transnational form – a process that had accelerated throughout the twentieth century.[22] Whether this transition was responsible for the creation of an international elite, whose members were drawn from leading industrialized nations, or whether, instead, the transition was the product of the emergence of such an elite, is impossible to say with any certainty. What is clear is that the two developments were clearly synergistic and anchored in economic forces – of which the United States was the principle catalyst. And, in contrast to the traditional state-centered interests of the foreign policy community, these new international elites were motivated more immediately by the interests of global capital.

Transnational elite networks

The development of what some see as the transnational phase of capitalism is, for neo-Gramscians at least, the result of the emergence of a powerful "historic bloc" – a constellation of material, ideological, and institutional forces capable of determining the nature of individual and collective action. This bloc was brought about by a faction within existing national elites using its positions of influence to inform and perpetuate a particular brand of ideology within society. It's possible to view the transition of this bloc from its multinational form, in the first half of the twentieth century, to its emergent transnational form of the 1970s and onwards. The multinational bloc is seen as emanating from the largest, most high-growth corporations in the US economy.[23] And, since it was led by industry leaders, with the most sophisticated management teams in the world at that time, it was able to dominate the major American foundations, which were themselves exercising significant influence over public opinion and elements of US domestic and foreign policy.[24] Indeed, it's been argued that the first transnational elite networks, in particular the transatlantic network, were initiated by an international congruence of these very same forces. Evidence, it's suggested, of the formation of a transnational capitalist class[25] – a class "whose locus of power is the global corporation."[26]

There are some differences of emphasis concerning the exact composition of this class. Some have identified the significance of corporate executives, bureaucrats, politicians, globalizing professionals, and consumerist elites.[27] While, elsewhere, the focus has been on the owners and managers of transnational capital who, along with politicians, charismatic figures, ideologically predisposed intellectuals, and a cadre that manage organizations of the fledgling transnational state (for instance, the International Monetary Fund (IMF), World Trade Organization (WTO), and World Bank) provide the hegemonic backbone of this emergent bloc.[28] There is, it should be said, a considerable question mark over how homogeneous this "class" is in real terms – something that critical researchers have acknowledged and are attempting to address.

What we can say with a degree of confidence is that a transnational network of business interests has undoubtedly formed in recent decades. And, at certain points, these business interests interconnect with, and form part of, a broader transnational policy community. When we look, for instance, at interlocking directorates, links created between companies by directors who sit on multiple boards, early research demonstrated a significant proliferation of such activity in the 1970s.[29] This research has been replicated in the intervening decades and provides evidence of the emergence of a transnational business network – albeit a network resembling a superstructure resting on top of entrenched national bases.[30] This transnational network of board interlocks, which consolidated substantially from the 1980s onwards, is largely characterized by "thin" ties.[31] These are connections formed by secondary interlocks – where the "inside" director of one corporation has an "outside" presence on the boards of other corporations – or by those directors who hold only "outside" positions on multiple boards.

The proliferation of this kind of interlocking has been especially pro-nounced in Europe and, in the broader context, between Europe and the United States.[32] Between 1996 and 2004, for example, almost half of the Global 500 corporations had a least one transnational interlocker.[33] Marxist researchers have cited the degree of asset accumulation within the USA and EU as a key reason for this development, and certainly, when one looks at measures of global inequality based on income or asset ownership, the weight of evidence is with those who suggest that glob-alist policies of economic liberalization are disproportionately benefiting wealthy states.[34] And, notwithstanding the emergence of challenger states, the EU and US economies represent almost half of the entire world economy, and one or other of them is the biggest trade and investment partner for every other economy in the world.[35] The EU and USA are also highly interdependent with, in 2008, $2.1 trillion of foreign direct investment in each other's economies.[36] And crucially, perhaps, from the perspective of considering interlocks, almost a quarter of all trade between the USA and the EU is comprised of transactions within firms based upon their investments on either side of the Atlantic.[37]

This economic Atlanticism, emanating from historical ties which con-solidated substantially during the Cold War period, clearly influences the composition, values and activity of the transnational policy community.[38] In April 2007, for instance, at the EU–US Summit, US President Bush, German Chancellor Merkel, and European Commission President Barrosso signed the "Framework for Advancing Transatlantic Economic Integra-tion between the USA and the EU" precipitating the formation of the Transatlantic Economic Council – a body designed to oversee and facil-itate ever greater integration of the EU and US economies. One only has to look at the rhetoric of EU political leaders to see how, despite varying levels of political engagement by the United States, the relationship remains fundamental for many within the European policy elite. Speak-ing at the Brussels Forum of the German Marshall Fund in March 2010, for instance, Commission President Barrosso suggested that Europe and the United States could build on what they had already achieved by combining their efforts to "reform the architecture of international cooperation."[39] Similarly, the EU High Representative for Foreign Affairs and Security Policy, Catherine Ashton, stated that the relationship was "fundamental for business and fundamental for people … [moreover, it would continue] forever".[40] When one considers the implications of these sentiments, it's not difficult to see how the central tenets of Atlanticism are viewed by members of its policy elite as a desirable basis for more extended universal values. The structural certainties of the Atlantic relationship may have withered somewhat during the post-Cold War period, but its underlying dependencies and values continue to shape transnational activity.

By situating elite transnational policy forums within a web of corporate interlocks, we're able to see not only how public and private elite communities converge, but also a possible function for elite transnational networks in world politics. Research in this area to date has been limited, but it nevertheless provides significant insights into the nature of public–private interactions in the transnational arena. Specifically, researchers have considered the proximity of corporate interlockers to five transnational policy forums: the International Chamber of Commerce (ICC); the Bilderberg group; the Trilateral Commission; the WEF; and the World Business Council for Sustainable Development.[41] With the exception of the ICC, which is viewed as performing a peripheral, integrative role between the transnational corporate network and its national fringes, the policy groups are seen as deeply enmeshed within the global corporate elite. They are substantially interlocked with each other as well as with common corporate boards, a small number of which account for two-fifths of all the corporate policy links.[42]

The elite policy groups act rather like hubs in a network, reducing the distance between disparate clusters of activity. In particular, they enable a fuller, and more profound, integration of the North American network with its Western European counterpart. Predictably, perhaps, a strong Atlantic corporate bias to the composition of these policy groups exists, although they do provide "portals" into the transnational network for corporations and policymakers that exist beyond its immediate orbit. In short, research supports the contention that a global corporate elite has, indeed, formed and that, in effect, a "few dozen cosmopolitans" at the heart of the network, drawn mainly from the United States and Europe, bind the transnational corporate-policy network together.[43] Beyond this small, or inner, core of the transnational network, most participants are seen as elite representatives of national interests.

Whether one subscribes to the view that the core group within this transnational network is evidence of transnational class formation is, in some ways, irrelevant to the question of whether the community exists at all. Of that, there can be little doubt. But this analysis of interlocking directorates and policy forums tells us only part of the story. Yes, it points to the existence of a global corporate infrastructure that is not only connected with transnational policy networks, but fundamentally embedded within them. An infrastructure, neo-Gramscians claim, that enables coordination and dissemination of a prevailing hegemonic culture – that of economic neoliberalism. One that, allowing for pluralistic differences within the neoliberal community, is loose rather than monolithic.[44] But how certain can we be that we're observing a transnational capitalist class or global ruling elite? After all, there may be a dense network of corporate interlockers who share similar values and interests, but what is the meaningful substance of these connections? How does the network function – if at all? And what do we really know about consensus at the heart, or inner core, of this transnational policy community? Answering these questions is a critical first step towards a fuller understanding of the significance of transnational elite networks in world affairs. And it's only by looking at the activities of transnational elite policy forums, and the people who participate in them, that we can begin to get close to such an understanding.

Coming to terms with the transnational elite

Perhaps a surprising feature of transnational elite policy communities, given their potential significance in world affairs, is that so little reliable information exists concerning their activities. We know, of course, that there are hundreds, if not thousands, of transnational policy groups, institutes, think tanks, clubs, talking shops, conferences, and ginger groups, but when one looks for material on what they do and how they function, there's a general paucity of data. This absence of information, and a more general lack of transparency, has led to the emergence of many conspiracy theories, notably related to those groups with the most elite participants. Why, after all, would such powerful individuals want to come together, often for days at a time, unless something of significance and value was taking place? And why, in the case of organizations such as Bilderberg and Le Cercle,[45] would they go to such lengths to avoid the glare of publicity? What possible explanation could there be, ask those fearful of such groups, other than that some form of conspiracy is being perpetrated by those in positions of power?

Given the disinclination of such groups to engage in discussion of their activities and, it must be said, a certain fetishism within elite circles for club-like exclusivity and non-disclosure, it's hardly surprising that conspiracy theories should have emerged and, indeed, become ever more fanciful. Weaving together a combination of political anxiety, observation, hearsay, historical truth, half-truth, and paranoia, these theories have been stoked by a small number of individuals – some well meaning, others less so. The problem for those with an interest in the subject is that, while the conspiracy theory community has done much to highlight the existence and activities of elite transnational communities – and must be commended for doing so – it is practically impossible to discern credible material from the incredible and nonsensical. Furthermore, the more speculative and hysterical the views propagated on the internet about elite groups, the less inclined serious journalists and academics are to associate themselves with the subject. This, of course, is remarkably convenient for the groups concerned. Despite some very real and important questions raised by the conspiracy theory community, the existence and activity of transnational elite networks has, for the most part, been ignored by credible journalists and academics.

Leaving aside the problem of association with the conspiracy fringe, academics have generally tended to avoid discussion of a global power elite or ruling class. The idea has been highly unfashionable since the 1970s, and is still viewed with suspicion and ridicule by many in academia.[46] As a consequence, there exists a rather perverse situation in the social sciences field, where the highest and most powerful echelons of society have tended to receive the least attention of all social groups.[47] Indeed, the study of elite groups within universities has become an increasingly marginalized activity existing, as it frequently does, in the critical departments of politics and sociology. This, in turn, has fuelled a sense of embarrassment among mainstream social scientists, keen to avoid being perceived in ways that might be detrimental to their careers. They have, in effect, self-censored research activity for fear that it might be seen as Marxist in orientation, lacking seriousness or, worse still, the product of a conspiracy theorist. In some senses, these responses are understandable, given the increasingly market-oriented research agendas of higher education but, ultimately, they represent an abandonment of criticality, principle, and courage on the part of the mainstream research community.

Despite this reluctance among academics to engage with the subject, a small number of studies have been published that shed light on the development and purpose of a number of transnational policy forums. Research into the post-war development of the Atlantic community specifically, and the circumstances that led to the formation of two elite policy forums, the Atlantic Institute and Bilderberg group, has demonstrated how a convergence of events and personalities was ultimately responsible for the creation and preservation of these groups.[48] Casting doubt on a number of well worn conspiracy theories related to the funding and control of such organizations, it has been demonstrated that the purpose of these forums was far less coherent and unified than some believe it to be. For instance, very early on in their development, the internal concern shifted from that of solidarity against Soviet ideological propaganda to a far more immediate concern for European anti-Americanism within the Atlantic community. This explains the historical and disproportionate presence of participants from the Netherlands and Belgium who were seen as a way of buttressing a "liberal democratic tradition not sufficiently rooted in Germany, Italy or France."[49] And while it's true that organizations such as the CIA were keen to cement relations between the United States and Western Europe at this time, and undoubtedly provided funding for many groups supportive of US foreign policy objectives, there is little evidence to support the view that they were the driving force behind such groups.

This conclusion has been supported by further archival research on the early years of the Bilderberg group, conducted with a view to understanding which, if any, of the conspiracy theories – CIA plot, global socialist conspiracy, or attempt to forge a new world order – is the most credible account.[50] The suggestion of a CIA plot is largely discounted on the grounds that, first, it substantially overstates the involvement of the organization; and, second, overlooks the crucial interplay between key individuals in the early years of the groups' existence.[51] At the same time, enthusiastic participation on the part of revisionists within the British Labour Party, and latent US power within the group itself, make the idea that it represented a global socialist conspiracy somewhat improbable. There is simply no evidence, looking at the composition and representation of attendees, to support the contention.[52] Of all the conspiracy theories, the suggestion that Bilderberg was, and is, helping to facilitate the development of a new world order is considered, in an extremely qualified manner, the closest depiction of actual outcomes.[53] Ultimately, however, we must guard against an overly simplistic and instrumental account. Bilderberg, in many ways, epitomizes the development of transnationalism and the conflation of traditional state boundaries in international politics and, in so doing, stubbornly refuses to lend itself to a simplistic reading of its purpose. As the respected historian Hugh Wilford puts it,

> "[Bilderberg] is neither an entirely European nor American invention, but rather the result of a highly complex process of Atlantic interaction. For that matter, it is equally difficult to tell whether Bilderberg was the creation of state agencies, specifically the Western intelligence services, or non-government actors. In the curious person of its principal founder, the wandering scholar Joseph Retinger, the distinction between the private and official realms, civil society and the state, seems to collapse altogether, as indeed does the very concept of nationality."[54]

Whatever the precise details of its development, evidence points to the fact that Bilderberg emerged as a significant event in the Atlantic political calendar during the Cold War period. Harold Wilson, by no means a member of the Gaitskellite revisionist Labour bloc attending Bilderberg meetings in the late 1950s and early 1960s, was sufficiently persuaded of its value and influence in international matters to give consideration to the formation of a Commonwealth Bilderberg group with Prince Philip as its figurehead[55] – despite the serious political consequences that would surely have followed had his support become known among the wider Labour movement.

Bilderberg conferences, and the Atlanticism they fostered between the policy elites of Western Europe and the United States during the Cold War period, is therefore of considerable interest to our understanding of US/West European policy consensus during this period. And, crucially, those consensuses related to security and the European community. In short, "the transatlantic proliferation of ideas, contacts, information and trade stimulated by the Bilderberg meetings has had a cumulative impact that any serious student of transatlantic relations should at least be aware of."[56] From the perspective of understanding the tangible influence of Bilderberg meetings, however, the precise nature of its impact is difficult to gage with any degree of certainty. The reason for this is rather more complex than the frequently cited policy of strict non-disclosure suggests. Instead, it is related to a hitherto limited appreciation of power and consensus formation in transnational elite circles – a key focus of this book. By better understanding the instruments of power within elite networks, and how they inform consensus within such settings, we can gain a more meaningful appreciation of the consequences of elite fraternization and networking. And only then can we begin to understand the cumulative significance of such transnational interactions.

When one considers the emergence of new economic and political powers towards the end of the twentieth century, a surprising feature of the Bilderberg conferences has been an enduring Atlantic composition and outlook. This Atlanticism has frequently, it seems, been out of kilter with broader international developments, suggesting that the preservation of it, and the conscious rejection of greater inclusiveness, remains an important concern for those involved. Certainly, the peculiarly Atlantic flavor of international consensus led to resentment as early as the late 1960s, notably among the Japanese and Chinese policy elites.[57] Calls for a broader representation within Bilderberg, specifically the inclusion of Japanese attendees, were led in the early 1970s by David Rockefeller. But, despite support, there was a general resistance among organizers and regular participants to the idea of diluting the Atlantic focus. This led to the formation in 1973 of Bilderberg's sister organization, the Trilateral Commission (TC), which was designed to foster greater understanding of the challenges and leadership responsibilities facing the leading industrialized nations of North America, Western Europe, and Japan. This difference of opinion, while far from acrimonious, coincided with what Stephen Gill has called a "crisis of hegemony"[58] among the advanced capitalist states. In short, many of the post-war political settlements began to disintegrate[59] and there was a rejection, in Western and Japanese policy circles, of what many saw as an outmoded and dangerous Nixon–Kissinger worldview.

Gill's own research into the TC between its inception and the late 1980s goes some way to demonstrating the fallacy of waning US influence in world affairs. Through interviews with 100 TC members, he contends that we need to move beyond traditional conceptions of declining US political hegemony, and instead consider the consequences of a far more profound, and less observable, economic influence in world affairs. Predictably, perhaps, given the intangible nature of this influence, his research was initially criticized for failing to provide concrete enough support for the contention of growing US hegemony but, with the benefit of hindsight, few would disagree with his overall analysis. Where others were to suggest that a "major component of trilateralism [was] the attempt to bribe, threaten, and cajole the people of the advanced capitalist countries into supporting the internationalization of capital,"[60] Gill's depiction of elite policy network activity emphasizes a much softer and more discreet form of influence:

> "Private councils are part of a much wider international process of elite familiarization and fraternization, mutual education and, broadly speaking, networking. This process involves both consciousness-raising and social intercourse. It is relatively indirect with respect to the precise contours of policy but it is nonetheless significant. Private councils provide forums for developing or reinforcing concepts of international relations and foreign policy which may diffuse within the nations represented."

Perhaps the most concrete example of the relationship between the activities of an elite policy forum and the foreign policy thinking of government is provided by the Council on Foreign Relations (CFR) in the United States. It's clear, from its formation in 1921, that the CFR has consistently espoused a form of Wilsonian internationalism – something that remains an obvious commitment of the group to this day. Two rather self-congratulatory accounts of the Council's history, published in the 1990s, tellingly reveal an attempt on the part of the group to reinvigorate the liberal internationalist cause in the face of an emergent foreign policy agenda driven by neoconservatives.[61] Most of the research on the Council's activity relates, however, to the heyday of CFR influence during the Second World War and through to the breakdown of foreign policy consensus around the time of the Vietnam conflict. It presents various perspectives on the nature of the relationship between the

Council and US State Department, and these have been compared for the purposes of defining the relationship more satisfactorily.[62]

In broad terms, there are those accounts that suggest a weak state bending to the intellectual will of the Council. Policies of post-Second World War reconstruction, and the formation of the Bretton Woods institutions, have been cited as examples of direct Council influence over government policy. Furthermore, the Council's wartime role as a trusted intellectual advisor to the government is suggestive of a similar, albeit softer, form of control.[63] Elsewhere, it has been claimed that the "respected advisor" relationship was more defined, with the government very much articulating its own agenda. Certainly, the state is viewed in these latter accounts as having special advantages that maintained its integrity and dominance within the relationship.[64] But both perspectives, it has been argued, fail to grasp the real essence of a relationship where we should, instead, think in terms of a "power shared by forces that transcend the public–private divide" – in short, a power wielded by parastate organizations.[65]

These few academic contributions to our understanding of elite policy networks go some way to illuminating a darkened corner of social science research. And, given a near absence of media coverage, they represent pretty much all that is available outside of the conspiracy theory domain. With the exception of high-profile, and somewhat fawning, media coverage of the glitzier aspects of the annual WEF in Davos, journalistic coverage of transnational elite networks has been virtually non-existent during the past fifty years. The suggestion of media complicity in the activities of transnational elite has become a subject in its own right for many conspiracy theorists. It provides evidence, if it were needed, that the news agenda is being controlled by powerful interests. For conspiracy theorists, the implication is straightforward: it is being controlled in order to ensure compliance of the world citizenry with the objectives of the global elite. Indeed, it has become impossible to read any conspiracy theory website, book or pamphlet without seeing the apocryphal statement attributed to the transnational elite grandee David Rockefeller, in which he seemingly substantiates the nature of media complicity to an audience of TC members in 1991:

> "We are grateful to *The Washington Post*, *The New York Times*, *Time* magazine and other great publications whose directors have

> attended our meetings and respected their promises of discretion for almost 40 years. It would have been impossible for us to develop our plan for the world if we had been subjected to the bright lights of publicity during those years."[66]

Notwithstanding the context, or general veracity, of this statement, it is an undeniable fact that coverage of transnational elite activity has been conspicuous by its absence in all of the major news media. When one considers the highly exclusive nature of participation during the Cold War and post-Cold War periods, and the possible implications of such elite activity, there is no disguising the conclusion that this is a startling journalistic omission. Admittedly, the absence of coverage may be the product of there "not being a story to report," as one Bilderberg attendee we interviewed suggested, but it's difficult to accept that such powerful and glamorous assemblages – as is certainly the case with Bilderberg – do not constitute a story in their own right. On the few occasions when the conference has received mainstream media attention, the emphasis of the story is usually on the more sinister claims of the conspiracy theory community, rather than on any meaningful attempt to question the legitimacy of these networks. That being said, a small number of interviews with elite participants have taken place and, insofar as they address the issue of a global conspiracy, provide important insights into the problems of such a perspective.

It's clear, for instance, that journalists who've interviewed transnational elite participants have, on the whole, discounted the idea that elite transnational networks constitute a sinister global cadre attempting to determine world events and rule the world. However, they've stopped short of completely discounting the significance or implications of such activity on the grounds that elite networks do provide opportunities for communication and high-level fraternization that undoubtedly have consequences. The potential benefits of association for business leaders, in particular in their relationships with policymakers, are cited as important issues by journalists, but the effects are perceived to be very "soft" and not necessarily deterministic. The importance of collaborative forums for global policymakers, who can associate freely and discuss issues without fear of reproach, has also been highlighted. Most significant of all, perhaps, has been the general impression that transnational elite networks represent some kind of parallel collaborative sphere in which ideas can be shared and consensuses formed. Again, journalists have steered clear of attempting to quantify the significance of such activity, but it seems that one consensus does exist among elite participants and journalists alike: that such activity is inevitable and, insofar as it contributes to the avoidance of conflict, is a potentially desirable feature of contemporary politics. The extent to which it does contribute is, of course, difficult to say, but credible journalists who have reported on the subject seem to concur with elite participants that transnational elite interactions play a small, if indeterminable, part in the overall milieu of world politics.

Conclusion

As world politics moves inexorably in the direction of ever greater interdependency, the notion of global governance has attained wide acceptance in contrast to the more immediate, and politically charged, concept of global government. Pascal Lamy, Director-General of the WTO and a prominent Bilderberg attendee of recent years, observes[67] that while both concepts are derived from the Latin word for rudder, implying "to steer," they are fundamentally distinct arrangements. Governance, he suggests,[68] is concerned with the unity, and not the uniqueness, of interests and, crucially, removes the political dimension from government. It is focused on the organization of power and emphasizes consultation and dialogue as a foundation for ever greater harmony. In short, he suggests that

> "Governance is a decision-making process that – through consultation, dialogue, exchange and mutual respect – seeks to ensure coexistence and, in some cases, coherence between different and sometimes divergent points of view. This involves seeking some common ground and extending it to the point where joint action can be envisaged."[69]

If a latent desire for perpetual peace underpins the philosophical and historical justification for liberal internationalism, then the language of governance, collaboration, and consensus formation provides its contemporary guiding narrative. Notwithstanding the seductive *reasonableness* of this narrative, there is – and has always been – a tension between the more radical aspirations of liberal internationalism and the immediate interests of national citizenries within liberal states. Progressive elite thinking is, in this regard, as much at odds with opposition in its own backyard as with anything that exists in its neighboring gardens. Balancing the need to placate national constituencies with a desire to forge ever tighter international harmonization is a precarious occupation. And it's primarily for this reason that elite transnational policy networks are far from transparent and have tended to foster a sense of enlightened elitism among those who participate.

It seems clear that transnational policy networks serve a useful integrative purpose in world politics, in that they informally draw together primarily regional clusters of business and political activity for the purposes of greater communication and understanding. There is a frequently presented assumption that such activity is conscious and purposeful, with consensus the natural product of like-mindedness and mutual self-interest. But, to date, there has been little substantive evidence to support such an assumption. The formation of consensus does not necessarily imply a lack of conflict[70] and, as some have identified already, consensus is often a loose description of elite network output. Furthermore, something important has been missing from our analysis of elite policy networks, and that is a recognition that they are comprised of people – people who cannot always be relied upon to do what they are expected to do. If elite network influences were simply the product of shared values and mutual resource interdependencies, we might reasonably expect to be able to predict the shape, tenor, and detail of such activity. As it is, we are unclear what tangible impact, if any, they have in world politics.

In order to comprehend the significance of elite transnational networks, we need to gain some degree of transparency on what is taking place within them. We need to understand the interdependencies and motivations of participants, as well as the relationship between power and consensus within such communities. And, crucially, we need to understand how consensus is formed and disseminated within, and beyond, elite networks of this kind. This book, like the academic research upon which it is based,[71] is concerned with power and consensus formation at the heart of the transnational elite network. The Bilderberg group is consistently cited as the most pre-eminent elite network in the world, and its attendees are, not unnaturally, among the most interconnected of all. They are uniquely placed to provide the most panoptic view of elite network activity in the transnational setting, and it's their comments, and only theirs, that inform this book.

2

LEGITIMACY IN WORLD POLITICS

New York, September 24, 2009. Before flying to Pittsburgh for the third Group of Twenty (G20) Leaders' Summit, UK Prime Minister Gordon Brown tells reporters that the G20 gathering will be institutionalized by global heads as the world's main economic governing council. "What we are trying to do is create a new system of international economic cooperation […] it's never really happened before. We've had the G8, we've had all these organizations – we've got this one chance to make a huge success of international economic cooperation" he said.[1] Originally formed in 1999, in response to the Asian financial crisis, the G20 represented an informal congregation of finance ministers and central bank governors from the world's leading economies. Almost overnight, following the events of the global financial crisis, the G20 was elevated to a position of pre-eminence in all matters related to the emergent – and faltering – world economy. According to the G20, it has already responded to this increased responsibility and is delivering significant and concrete outcomes.[2] Indeed, it has committed to implementing the "unprecedented and most coordinated expansionary macroeconomic policies, including the fiscal expansion of $5 trillion and unconventional monetary policy instruments; [to] significantly enhance the financial regulations, notably by the establishment of the Financial Stability Board (FSB); and [to] substantially strengthen the International Financial Institutions (IFIs)".[3] What Gordon Brown's comments exposed, albeit inadvertently, were the fundamental questions of legitimacy that exist at the heart of the G20 organization. Leaving aside its international membership criteria, which are highly arbitrary and the subject of considerable debate in their own right, the G20 had – and has – no obvious political mandate or source of institutional legitimacy. There is no international treaty or United Nations (UN) resolution related to its existence or functioning; it is not governed by charter or statute; it makes no pretence towards international inclusiveness; it is far from transparent; and it remains, to all intents and purposes, a private club of self-interested and self-appointed economies.

By "institutionalizing" the G20 during the 2008–09 global crisis, rather than, for instance, reforming the politically rather ineffective Economic and Social Council (ECOSOC) under the auspices of the UN, the G20 countries could be said to have succeeded in legitimizing an economic leadership function that exists beyond the formal decision-making processes of international economic institutions such as the World Bank and IMF. As if to emphasize this development, the April 2009 meetings of the World Bank and IMF, held in Istanbul, broadly accepted the proposals agreed by the G20 earlier the same month in London.[4] Even long-term proponents of the UN system of international cooperation found themselves pragmatically – and somewhat incongruously, it might be argued – accommodating this development. Kemal Dervis, for instance, Vice President and Director of Global Economy and Development at the Brookings Institution, former Administrator of the UN Development Programme, former Turkish Minister of Economic Affairs, and regular Bilderberg attendee of recent years, suggested that the

> "recent sequence of events should remind us that an informal meeting of leaders, even when they represent the most important countries, cannot replace the governing bodies of the international institutions of the UN system, including the IMF and the World Bank. Global cooperation requires burden sharing and coordinated action within the framework of these institutions. Progress on issues such as long term financial stability, climate protection, effective control of infectious disease and the peaceful management of nuclear energy depends on how the G20 will be able to provide

leadership, while recognizing that all nations and peoples must have a say and must be part of a legitimate international system".[5]

The difficulty with such a position is that, on the one hand, Dervis appears to be arguing that the G20 is informal and not part of a legitimate machinery of international cooperation while, on the other, suggesting that it might provide necessary leadership and direction to the international institutions of the UN system. For a pragmatist such as Dervis, however, it seems to be perfectly consistent to balance issues of legitimacy – in this case, legality, authority, sovereignty, and morality – with a pressing need for direction, efficiency, and action, and, in so doing, to claim that the resulting arrangement is in some way still itself legitimate. The very act of balancing, with its outward appearance of reasonableness, might be seen to reinforce the sense of legitimacy. Legitimacy is, after all, not some form of constant or objective reality – it is whatever we define or accept it to be in a given context. At a time when international cooperation and action are essential, it should be noted that legitimacy is a fluid, expedient, and purposeful concept in world politics.

Legitimacy in the transnational era

Before considering the role of legitimacy in world affairs, it's important to give some thought to obvious questions of legitimacy presented by current policy processes in world politics – questions appropriate to all spheres of policy development, but particularly acute where transnational policy networks are concerned. Due to the vagaries of transnational activity in world politics, however, and the absence of anything resembling a typical transnational group or network, such questions tend to be multi-layered and more complicated than they first appear. Take, for instance, the sheer array of groups, networks, and activities that are now described as transnational.

The term can be applied with equal measure to business corporations, whether they're financial service institutions or industrial conglomerates, as to religious movements such as Islam, Judaism, or Catholicism. It is applied to a wide range of non-governmental organizations (NGOs), including obvious campaign groups such as Greenpeace, Friends of the Earth, and Amnesty International, as well as charities such as Christian Aid, Oxfam, and Save the Children. In fact it can be applied to an enormous array of activities, including those of organized crime gangs and terrorist organizations; professional bodies such as the International Organization of Employers and BusinessEurope (formerly UNICE); trade union assemblies such as the International Trade Union Confederation and UNI Global Union; and a plethora of policy institute and ginger group activity. Increasingly, the term is applied to collaborative forums, talking shops, and policy networks that draw in representatives of some, or all, of these organizations (depending upon one's definition of criminal gangs and terrorist organizations); along with representatives of national governments and international organizations such as the UN, IMF, World Bank, and Organization for Economic Cooperation and Development (OECD). When one considers the scope of transnational activity, therefore, it becomes clear that questions of legitimacy vary significantly depending on the type of organization or activity assessed.

We must also recognize that, with questions of legitimacy, established or accepted conceptions are not always constructive or, indeed, a reliable barometer of overall legitimacy. After all, if we're faced with a choice, on the one hand, between the preservation of legitimate structures and practices that lead to almost certain mutual destruction and, on the other hand, engagement in activities with a less than satisfactory basis of political legitimacy which might lead to a greater degree of mutual security and benefit, perhaps we should accept the latter is, in some way, a more valid and legitimate course of action. Incidentally, this may seem a rather crude and simplistic example but, as we will show later in the book, it is frequently presented in transnational circles as justification for actions that many critics consider to be illegitimate. Whatever the veracity of the argument, it should be noted that definitions of legitimacy are, at times, highly subjective, conflicted, and multi-layered – a fact that is frequently overlooked. There is a tendency among the conspiracy theory community, for instance, to view the legitimacy of transnational elites in a rather two-dimensional fashion. Seen through the conspiracy theory lens, where accepted (and often selective) conceptions of political legitimacy are applied, the activities of the transnational policy elite have no legitimacy whatsoever – a view that is compounded by fears related to intent, transparency, and accumulated power. And, on the face of it, it is difficult to argue with such a conclusion. But to accept such a view without further qualification is to ignore entirely the subtleties and requirements of world politics at this time. It may be that the fears and anxieties of the conspiracy theory community are entirely justified, especially given the wall of silence that surrounds the activities of transnational elite networks, but without a fuller appreciation of the circumstances and motivations that surround such activity, such perspectives lack essential credibility.

What we can say with some confidence about transnational elite networks is that they are, self-evidently, premised on principles of cooperation and collaboration. If we look at the agencies and committees of many of the bodies of international cooperation, for instance, we find an ethos of multi-stakeholder cooperation that has permeated all levels of the international policy machinery. The pervasive logic of collaboration that has underpinned this development is to be found in practically every corner of the policy process – and, in particular, those corners that become ever more opaque as we move from the local, to the national, to the regional, and into the world political arena. This development, which is considered in greater detail in Chapter 3, reflects the role of collaboration and consensus, absent world government, in lending legitimacy to emergent forms of soft governance in world politics. The emphasis on collaboration and consensus in world politics, on pragmatism and realism rather than dogma and idealism, undoubtedly strikes a chord with those who view it as the only possible solution to complexity in world affairs. But such a view disguises a preoccupation with process rather than governance,[6] and conveniently sidesteps questions related to established conceptions of political legitimacy – in particular, questions concerning authority, consent, and accountability.

Authority, consent, and accountability

On what grounds can agreements or understandings formed between transnational actors make any justifiable claims to authority? In fairness, and before being accused of profound idealism and naïvety, we should acknowledge that, given the problems associated with a fundamental governance vacuum in world politics, transnational political activity has proven an invaluable mechanism for creating certainty where there might otherwise have been none. And, admittedly, certain transnational policy actors might claim that their understanding of the complexities of world economic, social, and political challenges makes them potentially legitimate participants in such policy discussions. But, if we take the consensus-formation activity of elite transnational policy forums such as Bilderberg, the World Economic Forum (WEF), the Trilateral Commission and the Council on Foreign Relations as cases in point, can it be right that those selected to participate, to contribute consciously or unconsciously – however modestly or tangentially – to the future terms of world governance, are those whose only claim to participation appears to be having achieved in their respective walks of life? How should we, as global citizens, respond to this reality? Is it enough to know that their participation is well meaning, or to be told that only the most naïve would imagine that it could happen any other way? Because, if so, we have somehow ceded authority to actors in world politics on grounds that many would see as running counter to principles they would never dream of compromising in national politics.

Next, in what sense are such activities based on the principle of democratic consent? Sovereign states can clearly make claims to a consent-based source of legitimacy – some more than others, admittedly – on the grounds that they are elected and represent the interests of their national citizenries. The proliferation of bilateral and multilateral government networks and the growth in numbers of international parliamentary assemblies,[7] notably during the years of heightened globalization activity in the 1980s and 1990s, can be seen to be very much an extension of the traditional international relations function of sovereign states. And, while such assemblies or networks may lack a direct mandate of their own, they can claim, through extension of the national mandate, some kind of reflective legitimacy – however strained the relationship at times. Transnational groups or networks, on the other hand, that transcend the formal constraints and definitions of state-based constituencies, can be seen somehow to distort many of the traditional notions of representation and pluralism. Within the context of world governance, they have ambiguous constituencies and are not representative in any coherent political sense. They have emerged as significant powers in world politics with the ability to influence policy through claims to legitimacy that have little or nothing to do with accepted notions of the concept at the nation-state level. This, of course, is not the same as saying that they are illegitimate actors; after all, we're still some way short of defining what constitutes legitimate and illegitimate in world politics. It is natural to apply accepted measures of political legitimacy to the activity of transnational groups and networks and find them wanting; but the fact is that meaningful political legitimacy in the world context is still very much a work-in-progress concept.

Finally, and related to issues of authority and consent, it's clear that there are enormous issues related to the accountability of transnational entities. In the first instance, there are few regulatory frameworks or mechanisms that are, at this time, capable of comprehensively controlling the activity of such organizations. In essence, the legislative mechanisms that might hold transnational organizations to account have either not yet been developed; exist in a form that allows considerable room for maneuver; or, just as importantly, are impossible to police effectively. Second, national governments are in a remarkably weak position when it comes to controlling transnational organizations, since the latter are capable of removing themselves from the immediate orbit of "unfriendly" regulatory regimes. This direct consequence of globalization has led to a waning of state power, the most obvious examples of which can be seen in the economic sphere. Multinational corporations, capable of generating significant inward investment for national economies, are effectively courted by individual governments offering preferential subsidies, tax regimes, and regulatory frameworks. The ability of multinationals to "play off" governments against one another has led to the rather unedifying spectacle of competing governments openly fawning for inward investment activity. In the words of two widely respected Bilderberg attendees, the first from the media community and the second a political participant, this has far-reaching governance implications in world politics:

> "I think there is a potential real conflict between the interests of multinationals and the interests of governments which, at the moment, is being settled in favor of the multinationals because, with modern communications, they can move around much more easily than they ever could. And, therefore, if they don't like the way, particularly on tax, that a country is behaving they can simply transfer their business, or parts of their business, to other countries that will treat them differently. And I think, therefore, that we're going through a phase when they are in a position to dictate their terms which is, to an extent, not desirable but to which I see no answer. If Europe, the United States, China and India all got together, I suppose they could dictate to the multinationals, but

I'm not sure of that. But supposing they could, that would require a degree of rapprochement between the major economic groupings of a degree it is very difficult to foresee."

"I think the idea of getting the United Nations to subject multinational companies to certain rules is, quite frankly, completely 'for the birds'. It's never going to happen. It was tried in the 1970s and was a complete flop – it won't work. It's safe to say there won't be [a global regulatory framework]."

In addition to problems associated with the subjugation of multinational corporations to regulatory control, governments also find themselves increasingly called to account by an emergent crop of powerful transnational advocacy groups, capable of stirring considerable anti-government sentiment. In short, not only are national governments incapable of holding transnational organizations to account but, perversely, they can find themselves held to account by many of the same organizations.

Third, given that many transnational organizations lack anything resembling a coherent constituency, an obvious question relates to who exactly they're supposed to be accountable to. It's true, of course, that multinational corporations have shareholders and are, therefore, accountable for their business performance. But, other than on grounds of share value, which is hardly a guaranteed determinant of altruistic political behavior, there is little in this arrangement capable of subjugating multinational corporations in any broader societal sense. Voluntary codes of conduct – such as the UN Global Compact – and a willingness to engage with the corporate social responsibility agenda may play well, in a legitimizing sense, with some stakeholders, but they are a far cry from enforceable compliance with the letter and spirit of a worldwide regulatory framework. Likewise, powerful transnational NGOs may have memberships to consider and reputations to protect, reputations fundamental to their political influence, but there is little by way of a regulatory mechanism in world politics capable of holding them – in a holistic sense – to account.

The challenge of legitimacy in world politics

Despite the fact that legitimacy has emerged as a critical concept in our understanding of post-Cold War international relations activity, it remains an infuriatingly difficult thing to define satisfactorily. It is frequently confused with those things that are seen to constitute it – such as consent, legality, democratic principles, morality, transparency, and account-ability – and some have convincingly argued that it doesn't exist in any meaningful sense without reference to them.[8] It is our contention, how-ever, that legitimacy does exist as a separate and identifiable concept in world politics, notwithstanding the difficulties and ambiguities that sur-round its use. The concept of legitimacy is so fundamental to our understanding of action in world politics that to confuse it with, or limit its meaning to, the more narrow concerns of its constituent components is to overlook the distinct, and somewhat transcendental, essence of legiti-macy. This essence relates to the cementing of beliefs that concern whe-ther the dictates of ideas, rules, people, or organizations are valid and should, out of respect to individual and collective interests, be observed. As a consequence, the term is inextricably entwined with those things that might constitute it, but ultimately expresses a subjective sense of validity that sees it transcend each. It is perfectly plausible, for instance, for an organization or institution to have authority, an authority that is no doubt enhanced by the perception of legitimacy. But authority does not equal legitimacy; indeed, there are many authorities that lack it almost entirely. Legitimacy in this instance, therefore, relates to the subjective acceptance of authority, based upon the application of normative beliefs that it is valid and should be obeyed.

The tendency to view legitimacy in terms of its individual compo-nents, or as some kind of externally verifiable condition, also overlooks a critical socio-political dimension to the validity of ideas, rules, people, and organizations in world politics. Legitimacy is the subject of definition and interpretation. The pervasive legitimacy of certain ideas or interpretations of world politics are of huge importance to individual and collective governmental action. It therefore follows that defining what constitutes *legitimate* within such a context will be of enormous significance to the shaping of future outcomes in world politics. It is because of this that the frequent characterization of consensus-formation activity in transnational elite networks as an attempt to grapple with complex, and otherwise insurmountable, societal challenges goes only part of the way to explain-ing the function of such activity. We must also recognize that it forms part of an essentially contested process in which the pervasiveness, or otherwise, of legitimate worldviews – structural paradigms – are cemented or challenged. The significance of such activity has become critical to our understanding of collective action during the post-Cold War period, as one government minister, and frequent Bilderberg attendee, notes,

> "there has been a dramatic change. The Cold War system was a structure. The reason structuralist schools were so successful during the Cold War period was that everything was inside the structure. Nothing could really move outside of the structure either in the West or the Communist countries. Even in the third world, even though their realities were very different from the industrialized countries of the West or the Communist world, it was still completely absorbed in the structure. But now we're living outside of this structure … [Take the Iraq invasion], you had two consensuses. On the one hand, [there was] a consensus around the position of countries like France and Germany; and, on the other, around the position of the United States and the United Kingdom. It divided, polarized, Europe and it polarized the United States, not at that moment but later. And it polarized the [UN] Security Council. It was not possible to reach a single consensus. But the consensus building processes – in think tanks and among the elite – continued to operate. It was mainly in these sorts of forums that we found legitimacy – or enough legitimacy. It was a very active period for many think tanks, institutions, foundations, academic circles, and media groups. For or against, but especially for – this machinery worked very well for."

The idea that legitimacy can be found, discovered, or negotiated emphasizes the fluid essence of the concept to those in international policy circles. It is not some kind of established or fixed point of reference; instead, it must be teased out, contested, defined, and articulated. And its significance to the exercise of power in the post–Cold War era should not be underestimated, as the same minister explained:

> "you have an asymmetric world at this time. You have moments in which you have to use power but the traditional instruments of

international relations – for instance, diplomacy – have completely changed now because of transparency and the need to be more accountable. If you use diplomacy, you have to use it in a different way and you have to explain what you're doing, what you're saying, and why you're saying it. When you use the traditional instruments of power you have to use them in a different way or you cannot use them at all. And, crucially, you have to use new instruments of power. The rules of using power, everyone has to accept them, even the United States, because of this transparency [...] Very powerful countries, who use traditional instruments, talk more and more about 'soft' power. They have 'hard' power – military power, diplomacy, pressure, sanctions, and so on – but then, they also have soft power, for instance, power related to cooperation, culture, development, scientific advances, and so on. This is the case for very powerful countries. Then you have a second group of countries, the UK, France, etc., and they have more difficulties when they try to use traditional instruments. Why? Because let's argue that the United States is an empire; it isn't but, given the way it works and acts, it is the number one and has to protect its position [...] everyone understands they will use everything [they can] to protect this agenda. But the others, they are not protecting such positions. They are less and less imperial from that point of view. Our societies are not asking us to protect hegemonic positions in the world; they want us to be good players, to be more and more ethical in our foreign policies. At the same time, however, each sector of our societies is asking us to protect certain national interests related to them. Corporations are asking us to protect their interests from an economic and trade perspective. Europe makes similar demands, etc. We will be less and less able to use the 'hard' instruments of power and will, more and more, need to use both hard and soft power."

The necessity to align legitimacy with the capacity to act is therefore of critical importance to states. The hard instruments of power and domination may continue to have relevance in international relations, but they have the capacity to backfire if not accompanied by hearts and minds.

Soft power

The concept of "soft power"[9] has featured prominently in international relations circles in recent years, and highlights the importance of attraction in compelling others to accept the logic of one's arguments, worldviews, or demands. Coined by Professor Joseph Nye – Dean of the Kennedy School of Government at Harvard University, former Chairman of the National Intelligence Council, Assistant Secretary of Defense in the Clinton administration, North American Chairman of the Trilateral Commission, and occasional Bilderberg attendee – "soft" power is distinct from "hard" power and

> "grows out of a country's culture; it grows out of our values—— democracy and human rights, when we live up to them; it grows out of our policies. When our policies are formulated in ways which are consultative, which involve the views and interests of others, we are far more likely to be seen as legitimate and to attract others. And certainly the style of the new unilateralists in the Bush Administration has decreased the legitimacy of American policy. So to restore our soft power, we need to change both the substance and style of our foreign policy. We also need to find better ways to present this policy. This country, the leader in the information age, supposedly the greatest communicating country in the world, is being out-communicated by people in caves. This is a bizarre situation."[10]

While the subtle instruments of soft power are often contrasted with the more coercive forces of hard power, it's important to note that both are concerned with domination of a subject in order to achieve one's ends. In essence, the *end* remains the same, the only difference is the *means* by which it is achieved. Within the context of twentieth-century international relations, hard and soft power are seen to have gone hand-in-hand, and establishing the right balance between the two remains critical to ambitions in the international arena. The attractiveness of a state's perceived legitimacy can have significant implications for its ability to exercise hard power, as Professor Nye made clear in the wake of the Iraq invasion of 2003:

"a country's 'soft' power can affect its 'hard' power. If you take the example of Turkey [in 2003], the Americans wanted to persuade the Turkish government to send the Fourth Infantry Division across Turkey to enter Iraq from the north. The Turkish government might have been willing to concede, but the Turkish parliament said, 'No,' because the United States had become so unpopular, its policies perceived as so illegitimate, that they were not willing to allow this transfer of troops across the country. The net effect was that the Fourth Infantry Division had to go down through the Canal, up through the Gulf, and arrived late to the war, which made a difference in the number of troops on the ground in areas like the Sunni Triangle. Neglect of soft power had a definite negative effect on hard power."[11]

The cultivation of relations with allies and enemies alike, the projection of principles that are widely considered to be attractive, and the attempt to maintain favorable public opinion and credibility abroad are all consistent with the notion of legitimacy as a basis for action in world affairs. Critically, and in recognition of the more "hierarchic" limitations of political and economic diplomatic efforts in international relations, this soft power strategy, designed to increase broad acceptance through *public diplomacy*, recognizes the flatter, more networked complexities of the transnational era. It also emphasizes the significance of the relationship between consensus and legitimacy to our understanding of transnational elite activity. For Viscount Etienne Davignon, former Vice President of the European Commission and Honorary Chairman of the Bilderberg group, this relationship is perceived to be about respect, trust, and an acknowledgement that legitimacy is a most desirable, if not absolutely essential, prerequisite to action:

"There is a necessity to have a minimum of trust. You need to have a capacity not simply to force people to do things because you are in a position of strength. That is not how the world is run. There is a balance of power and that [way of working] is not sufficient."

In contemporary world politics, consensus and legitimacy clearly share a bi-directional relationship. That is to say, ideas based in a sense of the legitimate may more readily lead to consensus than those that are not and, importantly, ideas that are shared – and represent an existing consensus – are perceived to be more legitimate than those that are not. To act without a consensus in support of action, while not necessarily the same as acting illegitimately, does have potentially devastating consequences for the longer-term perception of whether an individual or collective acts legitimately. And when applied in the international relations context, this can damage the accumulation of influence a state or individual has in determining a sense of the legitimate in future consensus-formation exercises. Commenting on the perceived debacle of the post-invasion Iraq settlement, for instance, a Bilderberg academic attendee went as far as suggesting that

> "the [George W.] Bush Administration has utterly wasted whatever legitimacy it had – whatever power it had economically, politically, and militarily. There is a shift from an Atlantic to a Pacific world and [the USA] cannot dictate to the rest of the world any longer. It will have to come to the table. The Washington Consensus is out of the way – I think we will have a much more regulated world. The global financial crisis is the last nail in the coffin. The US is weakened. If you need foreign capital to save your biggest institution, if you have to go to such lengths to prevent Bear Stearns from falling into foreign hands, you can hardly steer the world in the same direction. We will have to revitalize the Bretton Woods institutions and the United Nations will require refashioning for this new world. It's not going to happen overnight, but we will get there."

Others were more circumspect about the longer-term consequences for US legitimacy and the strength of its traditional alliances – in particular, the Atlantic relationship – suggesting that they continue to play an important role in shaping broader international consensus and, it follows, a sense of the legitimate in world affairs.

Ties that bind

It is particularly interesting to note the role of transcendental economic interests in the preservation of traditional alliances. In the words of two

Bilderberg attendees, the first a policymaker, the second Viscount Davignon,

> "[the differences have] been overstated. I think you'll find this transatlantic relationship has been transformed by the end of the Cold War in the sense that its automatic reflexes have gone, for instance, 'we'd better hang on to each other otherwise those horrible Soviets will overcome us.' But the need for it is about to make a big comeback and, with the forthcoming US presidential elections, it's already happening. You can see with the President [George W.] Bush trip around Europe right now that it's all about how we can work together. So I think the period between 2000 and 2006 will come to be seen as an aberration."
>
> "The misunderstandings between Europe and the United States have existed since the exercise of European integration started [...] There's always a caricature that Europeans believe the Americans are single-minded and *vice versa* [...] It seems that, whatever their differences, the Europeans and the Americans have a basic need for the World Trade Organization and that, whatever their other pre-occupations, the bigger picture will require them to go beyond their dissenting elements [...] It was clear during the Iraq saga [that] relations between some European countries and the US were not the best in the world, and the fact that the business community felt they would not be distracted from their long-term strategy in relation to this was a useful element. In other words, you don't translate a quarrel on point A into an across-the-line relationship. [This is] true between Europeans also. I think it was important for the Americans to see there was a degree of disagreement with Blair or a degree of Blair disagreement with the others [...] that being the case, life had to go on and [the] things which would still be there after Iraq I think were an important factor."

An obvious reason for the significance of the Atlantic alliance, aside from mutual economic considerations, is a continuing attachment, despite the end of the Cold War, to post-Second World War, security-based relationships. Bilderberg's role, during the Cold War period, in cementing relations between North America and Western Europe should not be underestimated. Along with other elite talking shops of the period, Bilderberg filled an important void created by the inability of alliance partners to agree a political function for organizations such as the North Atlantic Treaty Organization (NATO). As one Bilderberg member put it,

"the NATO Treaty envisaged that there should be a considerable amount of talk about political affairs between the allies. And this was really torpedoed by the French ... [They] collaborated very successfully in defense and refused to have anything to do with the rest of it – [they] nearly torpedoed it all because of their dislike, and jealousy, of the Americans. And so you had an organization – NATO – that was supposed to be rounded in the sense that they talked on political issues as well as on defense. But they really only talked about defense and I think that was an error. I think it was the only organization, at that time anyway, in which the Americans and the Europeans got together. There was no other organization, well there was the European Union but, otherwise, there was no way the Americans had any input into European thinking or that Europeans had input into American thinking. [Bilderberg] was a different sort of organization but it did have the benefit of having the North Americans and Europeans – it was confined to the same sort of people as NATO so, to that extent, it would do. [... After the end of the Cold War], the Americans got less interested in it politically; businesswise they didn't. I think they began to think that Europe wasn't quite as important – there wasn't going to be a nuclear war and therefore we were a lot of quarrelsome people who didn't matter very much. And, anyway, they'd rather go to China or wherever."

The decline of the perceived Soviet threat, disquiet concerning the pervasiveness of the Washington Consensus and the broader globalization project, significant international disputes over conflicts in Bosnia and Iraq, major advances in technology and communications, and the emergence of what some see as multi-polarity in world affairs have led to the suggestion that traditional transatlantic relationships are declining in importance. For those entering Bilderberg for the first time, however, or those – like certain Turkish delegates – who maintain an outsider's sensitivity to the cultural dimensions of the group, it is a mistake to underestimate the residual strength and exclusivity of these historic economic, social, and cultural ties:

> "I was struck by how Western European the whole thing was and I did say that to people. And they said 'well, we did try to have East Europeans in before but the size of it became too large.' But it struck me as quite an old-style alliance thing, you know, Western Europe and the United States. I mean, I can see the rationale from a scale point of view but, if you're talking about Europe, you can't talk about Europe [any longer] in just West European terms. But clearly that persists here."

> "Countries such as France, Holland, many other countries, look upon Turkey as the 'other' who doesn't belong in this club."

> "There is, of course, the divide that nobody wants to talk about between East and West. Here in Istanbul, this is where East and West meet. But there is still a feeling that a Muslim country shouldn't be a member of a Christian club. It's not discussed, but it's there."

Despite the broad commitment to Atlanticism that continues to characterize Bilderberg membership or participation, it's clear that the tensions of the post-Cold War period have revealed fault lines and differences – some of style rather than substance – in the way elites on both sides of the Atlantic choose to do business.

Contrasting means

In the run up to the Iraq invasion of 2003, the failure of American and British soft power initiatives, designed to foster broader consensus on the legal legitimacy for an invasion, led to a harder line from neo-conservative US Bilderberg representatives. As one European Bilderberg attendee confided:

> "Davignon acknowledged to me the change in the Democratic/Republican relationship abroad. Previously they presented a fairly unified front. He suggested that, perhaps now, the 'neocons' were too well represented."

Here, another member of the European contingent, recalling an exchange with Richard Perle, Assistant Secretary of Defence for International Security in the Reagan administration and Chairman of the Defence Policy Board between 2001 and 2003, describes his frustration at Perle's apparent disinclination to entertain counter-arguments:

> "We said 'what is your objective here? You want to get rid of Saddam, fine, but what are you talking about? If you go in there, with a huge force and occupational theories, you'll open up a Pandora's Box.' We know from history that all these maps were drawn hastily by our friends from Britain after the First World War and they are not natural maps – ethnically or in terms of national essence – it was not there […] And so, in the context of this, we said all the ethnic tensions will come to the surface, we tried to point out all the difficulties and how these might be managed, what kind of consortium could manage this, and Richard Perle came in and said 'well, sorry, but you don't know anything. We have all the intelligence. When our forces go in there, the Iraqi people will hug them, embrace them, and it will be a waste of time.' And this was a big difference of opinion, and we didn't like his style very much and the way he was."

It is particularly interesting to note the impact of style on the perception of legitimacy at this time. The perceived intransigence of the neo-conservative position, and a sense among certain European members of the transnational elite that the line was becoming less conciliatory and more revealing of a pre-existing agenda, reveals a curious aspect of elite engagement of this kind. There is a largely unacknowledged, but widely observed, behavioral code within elite communities. Disagreements are perfectly acceptable and, at times, rather encouraged, but there must always be a degree of subtlety, pragmatism, and mutual respect. Fundamentally, participants must be personally capable of transcending the conceptual limitations of their office and constituencies. While elite participants may look to explain their positions, to use such forums for the purposes of crudely promoting an agenda runs, in a sense, counter to the rules of personal engagement within such settings. While the consequences are themselves rather subtle, the impact on the perception of one's own legitimacy within such circles should not be underestimated. As another long-standing Bilderberg member rather nonchalantly revealed,

> "Things have changed, I mean when I consider the last ten to fifteen years, and the two Iraq wars, and so on, I know many – including myself – who have, in the process, changed their view. With hindsight, and knowing better perhaps, I think this is an indispensable tool that we must all use – to be critical with ourselves. I've always found that those who have a strong view on something and do not give, despite the world changing around them, were not the best people you'd like to talk to."

Notwithstanding the differences of style – and substance – that existed in the run up to the 2003 invasion of Iraq, it's important to note that most members of the transnational community were careful not to alienate political opponents during this period. A desire to maintain good relations, and recognition, perhaps, that the Bush administration was going to go ahead with its plans come what may, led to the formation of a temporary, and somewhat coerced, form of consensus among parts of the international community. Among the more profound consequences for those countries at the center of heated confrontations in the days leading up to the invasion, however, has been the varying degrees of political legitimacy enjoyed in its aftermath. While the United States has arguably paid a high price, in legitimacy terms, for its actions, countries such as France, a vociferous opponent of the invasion, have experienced a considerable increase in international political legitimacy. The perception of this has had far-reaching consequences for the incidence of international dissent and, crucially, has undermined much of the certainty that previously accompanied acceptance of international consensus. In short, the relationship between international consensus and legitimacy has been called into question and, in so doing, has created great uncertainty in world politics. As a frequent political Bilderberg attendee observes,

> "What the world has learned after Iraq is that, in the short term, not accepting a broad consensus is terribly difficult. But, if you're right, in the long term it becomes extremely important and very much reinforces your position [… Take the case of Kyoto], there

was more state pressure [on the United States] from the European Union countries. Angela Merkel, for instance, was not as strong in her opposition to Iraq as [Gerhard] Schroeder was, but the way Germany has positioned itself in the debate over Kyoto, the way it has been outspoken, just shows dissent today can be expressed in a different way […] Many of these actors, in the past, considered that their survival was linked to the acceptance of a consensus. Now, what Iraq has shown is that survival is not linked to this broad consensus […] the landscape of today is that nobody is convinced what is best for their survival. So we are in a moment where everyone is trying to find the best way to ensure survival, and this obviously creates a much more complex scenario. It's not clear what the best position is, and that's why we are in transition. It might be that after a few years there will be one way, one direction, but it will never be the same as it was in the past."

New realities

An interesting aspect of the uncertain realities of contemporary world politics has to do with the perceived relationship between consensus, legitimacy, and "survival". For those active in international policy circles, especially those representing countries with much to lose from getting it wrong, being on the right side of consensus, and those who drive it, is of critical importance. The problem is compounded by a need to pursue more immediate national interests while, at the same time, maintaining beneficial relations with all potential partners and allies. The rather two-dimensional idea that governments "come to the table" armed with their respective agendas and ready to negotiate is a somewhat sterile conception of how policymakers function in world politics. In the contemporary, post-structural era, the capacity of governments, or individuals for that matter, to wield power and exert influence is hugely complicated by the chaotic realities of world politics. In the words of two Bilderberg organizers, first Martin Taylor, a long-standing Secretary General of the group, and second Viscount Davignon, its Honorary Chairman:

"One of the most frightening things, of course, if you're anywhere near people who are in charge of governments or large businesses, is how they too are like 'corks' bobbing around on the stream of what's carrying on. I mean people hugely overestimate the ability of individuals to change the course of history [...] I'm absolutely convinced it's impossible for anybody to rule the world."[12]

"The margin of influence that leaders have on events, from the political, to the economic, to the social, bears no resemblance to what they had in the thirties. Life has become much more complex. The margin for maneuver, the capacity to act of democratically elected governments, has become smaller. And the problems have become larger with geographical dimensions that go way beyond anything that anybody could have invented before. So the world runs in a chaotic fashion, and will continue to run in a chaotic fashion."

This chaos and uncertainty is, to some extent, exemplified by the desperate spectacle of world leaders scrambling from one crisis to the next with no clear sense of whether, how, or on what grounds a meaningful consensus and coordinated policy response is likely. Couple this with the predictable forms of protectionism that characterize international politics and, rather than generating confidence in the legitimacy of emergent forms of international governance, collective efforts in world politics have tended, instead, to fuel awareness that the world's most serious challenges are currently beyond the scope and control of existing governance structures. Certainly, the many examples of collective strategic impotence and/or protectionism – such as the 2009 Copenhagen Climate Summit; the continued failure of world leaders to agree a collective governance structure for banks in the wake of the global financial crisis; or the June 2010 Group of Eight (G8) meeting held in Canada, where wealthy nations contrived to delay an agreement to conclude the Doha Trade Round in 2010 while simultaneously renewing their commitment to do so at some future unspecified point – do little to enhance public confidence in existing systems of international governance.

There is, however, some level of detectable disagreement within transnational policy circles on what these failures of collectivism mean for the perceived legitimacy of existing international policy processes; the legitimacy of governments as principle agents in world politics; and, crucially, the legitimacy of new, emergent forms of governance. Some firmly believe that power continues to reside with governments and that they remain central to any discussion of world politics. Two Bilderberg attendees, for instance, the first from the European political community, the second Martin Wolf, Associate Editor and Chief Economics Commentator of the *Financial Times* and Forum Fellow of the WEF, are clear that the exercise of political power in world politics is still very much the preserve of governments:

> "the shareholders of the international system are still governments and they decide collectively, more and more – multilaterally – to do certain things together mainly because these things can't be done by individual countries. So, in the UN, they decide to do a whole lot of things ranging from climate change to war, aggression, peacekeeping, world health, and any number of other things. In the IMF and World Bank, they decide other things, and in the WTO, they regulate international trade."
>
> "I think there's a tendency to believe, since we live in a very complicated world, that what you get is not what you see. In other words, the obvious stories of political processes – what makes for political success – are not the real stories […] Ultimately, political power rests with nation-states and with completely overt national political processes."

For others within the transnational elite, this rather formal depiction of international relations overstates the capacity of governments and, importantly, ignores significant developments brought about by economic globalization and the emergence of new, networked organizations in world politics. Here two more Bilderberg attendees, the first a prominent industrialist and the second a government minister, suggest that the networked and transcendental realities of transnational politics are rendering the formal shareholders of international politics – governments – increasingly superfluous in their attempts to establish workable governance solutions:

> "I think one outcome of networking, at least that's the way I've always seen it, has been the spreading of corporate governance standards across borders, across continents, even across oceans. I think that had a lot to do with networking and personal experience – [it was

done] by participants much more than by government action. It's fair to say that business totally accepted globalization – I mean, it's our daily life. We don't even discuss it, whereas politicians still, at least in this country, continue to discuss whether they should have it or not. As if they could make such a decision! I doubt it. I think [national] politics is totally at odds with globalization. Politicians do not understand how their old confirmed right – that whatever they said was binding within the borders of the national entity – is no longer true. They cannot escape the influence from abroad, and this makes them sick and tired."

"As I see international relations in the twenty-first century, I think the state is losing the protagonism it had during the previous system. We are now transitioning to a new system of international relations. And, in this new system, there are new actors taking power from the state – upwards, to the supranational organizations and institutions; and downwards, to communities, individuals and, of course, multinational corporations."

The situation is, of course, muddier than either perspective suggests – a point acknowledged by all. In the first instance, international and trans-national activities are not mutually exclusive; they are, instead, inter-dependent. That is to say, transnational policy activity has a significant bearing upon individual, and multilateral, governmental activity and, likewise, formal international relations activity plays a large part in determining the nature of transnational activity. Secondly, it's important to be clear about what constitutes power. For some, power is a "black-and-white" concept – unambiguous, observable, and based upon ideas of domination and compliance. For others, it can be more discreet and subtly affect the way we think and make decisions.

Transnational activities, with their networked capacity to find paths, logics, and consensus that exist beyond the capacity of international pro-cesses, have the ability to fundamentally and discreetly affect the way that problems are framed. As these new constructs or worldviews gain legitimacy, they are naturally spread – with varying degrees of success – through the various economic, political, and social communities of the extended net-work. It's important to recognize that these influences are not accidental in the sense that they just happen; instead, they are the product of discreet power relations within, and beyond, the elite transnational community. They might be unobservable, ambiguous and, arguably, unconscious, but that does not mean they lack power. Some of the differences, therefore, among members of the transnational elite are the result of fundamentally different conceptions of power. Since power is, on the face of it, exercised by governments or multilateral governmental institutions, it is the decisions of these bodies that have become the locus of attention for those who view the world in more black-and-white terms. For those concerned with questions of how such institutions decide what to do in the first place, power becomes a much more contentious subject.

Conclusion

Rather than leading to greater certainty and stability, the end of the Cold War has brought with it a much more fluid period of international cooperation – a period that has seen predetermined structural reflexes replaced with considerable ambiguity and anxiety in international policy circles. Talk of mutually assured destruction may have abated but, in place of the policy certainty that came from a world ruled by military superpowers, policymakers find themselves confronted by multi-polarity and the new contingencies of world politics. And, amid this new reality, the desire to find comfort and security is no less real than it was previously. The only difference is that the instinctive herding mentality that characterized alliances during the Cold War is now increasingly based on a vague, and shifting, basis of cooperation – that of legitimacy. Being perceived as legitimate, and being able to define what constitutes legitimacy in world politics, is critical to a nation's standing and its ability to steer the herd in a preferred direction.

For some people, the idea that legitimacy is found, discovered, negotiated, or even steered may be a little too far-fetched to comprehend. But when we stop to consider the impact of established ideas and worldviews on our capacity to think and act, it should come as no great surprise. The order that we take for granted in the social world around us is often confused with some kind of objective reality. But, when we pick away at the logic that underpins it, what do we find other than negotiated and legitimized agreements made over time and between people? There is nothing tangible about this order. It is not some kind of objective and everlasting truth ordained by the natural world or supernatural powers. These are orders constructed by people. They are the starting point for our conversations, for the way we see everyday challenges, for our sense of what is right or wrong, for our understanding of what is palatable and what is not. In short, they determine how we live our lives, and how we allow our lives to be run. And, within the chaotic context of contemporary world politics, negotiating their meaning is critical to unlocking the capacity for individual and collective action.

An interesting question relates to how ideas gain legitimacy, or remain legitimate, in contemporary world politics. To what extent are they consciously or unconsciously negotiated, and what role does collaboration play in this process? Specifically, what is the logic and nature of transnational elite collaboration? How does it legitimize ideas, and is it what it appears to be? Chapter 3 addresses these questions and makes clear the relationship between notions of legitimacy and collaboration. Chapter 4, on the subject of elite consensus, takes the discussion one step further and emphasizes the critical – and mutually constitutive[13] – relationship of all three concepts.

3

COLLABORATION AND PARTNERSHIP

Vienna, March 16, 2010. UN Secretary General Ban Ki-moon's report *Keeping the promise*[1] calls for a global action plan to accelerate accomplishment of the Millennium Development Goals (MDGs) before their impending 2015 deadline. The MDGs provide a framework for delivery of development and poverty eradication commitments[2] made by UN member states in the Millennium Declaration[3] of 2000, and have become a focal point for much UN activity in the intervening years. This is, perhaps, unsurprising given that the millennium, and the declaration that carries its name, were seen by UN member states as a "unique and symbolically compelling moment to articulate and affirm an animating vision for the United Nations in the new era."[4] Unfortunately, as consecutive MDG reports of recent years have identified, the rhetorical vision of the UN in the area of development and poverty eradication has not been matched by the actions of stakeholders. *Keeping the promise*, which was designed to act as a basis for discussion at the upcoming UN World Leaders' Summit in September 2010, identifies the considerable gap between the actions and words of members, and calls for greater accountability in the run up to 2015. Presenting the report to an audience of the UN General Assembly, Ban Ki-moon made clear that the proposed action agenda "should be specific, practical, and results-oriented, with concrete steps and timelines. And it must set out who does what, so that we can monitor our efforts and promote accountability for individuals and institutions alike."[5]

In many ways, the Millennium Declaration and its accompanying MDGs enshrine both the promise and paradox of transnational voluntarism. On one hand, they enable us, in principle at least, to act collectively and transcendentally in the interests of a greater good. On the other hand, they and the UN structures that underpin them, rather than inching us towards meaningful governance structures, have the perverse effect of prolonging the necessity for binding commitments – essential if accountability is ever to be properly established. Certainly, current UN agreements related to poverty and development lack any mechanism other than "naming and shaming" for ensuring compliance and accountability to stated objectives and commitments. And, given the tendency within UN circles towards constructive pragmatism, it seems unlikely that we'll see anything resembling a vocal and sustained criticism of member states and institutions. There is, therefore, little in the current arrangement, other than the capacity for greater levels of altruism, likely to generate a sudden improvement in MDG fortunes. After years of stressing that the MDGs "are still achievable, if we act now,"[6] and with the likelihood of further procrastination and prevarication as the deadline approaches, the UN continues to act as a legitimizing and sanitizing conscience for an international governance framework consistently failing to deliver on its promises.

Careful to praise successes and sugar-coat its criticisms, *Keeping the promise* treads a well trodden, fine line between the desire to maintain constructive participation and a fundamental, if veiled, call to move beyond principles of voluntarism. And the dilemma isn't limited to government participation. While restating a commitment, enshrined in the Millennium Declaration, to "give greater opportunities to the private sector, nongovernmental organizations and civil society, in general, to contribute to the realization of the Organization's goals and programmes,"[7] the report makes clear that there are significant implications of voluntary stakeholder collaboration and partnership as a basis for action:

"The Millennium Development Goals have triggered the largest cooperative effort in world history to fight poverty, hunger and disease. They have become a rallying cry in poor and rich countries alike, and a standard for non-governmental organizations and corporations as well. Nearly 10 years after they were adopted, they are alive and stronger than ever, which is a rarity among global goals. The world wants them to work.

   The shortfalls in progress towards the Millennium Development Goals are not because they are unreachable or because the time is too short, but rather because of unmet commitments, inadequate resources, lack of focus and accountability, and insufficient interest in sustainable development. This has resulted in failure to deliver on the necessary finance, services, technical support and partnerships. As a consequence of these shortfalls, aggravated by the global food and economic crises as well as the failure of various development policies and programmes, improvements in the lives of the poor have been unacceptably slow to achieve, while some hard won gains are being eroded."

Leaving aside obvious questions related to the principles that underpin voluntarism, cooperation, and partnership in world politics, there are also significant questions related to the motivation and nature of such activity. On the face of it, it sounds like a wonderful idea, playing as it does on our understanding of the problems and overwhelming complexity of world affairs. But partnership and cooperation, despite positive managerial overtones, are not always what they appear to be. In politics, for instance, they frequently disguise processes and motivations that are far from transparent. Take, for instance, the seemingly progressive attitudes of corporate stakeholders towards other parts of the Millennium Declaration agenda such as sustainability and corporate social responsibility (CSR). At first glance, one could be forgiven for thinking that, by sheer force of corporate social rhetoric and repetition, multinationals are at the heart of powerful and effective cooperative movement, reaching beyond the limits of international politics in the interests of common humanity. And voluntary projects run by multinational corporations under banners of sustainability and CSR have undoubtedly improved the lives of tens, if not hundreds, of thousands of people globally. But when we look more closely at this activity, we find that it is, on the whole, rather arbitrary, uncoordinated, and unmeasured. We also find that, in terms of the overall scale of the problem, it constitutes little more than a barely registered collective ripple in an ocean of human suffering. Most revealing of all, the rhetoric and goodwill that surrounds corporate engagement with the MDGs obfuscates the broader question of what role corporations, and the free market more generally, should have in our emergent global society. Even if we assume such an outcome to be accidental, there is no denying its convenience and desirability to the interests of global capital – especially given the strength of civil society demands for greater oversight and control made during the past twenty years.

The relationship between transnational civil society organizations (CSOs) and multinational business interests, set against a backdrop of rampant globalization towards the end of the twentieth century, provides a useful insight into the philosophical appeal of partnership and collaboration to certain parties. In 1976, a series of political commitments by member governments led to the launch of the Organization for Economic Cooperation and Development (OECD) Guidelines for Multinational Enterprises – an array of voluntary standards applied to multinational activities and their societal impacts. These guidelines, which formed part of the Declaration on International Investment and Multinational Enterprises, did little to stem a growing tide of civil society unease during the 1970s and 1980s at the perceived power and ethical deficiencies of multinational corporations. Underestimating the political implications of this unease, multinational corporations were caught off guard by the strength and influence of such sentiment at the 1992 Rio Earth Summit.[8] They responded, consciously or otherwise, by organizing a much more coordinated charm offensive for the 2002 UN World Summit on Sustainable Development in Johannesburg (Rio+10).[9] In the intervening years, business organizations convened a number of initiatives designed to curb the emergence of civil society – and hence governmental – interest in the activities of multinational business. The notion of CSR provided the perfect mechanism with which to demonstrate a newer, caring, socially integrated, and progressive business organization.

Coordinated efforts by business leaders led to initiatives such as the Caux Round Table Principles for Business – a forerunner of the UN's own Global Compact – and placed business at the agenda-setting heart of policy discussions related to corporate responsibility. Tellingly, perhaps, within hours of Ban Ki-moon's *Keeping the promise* being published, an open letter response, signed by 117 NGOs, recommended that

> "Civil society participation must be central to assessing progress on the MDGs and most importantly to achieving them. It is the key to making decisions taken by world leaders legitimate and effective and is at the heart of the global partnership for development [...] we urge you to support calls for the space for civil society to operate securely within a democratic environment and a legislative framework that allows autonomy over management and resources, alongside the freedom to express opinions without fear of harassment. We also welcome the June Civil Society interactive hearings but also call for broad civil society participation in the [September] summit itself, noting with concern the reduced space for civil society in the COP15 in Copenhagen and the 54th UN Commission on the Status of Women in New York. We call on you to make social dialogue a reality during this summit, to ensure that civil society including community based organizations, NGOs and Trade Unions assume their rightful place in the process."[10]

The implication should be clear: the perception among NGOs is that social dialogue has become increasingly peripheral to the so-called partnership. With the failure of the Copenhagen Climate Summit in 2009, the UN General Assembly's resolution to hold a (Rio+20) Earth Summit in 2012 has once again reignited hopes of international cooperation and binding commitments on emissions. The framing of the agenda, however, following the May 2010 Preparatory Committee meeting in New York, has raised serious questions among certain UN member states and NGOs – in particular, questions related to the focus of the agenda on a new, rather ambiguous paradigm of "a green economy in the context of sustainable development and poverty eradication."[11] Some clearly believe the goal of engineering a new global economy – one based on a unifying principle of sustainable development – is being replaced by a more superficial objective: that of "greening" existing economic realities. These suspicions are evident in the record of the Preparatory Committee's discussions:

> "[As for a] green economy, most speakers acknowledged that the international community had yet to reach an understanding of its scope, benefits, risks and costs, saying it needed to be further assessed [...] several developing countries said they thought the green economy approach did not offer a new way to address the disparity among nations, brought about by the current economic system. One speaker called it 'green neo-capitalism', because of the proposal by one developed nation to 'assess the value of ecosystem services' and to 'set the prices' on natural resources. Such speakers voiced concern over renewed protectionism by developed countries under the guise of economic greening, with one speaker asking that States engage in an 'upfront discussion of protectionist intentions'."[12]

Amid all the rhetoric of UN partnerships, cooperation, and collaboration, it's important to acknowledge that, as with any policy process, there are winners and losers. It just so happens that the winners in this process, as is the case with many great confidence tricks, are those who build trust by first appearing to lose.

The logic of collaboration

Collaboration between stakeholders has long been seen as a solution to problems associated with complexity[13] and, in particular, those problems where resolution is dependent on the acquiescence of all concerned. In the past thirty years, it has replaced traditional, more hierarchic systems of governance and become, in the words of Simon Zadek of the Harvard Kennedy School of Government,

> "this era's source of imagined hope [... underpinning] today's utopian visions of social organization."[14]

So discreet and persuasive has been the logic of collaboration that it's now a principle mechanism for dealing with complex problems in areas as diverse as economic development, regulation, administration, globalization, poverty, education, health, and the environment. And at all levels of policy formation, from local partnerships to transnational forums and networks, examples of collaborative governance are to be found. The types of activity vary considerably, of course, and reflect different challenges as well as different regulatory contexts. But the principle of engagement with non-state actors, most especially in the transnational context, is based on a set of largely unquestioned, pragmatic beliefs among the policy elite. These beliefs are theoretically justified on the grounds that large percentages of the world's population live in areas with weak state control; that there is a widespread crisis of confidence in state-centered forms of governance; and that, increasingly, collective challenges "in a complex, interconnected, information dense world – knit together by powerful market forces – simply cannot be accomplished (well, or at all) by government acting alone."[15]

There is also a rather managerial tendency, among those who seek to justify such activity, to stress the benefits of process rather more than outcomes – a convenient omission that emphasizes the degree of blind faith many have in multi-stakeholder collaboration and partnership as a superior system of governance. A blind faith, coincidentally, based upon pervasive neoliberal ideas related to the role and limitations of government in our globalizing world. In short, philosophical support for the concept of collaboration in world politics tends to be retrospective in nature. It provides a narrative for ideas that are already an embedded feature of political reality within, and between, liberal democracies. The extent to which these ideas have permeated the very foundations of transnational elite thinking was apparent throughout our interviews, and is epitomized by the response of one long-standing Bilderberg member who, when faced with the suggestion that multi-stakeholder collaboration might not always be a good thing, stated rather incredulously:

> "collaboration not being for the public good? The object of collaboration is, I hope, for the public good […] if there was no collaboration, you might not be able to get anything done."

Getting something done in world politics therefore requires collaboration, and if such collaboration is the cost of action, then so be it – it is a cost worth paying. But this thinking doesn't really do justice to a more fundamental acceptance of the logic of collaboration within such settings, where to question the legitimacy of such activity is to be laughably naïve in the ways of the world. For elite members, it's not only an indisputable truth that collaboration is a force for good in world politics, it is integral to their understanding of democracy itself. Here, three Bilderberg attendees – a business leader, a government minister, and the chairman of a bank – reveal just how embedded this belief is. The first equates collaboration with values he sees as being central to democracy; the second emphasizes that collaboration is, by its nature, democratic and good for transparency; while the third explains that nobody, within the policy circles he has moved in, has ever questioned its democratic legitimacy:

> "when you're talking about democracy, it's about a 'culture of grey', a culture of compromise, tolerance and coexistence."
>
> "there are two important sources of legitimacy: the first is that it's a more democratic system; and the second is that it is a more transparent system."
>
> "When I produced that [report for the government], I used individual business people to help out and I think that it's completely legitimate, if you're running something, to get anyone. You can get businessmen, academics, trade unionists – it doesn't matter, as long as it's properly done. I think it's legitimate. My point is that it needs to be done with some subtlety and thoughtfulness. I don't think anyone was really worried about the legitimacy of it and I don't think it's ever been a political issue – quite the reverse. The party [of government] would say it's rather good having an independent body."

These ideas are premised on pluralistic beliefs, where power is seen as dispersed throughout society into many competing groups, and where the role of government essentially becomes that of glorified mediator. They also reflect the emergence of a society-wide discontent with the seemingly closed and mysterious decision-making processes of government. Government is increasingly perceived to be, if not corrupt, then downright incompetent at decision making and execution. It follows, in neoliberal orthodoxy at least, that state control should be rolled back and complemented by forces that are better able to manage such responsibility – market forces. It is interesting to note in the final interview extract, for instance, the suggestion that multi-stakeholder collaboration was, in some way, more independent than processes that were traditionally government-controlled. Seen through this increasingly market-oriented, pluralistic worldview, government ceases to be the most appropriate arbiter of interests in society and, instead, becomes an interest itself. Its responsibility for decision making has, out of recognition for the superiority of collaboration, been outsourced to the collective – in which it is now a willing participant. As the same individual suggested, this development represents

> "a change that is largely for the better I think. I like the idea of it all not being contained in policymaking – not all being taken by government."

These sentiments are nothing new, of course. Seen within the context of twentieth-century politics, they might best be viewed as a natural continuation of the distrust in policy circles of ideology during the post-Second World War period. As Denis Healey, a stalwart of Bilderberg meetings from the 1950s to the 1980s, rather succinctly put it:

> "As you know, politics should involve people who are not politicians."[16]

The idea that, if left unchecked, ideologically charged politicians might, once again, be capable of steering the world in calamitous directions provided some of the post-war impetus for greater elite collaboration. From the 1970s, the notion of multi-stakeholder collaboration gained greater common acceptance as the forces of neoliberalism began to reshape notions of public and private and, at the same time, our understanding of the policy elite. Questions raised by these discreet forces have never really been satisfactorily addressed by elite networks and it's clear that, for Bilderberg participants – whether they're one-time or more established – there is some recognition of underlying tension in this area. Here, the political commentator and Vice-Chair of the Work Foundation, Will Hutton, a somewhat improbable Bilderberg attendee in 1997, and two more established Bilderberg figures from the 1991–2010 period, respectively, describe their perspectives on the precarious nature of legitimacy where collaboration in elite networks is concerned:

"I think these networks are rather ominous from the point of view of democratic accountability. Because you don't know who's saying what, why [they're saying it], and to whom they're accountable for what they've said. It's all done in private. I guess that's the upside of it. Because so much talking is done, and there are so many informal contacts, the risk of breakdown in the international system into war and protectionism is much lower."

"It has [a claim to legitimacy] in exceptional cases. At the end [of the day], we say it's so important that we [have to] do something. For instance, the issue of free flow of goods and the Doha round and so on – it was about three years ago when we had a panel on free trade at Davos, in the International Business Council. I mean it was so important for the world that we should issue a statement. So we issued a statement and we decided that each one, each member, should get in touch with their national government to say how important, on behalf of business, free trade would be. That is one I remember."

"I think I was very much aware of [the lack of legitimacy] and I always regretted it. What you're really trying to do is influence politicians [and] tell them what is happening outside of their view with stuff that is normally restricted to the edge of their plate. [As business people], we were forced to look beyond that. And so you turn it in very polite ways and try to tell them what you see there, being out there, what new developments are likely, and – whatever they might think – you help them to understand that this is going to hit us or reach us within the next weeks, months, years or whatever. That, if we don't prepare for it, we will be overrun, unable to respond successfully."

Again, therefore, collaboration is justified largely in terms of necessity. Will Hutton identifies the communicative value of elite networks in preventing international fractures, while the other participants suggest that collaboration – in this case between business and politics – is valuable, if not essential, in certain situations. Legitimacy, therefore, is based entirely on a subjective sense of the value of the intervention, and this value is considered by members of the policy elite to transcend concerns related to alternative sources of legitimacy. Questions related to accountability and democracy, for instance, can be overlooked – and, indeed, must be overlooked – in order to achieve more immediate and desirable world political outcomes. They are, in a sense, a hindrance to the creation of effective governance in the world context, since an insistence upon their requirement means an almost certain retreat to dangerous protectionist agendas. Multi-stakeholder collaboration within the context of elite networks is seen, therefore, as an indispensable mechanism for enabling those in the transnational policy arena to transcend the critical demands of their own constituencies – or, more pertinently, as a mechanism for protecting world citizens from the inevitable, and irreconcilable, consequences of their own demands.

In an early account of the Bilderberg group, founder Joseph Retinger described the significance of the meetings in this way:

> "statesmen, diplomats and politicians are bound by their instructions: they must defend specific interests and standpoints, even if they do not personally agree with them […] None of these disadvantages arises in […] Bilderberg […] Even if a participant is a member of a government, a leader of a political party, an official of an international organization or of a commercial concern, he does not commit his government, his party or his organization by anything he may say […] he can express his views on all the matters under discussion […] Thus, Bilderberg offers a framework of a unique kind insofar as it provides a platform for men from both sides of the Atlantic to exchange opinions and views."[17]

Retinger's emphasis on communication, and the suggestion that those in positions of power should be uncoupled from the burden of instructions and constituencies for the purposes of constructive dialogue, is a theme that is evident in the accounts of many Bilderberg attendees. When asked, a number of years ago, for instance, whether the characterization of Bilderberg as an organization focused on the formation of world government was accurate, Denis Healey replied,

> "I think it's exaggerated but not totally unfair. In the sense that those of us in Bilderberg really felt that we couldn't go on forever fighting one another for nothing, and killing people, and making

millions homeless. And, to the extent that we could have a single community throughout the world, it would be a good thing."[18]

The formation of a homogeneous transnational community, capable of transcending political divides in the interests of a greater good and, in so doing, facilitating the creation of a wider world community, was therefore a logical and conscious action for those involved in the early organization of the group. And it is an ideal that continues to consciously or unconsciously inform policy elite understanding of the role of transnational elite networks today. Here, four recent Bilderberg participants from the media and banking sectors provide further accounts of – and support for – the way in which elite networks establish personal paths through politically and culturally charged divisions:

> "It is very much in the public interest that powerful people get together in a private environment and exchange views. Are they [elite networks] in the interests of mankind? I think they are."
>
> "The first one I went to was the Koenigswinter – the Anglo-German one – which I think was quite literally to make sure that such terrific bonds were built up between the elites of both countries and, in so doing, make it less likely a war would happen. Its purpose is to get closer relationships between countries – genuinely, and I'm not being cynical. I have taken part in, or listened to, discussions between people of both countries where you see genuine cross-over of policies, and thinking, between countries."
>
> "In this world, that's why you need global networks, to really get people communicating and trying to find common wisdom, a common understanding; which will, of course, in no way eradicate clashes of countries, but will create some methods where clashes, conflicts, and wars can be resolved by working out more rational ways of overcoming misunderstandings and conflicts."
>
> "I think two years ago I sat between a Palestinian and an Israeli. Now, you know, this is all anecdotal evidence but I would say that these two guys not only got along very well, and had very interesting discussions, but I also started to understand why it is so complex, why it's not so easy […] I think it helps in many discussions you are having, and with all the other hundreds of

thousands of people on many different levels. So, I think it's adding to and improving the world – making the world better – overcoming barriers, cultural barriers, and religious barriers. I think that when we work together with people from different religions, and you start to appreciate each other and understand why certain answers are not as easy as you might think from a distance, it's quite amazing".

Listening to Bilderberg participants opine on this subject, it's tempting given the almost self-evident merits of elite collaboration to accept such logic unreservedly. After all, elite networking is hardly a new phenomenon and, provided it is demonstrably in the public interest and attracts the most appropriate individuals, we should perhaps recognize that there is a legitimate basis for such activity. As one self-consciously unapologetic Bilderberg participant put it:

> "usually, most people who are members of elites spend a lot of time denying that they are, and saying that elites are a bad thing. But, actually, they love them. I like them, but I don't deny that I'm part of them [and] neither do I think they are a bad thing, I'm afraid. I don't. I think that's the way the world works, that's the way. As long as they're meritocratic, that's the important thing. Are these people members of elites because they've got some real knowledge, or because they're prepared to put in some real service to the common cause? If they are, well [then], what's wrong with elites?"

This refreshingly frank question is, ultimately, at the heart of concerns related to the legitimacy of transnational policy networks. Apologists within elite networks may exhibit some sensitivity towards the issue of legitimacy but, clearly, it doesn't prevent them from participating. And when asked to explain their reasons for participation, they frequently attempt to justify it in terms of some kind of greater good. There may be substance to such arguments. But to accept such logic uncritically is to ignore fundamental questions concerning the precise nature and outputs of elite interaction. Without understanding their purpose, scope, composition, and impact, we can't possibly make judgments about underlying legitimacy.

The nature of transnational collaboration

In all accounts of the liberal democratic political model, it's clear that the idea of separated spheres of economic and political activity is absolute nonsense – the two are inextricably linked. Even if we allow for various interpretations of the significance of this relationship, it's difficult to escape the conclusion that business enjoys a structurally advantaged position, relative to other stakeholders, within such societies. In short, "much of politics is economics and most of economics is politics"[19] – an interrelationship further intensified by the onset of globalization forces in the latter part of the twentieth century. With the collapse of communism and the hegemonic spread of Western liberal democratic values, the fundamental desirability of market forces in contemporary world politics is rarely questioned. Indeed, the dictates of market forces provide much of the context for political debate. As a consequence, we're witnessing the redefinition of traditional governance structures, the increased prevalence of private authority in areas such as international finance,[20] and a more proactive participation of neoliberal institutions in shaping relations between state and market.[21] Take, for instance, the role of the World Bank and IMF in the latter part of the twentieth century, in demanding liberalizing economic reforms in return for financial assistance. States have effectively been compelled by debt dependency to align their political and economic regimes with the free-market demands of western liberal democracies. As one Bilderberg participant, a central bank governor, put it:

> "the international financial architecture, the framework of financial architecture in late 1980s – the very famous Washington Consensus – had been introduced for emerging market countries, for developing countries, in order [that they'd] implement their economic policy within the framework of market based neoclassical economics […] And [before] this framework, most of the countries except China or India, maybe for different kinds of reasons, hadn't followed the Washington Consensus principles. The IMF, of course, was the epicenter [-] the agency for imposing, for pushing, for urging, or for advising countries. Mainly because, in the whole financial system, the whole world economy, if these principles had been

applied, [they thought] stability in the international financial order could be established. And there were some [key] principles: for example, your budget should be in order [...], if you're in deep trouble with a budget deficit, and so on and so forth, it immediately affects your public sector debt, puts pressure on interest rates, interest rates concentrate the problem and you'll see pressure through your exchange rate system. And other principles [included], for example, central bank independence, [controlled] inflation, [satisfactory] public governance and so on. This is the international financial organization [and the] IMF is the centre for that kind of operation [...] The IMF, and also other international organizations – as well as the EU – had always said 'clear your house first and then let's sit and talk together' [Also, in return for their support in our international negotiations], the US Administration had one condition: first you have to correct imbalances in your economy."

It is important to understand the extent of such influences in world politics during this period of recent history and also the broader implications of liberal democratic dogma for contemporary world political discourse. If the market is no longer something that needs to be discussed, if it's the starting point for political discussion rather than a subject of that discussion, there are profound consequences for the breadth and nature of our policy responses. If, for instance, as Viscount Davignon asserts,

"Who questions the free market today? Nobody",

have we really witnessed the end of ideological inquiry? Is our state of ideological evolution really at an end? Is western liberal democracy, with its free-market infrastructure, the inevitable consequence, and crowning achievement, of human social organization?[22] Certainly, the assumptions that underpin discourse within elite networks would suggest that it is.

When we look, for instance, at the nature of collaboration in elite networks, we discover an obvious dimension to its composition: it is primarily between business and political elites, and concerns issues that are defined largely in business and political terms. Broader societal or cultural concerns tend to be addressed within the context of this macro-level elite preoccupation. Here, three Bilderberg attendees, an academic and two industrialists, emphasize the point. The first sees the business/political relationship as fairly explicit, the second makes no secret of what he sees as the function of the event, while the third highlights the lack of business/political integration with what he describes as a third field of "cultural" participants:

> "It seems to me to stand for 'what it says on the can' – it's business and political elites talking together."
>
> "Some of these events have politicians and business people together in the sessions. You have just as many ministers and prime ministers [coming] to these meetings to listen to what business leaders think [as the other way around …] I mean, basically, we want market liberalization, free trade [and] competitive environments with some regulation – I think that's the structure we want to see at this time. For me to be interested in this is just a natural thing because I believe in private enterprise."
>
> "It's business and politics. Strangely enough, these meetings have very little to do with the third big field, which I think is culture. That seems to be a different network. There are some [people from the field of culture] and you always run into someone who you know is active there; and you might make a meeting over breakfast to discuss something from this cultural view. But, normally, this isn't an official issue in meetings … [so it's] the economic/political, I would say. There is no good politics without economic backup. I mean you cannot be successful in politics if you're not successful, if there's not an economy supporting the political side [… But] there are different layers, I wouldn't say necessarily in importance, but in [this structure] you have the business layer of the network, then there is a political layer of the network, and then there is this cultural layer of the network. There's lots of horizontal networking [within the layers] but maybe not enough vertical, through these different layers, to interconnect them, which, I think, is sometimes so important."

The emphasis on business and political networking within elite circles highlights an important aspect of elite collaboration: namely that the interdependency that exists between business/political elites has, over time, created a shared sense of understanding and purpose. While each is seen as integral to the activity and success of the other, participants who exist outside of this core relationship occupy a peripheral or supportive role within the network. One aspect of the shared understanding that exists between the two core elites is, for instance, a belief that cultural or societal interests are understood and represented by a variety of participants within the network. In some ways, this belief is rooted in a sense that such perspectives are already understood as a pretext to discussion; or, alternatively, that members of the network work in the interests of society and therefore have a fundamental grasp of the issues without the necessity for expert contribution. As one well established Bilderberg participant, and recognized member of many elite forums, suggested,

> "business makes its interests and challenges more explicit to politicians, and politicians, of course, talk about their challenges. And business talks about its challenges – what it needs to grow. That is certainly an element [but] it's probably [happening] more outside the events, where you sit together and have a beer. But I don't think that it is characteristic of the meetings themselves. You have business people who are very often more political and more cultural – it's a much more intellectual debate than an agenda debate."

The idea that cultural and societal concerns are somehow factored into elite debate has also led to a rather warped sense of physical representation within the network. Administrators of the various networks, and participants from the business and political elites, are firmly of the belief that elite networks are hotbeds of opinion and diversity when, in fact, even the most cursory glance at invitee and membership lists reveals they are not. This could be an attempt to obfuscate the real membership and purpose of elite groups, but the widespread defense of diversity is so pervasive that it seems to have become an accepted myth within the extended elite network. Here, two prominent Bilderberg participants, the first Viscount Davignon, the second another member of the steering committee, provide fairly typical accounts of diversity:

> "I don't think it's a global ruling class because I don't think a global ruling class exists. I simply think that people who have influence

are interested to speak to other people with influence. But it can be an influence in business, and influence in research, and influence in education; for instance, we're going to have at our next Bilderberg meeting a real study on education because that is really a need of society. You need people who can contribute and be listened to by other people. And in a certain fashion, that is how the world works – it's a logical consequence."

"First of all, you have very mixed groups – on purpose. There's a steering committee and each year they invite many people from NGOs and you get a very mixed picture and very critical input. I mean, outside Washington, we had all these protestors standing around for three days and I said, 'we should invite them into this room – they'd be shocked to hear what we're discussing'. You know, there was more discussion of social issues and environmental issues than these people would ever have thought. So it's absolutely not the case [that there is not diversity]. Take last week, we had a meeting in Davos on corporate social responsibility; a very, very stakeholder-oriented approach."

There is, of course, a crucial distinction to be drawn between those who exist at the heart of the network, those who are aspirant members of the network, and those at the periphery, who probably fall into the category of invited guest or, rather more disparagingly, "entertainment". When members of the elite talk of diversity, they are not talking about physical membership of the group. Instead, they are talking about breadth of discussion. In the case of the latter, it seems likely that there is, indeed, diversity of opinion within elite forums. But this diversity is coming from transient attendees who are replaced on a regular basis. They are not full members of the network and do not exert personal influence within the established group. Part of the reason for the discrepancy is a belief among the transnational elite that CSOs have played a fundamental, and much broader, policy role in the development of hard and soft governance structures. Their presence in policy networks is something that business and political elites are consciously aware of, as they see civil society groups as responsible for significant parts of the global policy agenda. In the following interview extracts, a government minister, an international policymaker, and a financier acknowledge the perceived influence of such organizations. The first highlights the increased awareness of civil society sensitivity among policymakers; the second explains how civil society commitments are used by international organizations to leverage collective action among participant governments; and the third emphasizes the increased seriousness with which such groups are taken.

"Despite the strong position of very important think tanks, over the past few years the decisions now being taken reflect much more what civil societies are saying. This consensus […] there is probably a technical expression to describe how these groups work, but these lobbies are trying to influence decisions."

"It's an important [source of influence]. I mean it's driven, of course, by the fact that there are civil society pressures to live up to commitments; so showing that people haven't lived up to these commitments will have an indirect effect on electoral politics. It's not as simple as just shaming them in the sense of a schoolboy, you know, making somebody look bad in front of the rest of the class. It's more complicated than that but, in the end, it does work. [And, in the international setting], if you take examples like the landmine convention, that was driven almost entirely by civil society organizations. Now there's a second example with the cluster bomb convention, which is about to be signed by 120 countries – again, driven heavily by civil society. So security is certainly not off limits."

"A big change, now, in most areas of policy are the not-for-profit organizations who are seen whether it's [to do with] age, multiculturalism, youth [or] third world issues. Government takes very, very seriously [the] people operating in independent, not-for-profit organizations covering their patch. I've been involved in some of the developing world ones and, whereas twenty to thirty years ago we were seen as 'flower power' types, 'nice, lovely people', today I think you will find in Oxfam, for instance, seriously bright people. I see much greater, increased credibility of organizations that are independent of government, but who have enough money to be expert in areas covered by government."

While it is true that representatives of CSOs are to be found on the attendee lists of prominent elite networks, and are often familiar with members of the business and political elites, they do not tend to be established faces within networks like Bilderberg. Again, some of the perceptual discrepancy may be explained by the representation of international organizations such as the United Nations, but actual civil society participation tends to be from the guest list rather than the members' roster. This lack of "full" membership further reflects the parameters of shared understanding within elite transnational networks and, in a sense, the edges of legitimate thinking. The scarcity, for example, of trade unionists within elite networks is an obvious omission and, if nothing else, demonstrates a macro-level interest in market dynamics and corporate governance, rather than the more immediate concerns of labor. Again, members of the transnational elite would suggest that trade unionists are invited – as are more established centre-left politicians – but, in reality, union leaders are seen, for the most part, as rather two-dimensional political figures. Whether this is because their views are already known, or whether they have exhibited a resistance within elite networks to transcending traditional boundaries, is difficult to say. It is clear, however, that a boundary exists and certain perceptions prevail. Here, an established member of the Bilderberg steering committee describes his experience of trade unionists within such forums.

> "Some of it was very revealing because you suddenly realized that these people had very little to say. You realized that they had poor arguments, which meant that we would come out and say to one another, 'well, this will not do; you can forget about this'. This thought would stay with you for some while and you would say the same kind of thing to third parties, not referring to the person but saying, 'as I see it, this movement of French Labour and the French Unions is not going to make it – maybe a lack of good leadership or whatever'."

The lack of an established trade union or civil society presence within elite networks also demonstrates the way that external influences, those that do not sit comfortably within the existing consensus of the network, are further mediated by the shared understandings of the core group. Representation within elite networks, even if it were more obvious, is simply not evidence of influence. Trade unionists and representatives of

CSOs do not enjoy equal status within elite networks and, notwith-standing their significance to particular discussions, are likely to find themselves politely overlooked for selection in subsequent years. This is not necessarily a conscious act on the part of organizers, and they may, in fact, go on to invite different representatives from similar organizations. But there is a definite sense that everything that could have been gained from a particular individual has been gained. And while this might not always be a reflection of the individual's own personal qualities, it is almost certainly an indication that core members of the network see the views of certain types of attendee as rather predictable and, for want of a more appropriate word, unsophisticated. Especially when compared with the rather more pragmatic, worldly, and transcendental perspectives considered to exist within the network proper.

This issue of diversity is returned to in greater detail in chapter four; suffice it to say, elite transnational networks are not, by definition, representative or inclusive in any meaningful sense. In the words of one Bilderberg attendee:

"It doesn't represent public opinion, but that's not the point."

Moreover, the lack of diversity constitutes a significant determinant of eventual consensus within such settings because, not unnaturally, it exists in large part before the participants have even entered the room. As one long-standing Bilderberg participant put it:

"the point is that you're not always meeting a lot of people. Even if someone [is representing the poorest], he still tends to be living a good life. So whether he's really representative of the poverty of certain regions is another question so, maybe, you know, you are somewhat insulated in the people you are meeting."

These issues of selection and membership are hardly new observations of elite networks, but the fact that they are being played out in a transna-tional setting is of considerable significance. After all, they provide further evidence of elite homogeneity and possible class formation. In order to better understand their significance, we must consider in more depth the critical interdependencies of business and politics and, importantly, how this relationship plays out within the context of the elite network.

The interdependency of business and political elites

Given the almost self-evident nature of the interdependency that exists between business and political elites in liberal democracies, there is a considerable danger of oversimplifying the relationship. In particular, there has been a tendency to interpret it in transactional terms, with a focus on the dependency each has on the resources of the other, which has led to a rather limited appreciation of the personal dynamics that cement the relationship. Seen through this "resource dependency" lens, organizations naturally respond most acutely to those they depend on for resources and survival.[23] Where organizations need each other for stability and survival, mutual interdependency can lead to increased coordination and control over each others resources. When we consider the blurred distinctions between public and private in all areas of the liberal democratic policy process, it's easy to see why the depiction has been so appealing. But elite interactions are distinct, in a sense, from the more workaday forms of political influence – such as lobbying and domain-level policy networking – that characterize Western policy processes. Instead, it's been suggested that elite policy communities – at the local level at least – resemble tightly networked "coalitions" or "regimes"[24] with a focus on the more general, direction-setting nature of policy responses. Certainly, this depiction has considerable merit in the transnational arena although, unsurprisingly, elite participants are at pains to stress a clear demarcation between concerns.

In the first of the following interview extracts, Viscount Davignon, among other things a former European Economic Communities (EEC) Commissioner and Vice-President of the Commission, describes his motivation for business representation in policy discussions and suggests that it's possible to maintain a respectable, and objective, distance. The second extract, from an interview with a Bilderberg industrialist, attempts to dispel the idea that elite policy networks, and key individuals within them, have been instrumental in influencing the Commission's output. Of particular interest is the use of the terms "advisors" and "advisory" to distinguish this kind of influence. It's also interesting to note that Davignon discreetly justifies the need for elite representatives – or, in his words, *real interlocutors* – while the second Bilderberg attendee acknowledges the influence of *wise old men* over the decision making of the

Commission. All the time suggesting that the influence of prominent Bilderberg personalities is not what it once was:

> "The business side is not the total side, but there has to be an awareness from politicians of what [will] be the consequences [of their actions]. Politicians build a framework around the business. It is important that they have heard from business people. You need to bring them together for obvious reasons, business influences society and politics influences society. That's purely common sense. It's not that business contests the right of democratically elected leaders to lead. The democratic leaders should take the maximum amount of information. They can only work if there's a sufficient degree of discussion and trust […] At the end of the day, if people listen they must believe what they are being told in good faith. Business has limitations, politics has limitations. The European Commission is obliged under law to make proposals. I believe that if you make proposals you should research them as best as possible. Coming from a national environment, I was struck that what existed at the national level did not exist in the European environment. There was a void in the system and the justification [for that] was an old legal preoccupation, that if you discussed [policy strategy] with business leaders you lost your objectivity. I felt this was wrong. We didn't hear from the business people what they expected from the Commission. But it's always useful to know where their priorities are and why they are different from yours. You need real interlocutors who are going to speak their mind. And with your advisors you are a big enough boy to know when to take it and when to leave it. You should be big enough to know when to accept their counsel and when to leave it."

> "[On the influence of the European Roundtable of Industrialists …] Well maybe a few words from wise old men is considered to be valuable for the Commission but I still think the description would be advisory rather than a working mechanism [… And] people like Henry Kissinger and David Rockefeller have been around for years. They are much less influential now – twenty years ago they were much more influential, ten years ago they were still influential."

Implicit within these accounts, of course, is a ready acceptance of the principle of elitism and, moreover, an acceptance of elite regimes that provide context, advice, and counsel to those shaping policy strategy. But it's important to state that the transnational elite regime is not perfectly homogeneous. Participants don't all think the same things, and they don't all get along out of shared values and motivations. Indeed, some fairly crude distinctions and stereotypes are used by business and political elites to describe the activities of the other. Business people expressed bemusement and incredulity at what they saw as the idiosyncrasies of politicians, especially when juxtaposed with what they see as the straight-talking and business-like characteristics of their own participation. Here, an industrialist steering committee member and two bankers highlight some of the prevailing business conceptions of political participants. The first describes his frustration with policymakers and their publicity-seeking behavior; the second expresses suspicion that politicians are less honest and up-front about their objectives than business people; while the third describes the degree of reverence with which policymakers view business and its capacity to solve political problems.

> "I am a member of the board of this gathering [a collaborative forum in the communications industry]. We try to keep a minimum level of politicians because if you get too many politicians involved it is good, but sometimes they don't express their views – and they always want publicity from the press. There were eleven people from leading telecommunications corporations, all of them CEOs, but the moderator was another deputy of the Prime Minister. These people are just taking notes, preparing a report, and they'll later submit it to the Prime Minister."

> "Politicians live in a different network, and my suspicion is that when they are amongst themselves they talk differently on different issues. I think we are, coming from business, much more at ease on some of these issues. Foreign policy is a byline for what we do. We want an open market and we're all anti-protectionist and so forth, but we're talking very simple lines of thought. While I think politicians, particularly when they are active in their own field, for them it's all very complicated."

> "I do think that politicians and civil servants have always tended to romanticize about businessmen as though they're the answer to

everything. I remember once having lunch with a very senior civil servant and explaining to him that the guys who are running the FTSE were the people who failed the civil service exam when he passed it. I do think businessmen have things to contribute to government but I think they need to be handled quite subtly […] I read in the newspapers that business is getting a bit disaffected with Mr Brown. The fact is that everyone knows he believes in the market and he is continuing to get businessmen to do jobs for him of one form or another, so I don't think things have changed. I'm just a bit skeptical – I think businessmen have to be used quite subtly."

Similarly, the thoughts of politicians, media representatives, and even prominent business members of the network suggest a rather two-dimensional depiction of general business participation. While, as will be seen later in this book, some members of the business community clearly transcend the business/political divide, on the whole, business people are viewed as being not that interested in matters beyond their immediate sphere of influence.

"Business people are technocrats; they're interested in running their company but they're not interested in talking about Afghanistan, the ageing society in Japan, or whatever else. If it's not business-related they don't want to come."

"Business interest, when you look at it from a very objective angle, it's very sane. Nobody wants fights, nobody wants instability, nobody wants a fluctuating currency, nobody wants wars, nobody wants bitter conflicts, nobody wants to create trouble here, there or anywhere."

"At the most general level, business leaders want stability; they want open markets, they want a generally supportive environment, and, usually, they don't want to be bothered by too much regula-tion and a whole host of other things that come up in the political process. It's perfectly obvious that this is what business leaders want […] I think the main function of these things [elite networks and forums] for business leaders is to find out what the policymakers, who make the world they live in, think. They want to know how policymakers view the various problems and crises in the world, how they are likely to respond, the extent to which there is agreement among policymakers in different countries – this makes the world in which they live."

This distinction between business and political also has some bearing on the general inclination of participants to contribute to discussions. While business matters are discussed, the topics of discussion are more geopolitical in nature, which has the effect of dissuading less confident business members of the network from participating in discussions. This reinforces the view, of course, that business participants are interested only in matters related to their business. As two Bilderberg attendees from the media and academic communities observed:

> "The issues that interested participants were primarily political issues; the business sessions were, more or less, an afterthought [...] business people tend not to participate in political discussions."
> "The economic elites were slightly quieter than the politics people about politics and *vice versa*. They weren't heavily weighing in there."

An interesting characteristic of transnational elite networks, therefore, is the ongoing interplay that exists between distinct groups. These differences are very conscious, for those who perceive them, and may result in feelings of insecurity and alienation. One business participant, who had affinities with a wide variety of bilateral groups and security networks, classified himself in a category that seems to suggest the, at times, superfluous nature of business participation in what he perceived to be largely political networks:

> "I've always accepted invitations to join. I mean, I went to Koenigswinter, which is the Anglo-German bilateral, for many years, and then the Collot (the Franco-British one), Bilderberg and the Anglo-Spanish one. People ask me why I go [because] they're fundamentally political gatherings. You have current or recently retired politicians, senior civil servants, political journalists, political academics, and I always say there's a category called miscellaneous.

And I'm one of the miscellaneous, and my view is that it's always much more interesting for us in miscellaneous than the rest because they talk to each other all the time about the same subjects."

An interesting question, if we are to accept the suggestion of demarcation within the network and the idea that business leaders are not generally interested in broader geopolitical debates, is why they would bother to invest so much of their time in such activity. After all, participation in these networks, which is expensive and time-consuming, is not something that can be justified by its immediate value to most businesses. One possible explanation relates to the veil of privacy and the opportunity it provides to fraternize, unseen, with other business participants – often from the same industry. At the suggestion, for instance, that business leaders must speak all the time, one respected newspaper editor observed,

> "they don't really. If you were, say, the chairman of a major oil company, obviously you would occasionally have industry-wide functions, but very rarely I suspect – because they're afraid of being accused of colluding over trade practices, cooking up prices or whatever. They would be rather careful from that point of view. And there aren't all that many functions – industry-wide 'get-togethers'. So I think one motivation might be to meet colleagues from competing companies without it being criticized."

Another obvious explanation is that being present is of some interest, both personally and professionally, to those business participants with considerable international business exposure. This may be a straightforward desire to remain abreast of international developments, and the political thinking that surrounds them, or it may be borne of a belief that it's useful to participate in order that business interests are represented at the consensus-formation stage. Here, two participants, a steering committee member and a one-time attendee, respectively, both from the financial sector, relate their thoughts.

> "There are people who are not interested in [it], it's as simple as that. Who ask themselves is there any benefit, any added value for me, and maybe come to the conclusion [that] its not. On the other

hand, I must say, if you become part of [the network] it makes you much better informed and it's a very enriching experience [... I] went to this one conference, a very good one run by the American Enterprise Institute, it was a small circle and a little bit right-wing, Republican, but they invited people from other parts. This was under the Clinton administration many years ago, when [XX] opened the discussion. We talked not about the 'axis of evil' but Korea, Iran, Iraq, and so on. And, for the first time, as a European, I felt something was going to happen. They were building up a momentum in the United States, and this was before Bush. And, you know, to hear that and to get somewhat familiar with this kind of thinking was very important – to have this feeling in the United States long before anyone talked about it in Europe."

"I went there and saw the politicians talking over two days; speaking about stuff that was not part of my world, and I was quite privileged [...] I think its probably a rather good thing that people like me get involved, in a mild way, through things like the Anglo-French Collot."

Business representatives from countries with traditionally less favorable trading environments also recognized the possibility of exerting domestic pressure through their associations with international and transnational policy forums. International consensus, for instance, has been hugely important to Turkey's financial needs and trading aspirations. It has been dependent on the IMF and World Bank at critical junctures in recent history, and needs continuing support for its desire to join the European Union. Bilderberg, and other important elite policy networks, are of great significance to business and political participants keen to align their domestic economic trading environments. For their part, some internationalist members of the Turkish business community appear to have been attempting to legitimize many of the demands that have been placed on the country. In the following extracts, from interviews with two Turkish Bilderberg delegates, the role of Turkey's most important business association in facilitating changes to its national trading environment is highlighted.

"With the 1980s, as the whole world was rolling along with the globalization bandwagon, Turkey was bound to be left behind if we weren't part of a liberal economy. Given the previous narrow-minded approach to economic problems, you can't bring about any major changes in the economic structure, and life [generally], if you're lost somewhere out there. That's the point where TÜSAD[25] started forming a good number of committees [… It's different to a] think-tank situation, they're usually just 'thinkers', not 'executors'. TÜSAD represents about 50 percent of the Turkish economy, all the blue chips are there, very heavy boys who can lean quite strongly for some of these things to happen."

"[TÜSAD] doesn't drive foreign affairs, but it does have quite an impact. For instance, it had a significant impact over the change in policy in Cyprus. [It does this] by adding legitimacy to the decision. When nobody can diverge from existing policy or entrenched positions, they legitimate an alternative direction […] when 46 percent of Turkey's GDP speaks, people listen."

While not all Turkish Bilderberg delegates are members of TÜSAD, and not all consciously pursue internationalist agendas, it's important to bear in mind the significance of transnational network membership to some members of the Turkish policy elite. It has provided an opportunity to influence international opinion, and, more importantly perhaps, it has provided an opportunity to garner international support for domestic policy demands. This type of support may be relatively indirect but it should not be underestimated.

Conclusion

This chapter highlights the prevailing dogma of collaboration and part-nership that exists in elite transnational circles. The focus has been pri-marily on the business and political relationship and the assumptions that underpin it. Perhaps the most significant discovery is the one that escapes immediate notice – that the relationship is so seemingly natural for all concerned. The idea that this is simply the way the world "wags," to quote one interviewee, is so entrenched that questioning it is tantamount to lunacy. When asked whether they felt it was right that private elite networks or forums should exist, the responses weren't related to philosophical questions of legitimacy. They were, instead, pragmatically linked to the suggestion that it's bound to happen anyway. The following extracts, from a variety of Bilderberg participants, demonstrate precisely this point.

> "Do you think they wouldn't have these conversations in other forums?"
>
> "But does anybody suppose for a moment that these people don't meet all the time anyway?"
>
> "I should imagine that this happens all the time. I'm sure the head of x bank or x global company can get access to a foreign minister, an energy minister whenever they want, and *vice versa*. I'm not a conspiracy theorist, but I'm not naïve either. So it didn't strike me as that unusual, in fact, if you want to push me I would say the network I witnessed did not spontaneously come out of this, but existed in other ways. I'm sure these people see each other in other fora."
>
> "Of course, there was a higher concentration of important, influential people than there might otherwise be, but I've met these people in many other forums and events."
>
> "There always has been [collaboration], whatever government is in power […] now everything is so easy and people are so easy to get hold of, isn't it bound to happen that people collaborate more and more?"

Given the almost universal belief in the logic of collaboration among elite participants, it's important to point out that this, not unnaturally, has some bearing on the type of participants likely to engage and prosper within such environments. "Old-fashioned" political types, those who believe in something ideological (other than the free market), may find themselves excluded from the network. Pragmatists, those who are able to transcend the personal limitations of their professional calling in the interests of a "third way," will undoubtedly be more at home with the subtle consensus-forming contours of the transnational network. Most important of all, an appreciation and acceptance of the structural requirements of the global market, as a precursor to political discussion, is an absolute necessity.

4

CONSENSUS AND WORLD AFFAIRS

Washington DC, August 5, 2010. The Federal Communications Commission (FCC) announces that it is abandoning efforts to reach a compromise agreement between industry stakeholders on the thorny issue of "net neutrality" rules. In a statement, FCC Chief of Staff Edward Lazarus tells reporters that

> "We have called off this round of stakeholder discussions. It has been productive on several fronts, but has not generated a robust framework to preserve the openness and freedom of the Internet – one that drives innovation, investment, free speech, and consumer choice. All options remain on the table as we continue to seek broad input on this vital issue."[1]

Rules on net neutrality are considered necessary by many to ensure that telecommunications businesses do not use their control of broadband infrastructure to discriminate between forms of internet traffic for anti-competitive purposes and, ultimately, profit. Critics argue that a regulatory framework is urgently required to ensure that such corporations do not slow, or entirely prevent, services such as internet telephony, online video distribution, and a raft of emergent technology innovations from competing with their core businesses. The bigger fear among campaign groups, mindful of corporate self-regulation in the sector, is that broadband providers could use their positions to create premium services or internet "fast lanes" that, in effect, create a two-tiered internet, delivering priority services to those who can afford to pay. The issue is highly charged and politically contentious, with powerful advocates and lobbyists on both sides of the argument. President Obama placed the issue of net neutrality at the heart of his campaign for office and, until recently, had been a consistent and vocal advocate of the principle. In a post-State of the Union interview in 2010, for instance, he stated:

> "I'm a big believer in 'net neutrality'. I campaigned on this [and] I continue to be a strong supporter of it [...] we've got to keep the internet open. We don't want to create a bunch of gateways that pre- vent somebody who doesn't have a lot of money, but has a good idea, being able to start the next *YouTube* or the next *Google* [...]. So this is something we're committed to. We're getting pushed back, obviously, by some of the bigger [broadband] carriers who would like to be able to charge more fees, and extract more money, from wealthier customers, but we think that runs counter to the whole spirit and openness that has made the internet such a powerful engine for not just economic growth, but also for the generation of ideas and creativity."[2]

After the failure of the FCC discussions, however, some began to note the conspicuous absence of Obama administration commentary on the issue.[3] White House aides responded to growing criticism by citing the ongoing nature of FCC efforts and, in a statement closely reminiscent of that of the FCC itself, spokesperson Amy Brundage commented "The President supports an open internet that drives innovation, investment, free speech and consumer choice [...] We support the FCC's process to establish balanced, sound and enforceable rules in this area."[4] What she did not say, however, was whether the President supported an alternative legislative framework proposal, formulated while the FCC talks were still taking place – and almost certainly undermining them – by industry giants Google and Verizon.[5] According to a source close to the FCC talks, and prior to the release of the Google/Verizon legislative "sugges- tion," officials of the FCC were concerned that any such proposal would not go far enough to prevent phone and cable companies from using their control of broadband infrastructure to become powerful internet gatekeepers.[6] The release of the Google/Verizon proposal on August 9, 2010, with its *carte blanche* recommendations for wireless infrastructure, and "light touch" recommendations for the FCC itself, appears to suggest that their fears were well founded.

This particular episode in the development of a governance regime for the internet is the latest in a long line of stakeholder conflicts that epitomize the US government's belief in, and desire to promote, internationally effective self-regulation for the still emergent internet sector. The policy, heavily influenced from the outset by established business interests, has led to subtle forms of protectionism as well as a steady and gradual erosion of user freedoms in the name of consumer protection, intellectual property rights, international standards and, of course, security. More worryingly, perhaps, the strategy of brokering regulation or binding accords between business stakeholder interests appears to be premised on the rather questionable belief that a consensus agreement forged by competitive organizations is in the long-term interests of individuals. Certainly, the argument that government regulation would cost people their livelihoods has become a popular, and frequently cited, mantra among those keen to avoid government intervention. As things stand, eventual accords are almost entirely dependent upon the voluntary subjugation of participant organizations – something that fundamentally weakens the position of third-party brokers. And, despite the ever constant threat that government will step in to regulate if stakeholders don't do it themselves, few believe that government has the appetite or wherewithal to do so. As a consequence, internet governance has been characterized by considerable industry direction and a significant business presence in multi-stakeholder governance projects. Obvious and high-profile examples are the proactive roles of organizations such as MCI Worldcom and IBM[7] in the formation and organization of the Internet Corporation for Assigned Names and Numbers (ICANN).

ICANN, seen by some as a fledgling World Trade Organization (WTO) for the internet, is globally responsible for managing and coordinating the internet's domain name system. From its inception, it has benefited from private sector donations, motivation, and support to ensure its survival and, to this day, espouses a particular brand of public–private partnership – one that sees private decision making influenced by public interest, rather than the other way around. In guiding its decisions, for example, it states in its core values that:

> "While remaining rooted in the private sector, [we recognize] that governments and public authorities are responsible for public policy .and duly [take] into account governments' or public authorities' recommendations."[8]

Moreover, an underlying belief in principles of collaboration, consensus and, of course, maximum self-regulation, are plainly spelled out for all to see:

> "Within ICANN's structure, governments and international treaty organizations work in partnership with businesses, organizations, and skilled individuals involved in building and sustaining the global Internet. Innovation and continuing growth of the Internet bring forth new challenges for maintaining stability. Working collectively, ICANN's participants address those issues that directly concern ICANN's mission of technical coordination. Consistent with the principle of maximum self-regulation in the high-tech economy, ICANN is perhaps the foremost example of collaboration by the various constituents of the Internet community."[9]

An interesting aspect of this tendency towards self-regulation is the suggestion that the internet sector is, in some ways, too important to be regulated by government alone. That, unlike the world of bricks and mortar, the immense pace and complexity of change, as well as the scope and impact of technological innovation, is somehow beyond the comprehension and capacity of career policymakers. That, if left to politicos and government institutions, the internet revolution would find itself choked at source and unable to drive the kind of economic growth that is required in the twenty-first century. And, perhaps most prosaic of all, that clumsy government intervention would cost US jobs and competitiveness. All of these suggestions, at a time of great uncertainty and changing global economic realities, have helped to fuel a pervasive consensus based on a need for self-regulation in the internet sector – even among policymakers.

Part of the reason for this has to do with the transnational nature of the medium and a fear that domestic regulation could gift competitive advantage to overseas organizations that are not subject to it. As a consequence, anti-competitive or monopolistic practices that might not be tolerated in other industries are, in the internet sector, commonplace and, more tellingly, vigorously justified and defended. Here, Peter Thiel, co-founder and former CEO of Paypal, President of the hedge fund Clarium Capital, Managing Partner of venture capital business The Founders Fund (which took a very early stake in social networking website *Facebook*), and a now regular presence at Bilderberg meetings, suggests that

> "Any sort of regulatory response that penalizes the sector, hurts it collectively, is an extremely bad idea [… We] should think of [these companies] as a critical strategic asset that the United States has in competing effectively in the world. Not as this sector that's growing and we therefore have to regulate [it] to death before it's even taken off […] I do think, in thinking about anti-trust and monopoly powers on the internet, we have to think very hard about the […] questions it raises […] There's a tendency in these large discussions to always frame things as corporate power versus US government power and, I think in a global world, you need to think of it as these corporations relative to other governments in the world. With respect to Google, the question would be "do you prefer to have Google with all your information or do you prefer the Chinese government? […] Do we prefer *Facebook* to try to maintain very stringent privacy rules internally or do we wish it to be turned over to Iranian clerics [or] the Russian government […] If we end up with an anti-trust regime in the US, where we penalize these companies that are key American assets in this global competition […], what you will have happen is that it will shift the issue to countries like China, Russia, [and] various countries in the Middle East. Whatever civil liberties issues you have, you have to weigh them [not] against whether the US government will do a better job regulating – which I'm skeptical of but it's conceivable – but whether you trust governments that have no history of respecting civil liberties."[10]

While it is undoubtedly true that the US technology and communications sectors represent a strategic asset of the US economy, it is its control over the direction of governance related to the internet – and the subtle effects of this control – that present the greatest strategic asset of all. The capacity to determine the shape and tenor of regulation, or non-regulation, in ways that naturally favor dominant existing organizations and practices, will undoubtedly bestow long-term global competitive advantage. The idea, therefore, that the US government is in some way likely to disrupt such an outcome is, frankly, laughable. In favoring a soft governance approach, based on a consensus driven by US business interests, and attempting to balance it with a principled – dare we suggest quasi-constitutional – stance on the inalienable rights of citizen users, the government might be said to be demonstrating admirable pragmatism. Ultimately, with no agreement forthcoming, however, its priorities are becoming clear for all to see.

In August 2008, US-based internet service provider (ISP) Comcast was sanctioned and barred by the FCC, on grounds of net neutrality, from interfering with its customers' peer-to-peer (P2P) internet traffic.[11] However, a US Federal Appeals Court ruling in April 2010 effectively stripped the FCC of its oversight responsibilities, arguing that the commission did not have the "statutorily mandated responsibilities" to "regulate an internet service provider's network management practices".[12] The ruling, based on the US Communications Act of 1934, argues that, while the FCC has the right to regulate common carrier services such as "landline telephony, radio transmissions, cable services, and broadcast television," its responsibility does not extend to broadband services. The FCC's announcement in May 2010,[13] therefore, that it would open net neutrality talks in June was greeted with relief by open internet advocates and barely disguised consternation by many industry stakeholders. It was clear that the FCC did not agree with the decision of the Appeals Court and was determined to act quickly to ensure that the principle of net neutrality be preserved at a critical time of virtual non-oversight. While the legal position remained ambiguous, in public the FCC's actions received the support of the Obama administration. After all, if a "third way" consensus could be reached with all parties satisfied, a rather inconvenient impasse could be ended and the requirement for reluctant further government intervention avoided. Added to which, the administration was publicly committed to the policy, and failure to support the FCC, an independent government agency widely seen as the guardian of the public interest in such matters, might have embarrassing political consequences.

Press reports of the Google/Verizon parallel track on net neutrality were clearly felt by FCC representatives to have destabilized FCC proceedings at a delicate stage of negotiations. In a short and unequivocal response, FCC Commissioner Michael J. Copps stated that

> "Some will claim this announcement moves the discussion forward. That's one of its many problems. It is time to move a *decision* forward – a decision to reassert FCC authority over broadband telecommunications, to guarantee an open internet now and forever, and to put the interests of consumers in front of the interests of giant corporations."[14]

Within days of the release of the Google/Verizon proposal, the FCC announced that it would delay its own decision on net neutrality while it sought further public consultation on questions related to specialized services and wireless access.[15] Given the ambiguity concerning the FCC's legal position, and the collapse of the initial discussions, FCC Chairman Julius Genachowski continued to assert his earlier commitment to a third way solution. In doing so, he appeared to accept one of the major objections to an earlier agreement from industry stakeholders, and a central plank of the Google/Verizon proposal – namely the principle that wireless services should have special exemption from any such agreement. In a statement, he said that the

> "FCC wants additional feedback on how to handle specialized services and mobile broadband. The information received through this inquiry, along with the record developed to date, will help complete our efforts to establish an enforceable framework to preserve internet freedom and openness."[16]

In short, the FCC was attempting to reassert its authority with the suggestion of a proposal that would, potentially, fudge the principle of net neutrality for emergent wireless platforms. According to the *Wall Street Journal*,[17] the time taken to solicit further feedback meant that an announcement from the FCC would be unlikely before the US mid-term elections in November 2010. Predictably, the FCC's statement was welcomed by industry stakeholders, with Steve Largent, President and CEO of CTIA – The Wireless Association, stating that

> "We are happy the Chairman and Commissioners realize that wireless is different. We will continue to work with them to explain why these rules are unnecessary and should not be applied to the wireless ecosystem."[18]

This movement on the part of the FCC, which clearly paves the way for a consensus agreement among industry stakeholders, might be viewed as a constructive response to an ongoing impasse. After all, public concerns are at least partially addressed by such an agreement, and the FCC will likely find itself supported, once more, in its capacity as regulator. In general terms, industry and political stakeholders will be able to claim that they've responded collectively to issues of openness and transparency while, at the same time, balancing a need to allow businesses to invest in, and benefit from, lucrative emergent technologies. For anyone who knows anything about internet access trends, however, the outcome is more unequivocal: the principle of net neutrality will become a thing of the past within the next three to five years.

Consensus is a wonderful thing, isn't it? In contemporary world politics, what could be more reasonable, and provide greater legitimacy, than a consensus? Where adversarial forms of politics, with their ideological demands and zero-sum confrontations, promise conflict and stand-off, collaborative forms of world governance promise cooperation, shared understanding, and progress. In place of division, opponents, winners, and losers, we find stakeholders, understanding, compromise and, of course, the promise of a "third way". But look beyond the platitudes of consensus formation and we discover that, far from simply emerging, consensus is given form by the subtle, and ever present, dynamics of power. It is not some kind of transcendental truth or realization waiting to be discovered; instead, it is the negotiated, amplified, and persuasive assertion of the motivated and powerful.

Consensus formation in elite networks

For the most part, elite policy networks are seen by participants and observers as mechanisms for the formation and dissemination of consensus in world affairs. The extent to which members of transnational elite networks believe this happens varies considerably and reflects differing attitudes towards the purposeful nature of such interaction. Some see it as an instrumental activity, consciously designed for the purposes of delivering outcomes; others see it as a by-product of more benign social interaction within elite circles. In the following extracts from interviews with Will Hutton, a government minister, and an international diplomat, respectively, consensus formation is clearly viewed as an intended, and far from accidental, consequence of elite interactions.

> "You get access to other decision makers. It's an opportunity to play a part in, and find out what the *common sense* is. So, on every issue that might influence your business – oil price, regulation, tariffs, China – you will hear, first hand, the people who are actually making the decisions. And you will play a part in helping them to make those decisions and formulating the common sense. At the moment there are a number of common senses: that the EU needs reform; that it needs more flexible labor markets; that its welfare states hold it back […] there's less international common sense about what to do with the Muslim world. In all these areas, the politics and economics have been hammered out in private sessions in these kinds of places. Now sometimes the common sense is right and sometimes it's wrong, but you can't deny that there is such a thing."

> "You have some forum, the Trilateral or something else, where you have this small world of officials, politicians, and [the] managers of public companies meeting [and] exchanging views – this was the way to create consensus in international relations in the past, which is still alive and very important today."

> "You can't deal with trade, you can't deal with climate change, you can't deal with the Millennium Development Goals, you can't deal with peacekeeping, you can't deal with the proliferation of weapons of mass destruction and so on, other than on a global

basis. You have to have a global dimension to policy, otherwise it won't work. So, how do you set about that? Well, you set about creating consensuses around certain policy objectives."

The "hammering out" of consensus is seen by some, therefore, as a pre-requisite to political discourse. Without agreement on first principles – agreement on the definition of the problem – it is impossible to engage meaningfully with world issues. To that end, elite networks are perceived by some to be organizations capable of enabling a consensus based upon shared definitions of the problem. Indeed, this is seen as their purpose. Other participants, however, are clearly uncomfortable with the suggestion that consensus is the intended output of elite interaction. As one journalist attendee rather succinctly put it:

> "The formation of elite consensus is a by-product rather than a goal."

In a similar vein, the following three extracts from interviews with Martin Wolf, a financier, and a politician, respectively, highlight difficulties with such a perspective. Wolf explains that consensus is just one possible output of elite interaction, while the personal and social dynamics of consensus formation are emphasized by the other two participants:

> "It can help with generating a consensus; it can also help with clarifying and sharpening disagreements. If you disagree, you go away with an even better understanding of why you disagree and, where you agree, you have a better understanding [and] basis for cooperation. In a sense, what you're doing here is making the process of thinking that is driving policy more transparent, and that can be the basis either for better cooperation or more perfect disagreement."
>
> "[Consensus formation] or *definition of differences*, I would say. I would observe, and I don't want to exaggerate, that people narrow differences which is, I suppose, the same as consensus formation. I mean, it's not insofar as it is implied that consensuses are reached on things […] It was mutual consensus, mutual education, the swapping of ideas; I can't place a value on it but I think it's real."

"I wouldn't say a consensus; a consensus implies that everybody subscribes to it, but I do think, yes, certain *thinking crystallizes*, views emerge from these things. How they emerge, well it's very difficult to say. They emerge from what people read in the newspapers, what they hear on the radio and television, what they read in books, what they hear when they go to conferences. It's a process that most human beings would find hard to describe with any degree of precision."

In some senses, therefore, and despite the lack of a better description, consensus formation is rather misleading as an explanation of what is taking place in elite networks. It implies a conscious objective and process when, more accurately, it has more to do with the underlying momentum and consequence of such activity. In the following interview extracts, the first with Viscount Davignon, the second with another long-standing member of the steering committee, there is also the suggestion that a desire to address complex problems, and come to terms with the implications of long-term challenges, can result indirectly in a certain kind of consensus. A consensus related to the overall nature and framing of global political and economic challenges. Both men deny that consensus formation is the purpose of such activity, and in the case of Davignon, that it is within the strategic capacity of individuals to shape it. At the same time, however, he makes clear that a consensus related to the need to act can result from such activity – a point that is supported, in part, by the observation of the other steering committee member that elite networks are useful for identifying issues that exist on the horizon. It seems reasonable to suggest that raising the saliency of an issue, within the context of an elite network, will likely result in its appearance on more formal political agendas. Added to which, a discussion aimed at defining an issue within the elite context will almost certainly have some bearing upon the way it is framed for consumption by more formal policy processes.

"[The Bilderberg group doesn't reach a consensus agreement …], because the problems we deal with are of a general nature and don't adjust to simple answers. What can come out of it is [an acknowledgement that it is] wrong not to deal with a problem and that we should go home and encourage people not to leave it on the table. But a real consensus, with an action plan: one, two, three? The answer is no, people are much too sensible to believe they can do that [... But, it can create] some kind of consensus about why some things have to be addressed. However difficult, one can't just trust to fatality."

"I have a little problem with the word consensus. I can't remember participating in anything we went to in order to reach a consensus. Normally these informal meetings are very good, not because they are consensus building, but because you get to see things on the horizon. This may lead, in the end, to a certain similarity in thinking – within a network and even across borders – but it was not originally intended to build consensus."

Interestingly, perhaps, both men recognized that a distinction needed to be drawn between political and economic issues, and acknowledged that consensus tended to form more readily around the latter (Viscount Davignon's comments appear first):

"I think the consensus is much greater there [on trade] because automatically, around the table, you have internationalists. People who are not internationalists would find they are losing their time and overplaying the importance of the international component of domestic problems. So you have internationalists and, from this point of view, you need to have a degree of rules, a degree of references, and every business is interested in these types of references [...] I think that there [on trade], the consensus was always very powerful."

"Well, the broadly accepted vision was the market economy, no doubt about it. Absolutely. You may even say the good old traditional values of proper capitalism which, maybe, fifteen years ago, wasn't a dirty word like it is now."

The internationalist outlook of business participants, and the obvious absence of overt protectionists within transnational elite networks, almost certainly has a bearing on their propensity towards economic consensus. Curiously, however, established Bilderberg attendees were reluctant to accept a direct relationship between the representation of economic internationalists in the transnational policy elite and the formation of particular brands of political consensus. Despite Viscount Davignon's earlier observation, for instance, that strategic, long-term business relationships were useful during a fractious political period at the time of the second Gulf War, he was careful to avoid the suggestion that they facilitated subsequent political settlements although, clearly, it is difficult to escape the conclusion that they did. The relationship between economic and political realities means that it is impossible to speak of economic consensus without recognizing the political implications of such understandings. At the same time, political consensus is of little value if it fails to inform the finer detail of national economic bargaining. As a regular Bilderberg industrialist observed, the level of political consensus within elite networks varies by issue, but, even where there is general consensus on the nature of a macro-level problem – as there is with global warming – this doesn't necessarily result in transcendental policy arrangements:

> "The one area where probably there is the least debate and most consensus is, of course, global warming and environmental issues. There you don't see a negotiating position except when you get down to specific agreements like Kyoto. But there is a lot of consensus [regarding] what the world should do and what that means for politicians and business leaders."

Another point to make is that political problems are invariably multi-layered, and this fundamental complexity may result in conflicts related to different aspects of the same macro-level issue. This doesn't just mean a multiplication in the potential for conflicts between individuals; it can also create conflict at the level *of* the individual. If we take global warming as a case in point, for instance, it's perfectly conceivable for an individual to profess support for the idea of reducing global carbon emissions while simultaneously resisting carbon emissions targets that are perceived to be detrimental to economic growth. A resolution that allows individuals or collectives to balance these beliefs – and carbon-trading initiatives are one example of how this was achieved in the global warming debate – is clearly more appealing than having to make a difficult choice – or no choice at all. In many ways, the appeal of the third way is very easy to understand: whether the solution it offers proves to be satisfactory is, in a sense, of secondary importance to its capacity to salve a greater immediate anxiety of conflict and, thereby, provide the comforting reassurance of progress.

For some Bilderberg attendees, such compromise is part of a seemingly never-ending process that has very little to do with the notion of consensus. It has, instead, to do with an evolving political reality that is based less on shared understanding and more on basic principles of power, negotiation, trade-off, and settlement. In the following extracts, for example, an academic and a senior media executive explain the dynamic nature of negotiated settlements. The first stresses what he sees as the reality of political existence – namely the chaotic power play that underpins resolutions of any kind. The second takes a rather more pragmatic view of opinion formation, seeing it as a negotiated settlement between individuals and their social world. In both cases, there is a transitory and evolving sense of reality – a reality that does not exist in any permanent or concrete form:

> "Politics is about conflict! It's not about consensus [and] it's not about norms. Politics is about conflict and trade-offs […] we don't get to consensus, we get to settlements and settlements constantly change. It's not static, it's always moving as a result of events – and also because those settlements are constantly in flux."
>
> "I mean, bread has been produced in this world for around 6000 years now, since the inception of agriculture, but they're still experimenting with it: trying to introduce new types; new tastes; new ways to preserve it; better ways to preserve it; healthier breads – there's no end to developing taste, and I don't see any harm in testing your idea with new people to see how they react to it [… And then] seeing the reaction and making some amendments, if necessary, or adding interesting components to take it further."

Whatever the precise nature of elite community outputs, and allowing for participant differences of both substance and semantics, Bilderberg attendees do seem to believe, or accept, that elite fraternization has the effect, consciously or otherwise, of narrowing differences between members of the network. Whether this is the product of deliberate or accidental consensus-formation activity, or whether it is produced by power dynamics within the group, remains to be seen. What is clear, however, is that the development of shared understanding is definitely related to dynamics of social interaction at play within the elite community. We know that many of the political issues addressed by elite networks are multi-layered and far from straightforward, and yet agreement over the basic nature of such problems appears to emerge within such communities. What is it about these elite interactions that facilitates and drives agreement, settlement, or consensus? Is it simply the product of undirected and collective intellectual inquiry, or is something far more deterministic and motivated shaping elite consensual outputs? Only with a better understanding of power within elite circles can we get anywhere near to answering these questions.

Bias in elite networks

At first glance, interactions within elite communities don't seem to provide an obvious setting for an analysis of power relationships. After all, they take place between the *powerful* rather than between the *powerful* and the *powerless*. The lack of an obvious subject of power, and of competing factions and interests within the networks, might be seen to render the whole exercise somewhat pointless. But as tempting as it might be to view the absence of factionalism or diversity as evidence of interest homogeneity, or to view this activity as preceding the idea of interests altogether,[19] we should avoid rushing to conclusions of this kind. After all, a lack of conflict is not necessarily the same thing as an absence of power – it might just as easily be an indicator of its presence. Similarly, power does not have to be consciously exercised, or consciously observed, in order to be at work; indeed, the most insidious forms of power are those that induce compliance without our stir, question or, even, awareness.[20]

If we take, for instance, the selection criteria for membership of elite networks, and the processes that drive policy agendas within such circles, it becomes clear that discreet forms of power are at work – shaping the nature of discourse and eventual consensus within these communities. This suggestion is fiercely resisted by Bilderberg participants, not because they are attempting to disguise a hidden truth, but because they simply cannot see the processes at work. They are so discreet, and central to the functioning of the transnational elite network, that they now form part of an established cognitive worldview. The idea that power need not be conscious is important, therefore, because it explains why members of elite networks see the outcomes of such activity as, in some way, accidental. No distinction is being drawn between the randomness of accidental outcomes and outputs that are shaped, albeit unconsciously, by the functioning of pre-existing processes and relationships. So, while consensus may not be a conscious product of elite interactions, it should be noted that it is far from accidental. More accurately, elite networks are unconsciously deterministic when it comes to the formation of consensus.[21]

In the following extracts from interviews with five Bilderberg steering committee members – referenced continuously in this section of the chapter – past and present grandees of the group cite the existence of participant differences and the lack of conclusions as evidence that the group plays no deterministic role in swaying the opinions of members or policymakers.

"There's no such thing as Bilderberg thinking. We have people from both sides of the political debate. If you take the two steering committee members from the UK, me and Ken Clarke, we have diametrically different views on the desirability of British participation in the Euro, for example. Generally speaking, there are more people at the Bilderberg conferences who would be, in UK terms, highly Europhile, but that isn't surprising because the elites on the continent are 90 percent highly Europhile."

"This doesn't mean that you reach any agreement on policy – that is clearly what this group is not about. But you have a better idea what people are thinking about [...] Bilderberg does not try to reach conclusions, it does not try to say what people should do. Everyone goes away with their own feeling, and that allows the debate to be completely open and quite frank. You see what the differences are, and the only conclusion is that, whatever the differences, the world works better if the Americans and the Europeans get along than if they do not."

"It doesn't have a political relevance and it doesn't come to conclusions. I mean, you have a debate on whatever it might be, and that's the end of that. It doesn't come to any conclusions. You can draw your own conclusions from it, but the organization doesn't draw a conclusion [...] that was what it always sought to avoid. The conspiracy theories are terribly difficult to refute because, if you don't actually produce any results, people think you're hiding them. In point of fact, there weren't any."

"There is an even smaller elite business group in this country, twenty to twenty-five people, and we once issued a pamphlet on 'the market' but I don't think it had any impact. But that [kind of thing] is very rare. Bilderberg never does that on purpose. That's a clear decision – they don't issue any statements. And it's really not possible at Bilderberg to have one voice because you have so many, as I said, people from different constituencies that would never agree to say something [collectively] about free trade. You would almost certainly have someone from the emerging economies or from Western Europe who was opposed."

"But we never discussed this as a way to go and 'have a consensus'. All issues were hotly debated, I tell you they were! The most pleasant thing that we could imagine at Bilderberg were two parties up there on the stage almost hitting one another because they had totally different views on what is right – how to deal with the Arabs, or I don't know what. And we specifically looked for people to make speeches with widely different views and there was never an endeavor to reach a common view. It was about opening the mind to two totally different views. And then everyone worked it over in his own brain, what to make of it."

There is more to these responses, however, than first meets the eye. In the first extract, from an interview with Martin Taylor,[22] he attempts to suggest that the pro-European (pro-trade) tradition of Bilderberg is a product of the presence of a highly Europhile continental elite. This may or may not be the case, but the perception is almost certainly reinforced within the group by the invitation of only those who support such a position. Elite Euro-skeptics are an increasingly marginalized presence in transnational elite circles and tend not to be invited because their views are both unpopular and unwelcome. Here, two rather more infrequent Bilderberg attendees, one an ardent Euro-skeptic, the other an expert in European policy matters, describe what they see as a clear bias to group activity.

"I tended not to get invited to these things because I didn't share this consensus and was vaguely felt to be unsympathetic – and this was certainly true with Bilderberg. The first time I went to Bilderberg, I was a perfectly respectable European; by the second time I went, I had become increasingly critical of the European consensus as it existed at that time and I've become even more critical since […] I certainly felt it [a bias]. And I think the fact that, after the first time I went to Bilderberg, they didn't ask me again for some time; and after the second time, they haven't asked me since, reflects the fact that I wasn't one of them. I mean, they were perfectly polite, and it was very agreeable, and I wasn't made to feel that I was being 'sent to Coventry' or anything of that kind. […] but I think they did feel that I wasn't one of them and that probably was the reason they didn't invite me back again. They were recruiting, looking for recruits, for a particular kind of view, basically a strong Europeanist view in the case of Bilderberg. And if you didn't hold those views, you were never going to hold them. They sensed it, and they were more comfortable with people who were orthodox in that sense."

"There are certain issues where consensus is formed before they even turn up […] the people who turn up are almost all the sorts of people who believe in structural reform of the European market. I mean you're not going to get the revolutionary communists there […] It's not really consensus formation, I would say it's consensus reinforcement."

The idea that broad agreement is already built into elite interactions through the discreet – and largely unconscious – process of selection is of considerable relevance to the discussion of bias. A pretext of free trade, and broad support for regional trade blocs, almost certainly has some bearing on who is selected for inclusion and, by default, on the way issues are addressed in the network. Moreover, this bias has the effect of subtly reinforcing a sense of collective rationality that might potentially influence the interpretation of many other policy issues. Again, long-standing Bilderberg participants would dispute this implication and, no doubt, point to forces of pervasive logic that exist in the wider society as explanations of any such bias. They would certainly refute the suggestion that the group reaches any meaningful accords or resolutions of its own, although, as the second, third, and fourth extracts from interviews with steering committee members demonstrate, they do acknowledge that individuals draw conclusions from what they see and hear.

If we take the second and third steering committee interview extracts, for instance, from Viscount Davignon and another prominent Bilderberg figure, respectively, it is suggested that participants make up their own minds after exposure to arguments, debates, and protagonists. At the heart of this conviction is the idea that decision making is the product of rational choice rather than the more complex result of personal interaction within the social context of elite networks. Indeed, this rational choice explanation, with notions of information sharing and learning at its core, is a common explanation of the influence of elite networks – as these further four interview extracts from established business and political members of the group demonstrate:

> "I mean, there's no consensus-forming agenda; it's more information-sharing activity. Everybody leaves with a new sense of understanding."
>
> "Nobody is going to change my way of thinking, my approach, my wishes [but] I learned lots of things. Maybe there are some effects of that but, for my part, I got lots of benefits."
>
> "It doesn't mean that you go left and right and then change your opinion every other day, not at all; but I do think we all must have the ability to learn and to improve our thinking with more information."
>
> "What is very difficult to quantify is that you get somewhat familiar with broader topics and you hear, at an early stage, what might happen to water, to energy, to commodities, to geopolitical conflicts, and to many other things. So I think it broadens your horizons at a very early stage. It's not a direct result, but it helps you to better understand different aspects or different interests; that is for me the key."

It became clear during the interviews conducted for this book that Bilderberg participants were extremely reluctant to concede the point that their opinions and worldviews might be being influenced by elite networks. A collective desire to avoid suggesting that such communities are politically instrumental might explain this but, given the generally frank nature of the interviews, it seems likely that this was related more to personal defensiveness – a disinclination, perhaps, to admit to a personal weakness of some kind. It was easier for them to talk in rather managerial terms about the value of *learning* and *information* than to admit that they, like all of us, are influenced by the social dynamics of group membership. These dynamics are explored in greater detail in the following chapters but, suffice it to say, learning is not a value-neutral experience – it is inextricably related to the motivation of those who do the learning and, crucially, the biases and motivations of those who supply it. This point is acknowledged in the following two interview extracts, the first from Viscount Davignon, who cites the lack of objectivity within any social context, and the second from another stalwart of the group, who hints at the influence of individuals rather than arguments.

> "There is no objective discussion. A discussion is related to the opinion you have of your interlocutor. Do you think he's honest? Do you think he's speaking true language? And, even if you believe he's mistaken, do you still believe that he's somebody that you can speak to? And, if one believes that the world is not influenced by how people get along, that is not true. It's true from the simplest aspects of life to the highest. And this is nothing new. If you look through history, then you see major mistakes being made because people did not believe the person telling them."
>
> "They come together and the idea is to exchange views and learn about things. Now, there again you see, I think that it's probably useful because people get to know one another but I'm not sure the discussions are all that useful. Probably sometimes they are and sometimes they're not […] I think that people are better informed as a result of the discussions. People, particularly business people, come with not much idea about the Middle East problem, and they're very much better informed. And I suppose, to the extent that whichever speaker they agreed with, they'd come away feeling that man is right. But that's about all I think."

A couple of final observations related to the earlier steering committee extracts concern the subtly implicit sense of cultural identity within the

Bilderberg group – an identity that almost certainly has some bearing on power relationships within, and beyond, the elite network. Davignon, perhaps unsurprisingly given the Atlanticist tradition of Bilderberg, emphasizes the American/European relationship and articulates the widely shared belief, among Bilderberg attendees at least, that the world "works better" when they get along. Elsewhere, however, the throw-away comments of interviewees reveal something more about power and identity within the group. In the fourth steering committee extract, for instance, there is the suggestion that obstacles to a consensus on free trade are likely to come from emerging market representatives or certain European countries. While these countries remain unnamed, the implication is that a broad consensus is conceivable – and, indeed, may exist – elsewhere in the group. At the very least, it's fair to suggest that this member of the steering committee has a sense of where the consensus lies and where it does not. Of course, this might be nothing more than an "insider's track" on the ongoing Doha free-trade talks but, nevertheless, the grouping of non-cooperative countries, and participants, in this way is of some interest.

Another example of this sense of identity is provided in the fifth steering committee extract, where a long-standing member of the group stresses the merits of diversity and points to the differences that exist on questions of, for instance, "how to deal with the Arabs." It seems reasonable to conclude from this that "Arabs" are not fully paid-up members of the transnational elite network – even beyond the transatlantic net-work – and, crucially, exist beyond any readily acceptable definition of diversity within such settings. It's suggestive of a strong sense of cultural identity within the group – an identity rooted in more than shared beliefs related to globalization and US/European relations. Indeed, the presence of increasing numbers of Islamic Turkish participants at Bilderberg in recent years has brought some of these cultural issues into sharp relief.

On the face of it, a pragmatic recognition of Turkey's strategic position in matters of security, of its desire to ascend to full membership of the EU, and of its attempts to come to terms with years of economic turbu-lence, make its senior business and political leaders obvious recipients of invitations to Bilderberg conferences. But, leaving aside the increased significance of Turkey in international policy matters, there remains the suspicion among Turkish attendees that "Western" agendas are very much driving the nature of such participation. Here, a frequent Turkish attendee expresses a view that is fairly typical of other Turkish participants within the network:

> "These forums, they're not official forums, but they do have orga-
> nizers or a group of lead people who usually set the agenda. These
> people tend to be from western economies and they come to
> the table with an agenda which looks at world issues – whether they're
> related to the Middle East problem, the Iranian situation, or
> the emergence of Russia as a new power (and the different angle
> that Putin brings to it) – [through a certain lens]. But then, as I
> said, most of these forums are created by western business or poli-
> tical leaders so the agenda, and the views, are slanted towards that
> western view."

It's worth pointing out here that Turkish Bilderberg delegates do not represent, in any sense, a hotbed of Islamic fundamentalism. They are all, without exception, free market advocates and "progressives" within the Turkish policy community. Central to the description of agendas as "Western" is the implication that they still reflect the interests of a largely Christian club – motivated by a particular brand of liberal inter-nationalism. That internationalists within the Turkish business and policy communities should highlight this aspect of Bilderberg membership is especially interesting because it suggests that some of the ties that con-tinue to bind the transnational elite together are, to this day, culturally exclusive. This has implications for the sense of standing enjoyed by certain participants which, in turn, has implications for the influence they wield within the elite network. At the very least, the ties appear to pro-vide a continuing, and significant, cultural bias to the interpretation of world political issues.

Bilderberg people

Not everybody gets to be invited to a Bilderberg conference. And with roughly half of all participants only ever attending one gathering, even fewer get to go back again. So what makes a Bilderberg person? What qualities do aspiring individuals have to exhibit in order to be invited and, more importantly, to remain *bona fide* members of the most elite organization of its kind in the world? Understanding the highly personal selection processes, and rules of engagement within the elite network, provides further critical insights into the discreet mobilization of bias in such arenas.

Responsibility for identifying new attendees generally falls to members of the Bilderberg steering committee. This group of approximately thirty-five individuals, typically comprised of two long-standing participants from each of the main countries represented, provides personal introductions to the annual conference. In the words of one former, well established, member of the group:

"You just decided who would be a good person to have."

This judgment is, of course, based on certain criteria and, after listening to other steering committee members opine on the subject, one could be forgiven for thinking that the process is highly meritocratic. Here, Martin Taylor, Viscount Davignon, and a financier, respectively, describe how they see the process working:

"People come to one's attention in all sorts of ways. I mean, sometimes, you see them somewhere at a meeting, they're very bright; sometimes you read something they've written[23] […] We're looking for people who are thoughtful or who are going to be influential. I don't think we're as good at talent spotting as you suggest."[24]

"So the way in which we pick people follows two simple principles: Firstly, we have to have enough people who have never been before so that we keep a momentum and don't simply have an old boys' club. And [we have to have] enough people who *have* been before who understand the format i.e. that you speak briefly, that you speak your mind, and that nothing will ever be quoted. Secondly, and taking into account the agenda, and knowing that ministers are very occupied and might call off at the last minute, you then try to look for people who would be interested in relation to their own ambition to share thoughts with others […] I don't think it's an accident because, when you ask a German, 'who do you think would be interested and who is going places in

German politics?' he will make his best assessment of the bright new boys and girls – people who are in the beginning phase of their career and who would like to get known – and the other people who would like to know them."

"It's not everyone who goes but there are a group of people who are more active and, of course, if you're one of the guys who is perceived as being interested, and over time you add some value, you are asked and invited by everyone. It's almost a self-fulfilling process."

What is surprising, perhaps, is the emphasis on intelligence and thought-fulness rather more than expertise, influence, and prominence, although these are, of course, required attributes. While accepting that the process is far from perfect, there is an underlying assumption that, in some way, those most able and suitable will emerge as obvious candidates for inclusion. This process of elite natural selection is facilitated by knowledge of the activity and interests of those concerned, and superimposed with judgments related to whether the individual is inclined to participate in personal networks of this kind. What is less frequently cited by steering committee members is the significance of personal contacts but, as the interviews revealed, new attendees are invariably known in some way to members of the steering committee. Here, two attendees explain how personal relationships were very much behind their invitation to the group:

"I know perfectly well why I was invited. Because Bilderberg was run by Peter Carrington, who I knew and who obviously thought I could contribute. When it ceased to be run by Peter and was run by somebody who I knew less well – Étienne Davignon – I wasn't invited."

"The steering committee member selects who will participate from each country. We have two or three participants – there is a limited number from each country […] I liked Selahattin Beyazit very much for our relationship and for bringing me into the group."

This process of personal recommendation is typical of most elite net-works. In fact, the clue is in the word *network*. There are no formal application procedures. Participants are selected because of the circles they move in and, depending upon their levels of personal influence within these circles, may find themselves progressively elevated into more prestigious and influential networks. It is a highly idiosyncratic process that, at each stage, is heavily dependent on elite "gatekeepers" whose role, it appears, is to preserve the *quality* of membership and ensure that the *right* people are selected. The following interview extract, from a Bilderberg attendee heavily involved in the organization of other elite network events, demonstrates the considerable discretion and power exerted by such people:

> "I form an arbitrary committee [to select participants] and I make sure the committee meets […] I think I play a greater role in this than anyone else. The trouble with these forums is that they get old, the same people go again and again, and you have to be ruthless and disband them. I mean, like this last time, there were half a dozen members of the current cabinet, three or four members of the shadow cabinet, the heads of the security services, and editors of the leading broadsheets, blah, blah […] I mean it's serious, if you want to talk about power elite. I played a big role. If I wanted to, I could invite everyone, but I don't."

Personal discretion, as a basis for participant selection, has obvious implications for bias within the elite network. It creates the potential for practices that may, for the most part unconsciously, lead to an alignment of preferences between elite participants. These practices might possibly include: aspirant members of the extended network attempting to ingratiate themselves with established members and gatekeepers, by adopting what they consider to be acceptable beliefs and worldviews; gatekeepers favoring personal contacts, whose opinions they know, and who are unlikely to reflect badly on them within such circles; and gatekeepers projecting a subjective sense of what they believe the network to stand for – a projection that would naturally result in the invitation of certain types of people. In short, forces of bias on both sides are likely to incline the membership of elite networks towards the maintenance of a general, and prevailing, form of consensus.

To some extent, the selection process is successful in muting certain forms of dissent even if that is not its purpose. And, notwithstanding a generally convivial atmosphere at such gatherings, it is clear that there are unspoken, and widely understood, limits to what is considered acceptable or otherwise. As one media participant observed:

> "I don't think there was anything people couldn't say, or didn't feel they could say. But if people did say radical stuff, the others would think, 'why the hell are they here?'"

When coupled with the norms, rules, and rituals that characterize elite engagement of this kind, it's easy to understand how one's personal capacity for conflict might be dampened. Adapting to the subtle requirements of elite engagement, and learning to present one's position in ways that are considered constructive, rather than confrontational, is a political skill that proves critical to long-term survival within elite circles. In the following extracts, two experienced Bilderberg politicos describe first, the value of personal diplomacy, and second, a more discreet and gentlemanly form of criticality – a criticality that is, in a sense, all the more damning within the confined and knowing context of the elite network.

> "I've always been on the inside, not the outside. I've pursued my arguments over policy within a policymaking framework, whether it's the government or the European Union. So I've always been on the inside, but I don't think that's deprived my views of their sharpness or edge, but you are playing by certain sets of rules. So you can't be completely iconoclastic and remain inside; if you are, you won't be inside for very long. So, to some extent, the people who say these organizations and networks muffle dissent, they have a certain something on their side. But they only muffle what I would call extreme dissent […] I believe in a consensual approach to things, to dialog, to talking things through, to try and reach broad agreement on the way ahead […] I speak diplomatically because I'm a diplomat. I've found, funnily enough, very often it works better than speaking in a highly hyped way."
>
> "[The debate] was never heated. It's an extremely urbane and sophisticated lot of people after all. I mean they're not the sort of people who are going to make a fuss. They'll probably go out

> muttering if they disagree […] 'did you hear what that fellow said,
> absolute rubbish', but they wouldn't say so in the forum.'"

Unwritten rules and informal codes of conduct are of particular interest
when considering the ways in which bias permeates elite organizations.
Ultimately, and consciously or otherwise, elite networks are discriminat-
ing based upon a collective sense of what, and who, is acceptable. Certain
approaches, and types of thinking, have become embedded in the collective consciousness of the inner network and their pervasiveness is
unquestioned by established members. Instead, they act as a subtle and
ever-present reference point for elite discourse and interaction. Network
survival and advancement is based less on the acceptance of such bias than
on the fundamental belief and absorption of it. Many of these beliefs are
attitudinal in nature, rather than ideological, which allows for a degree of
political diversity to exist. They are nonetheless significant to the substance of individual interactions and, specifically, the way ideological and
political differences are reconciled.

While some members of the elite network appear to have effortlessly
traversed the demands of membership, for others the process is seen as
more of a test. In the following interview extracts, two established
members of Bilderberg and numerous other elite networks describe their
perspectives of this process. The first describes how he feels he was initiated into international elite network via the social core of the Bank for
International Settlements – the formal and informal network for central
bank governors. The second describes the process in broader terms,
emphasizing the importance of cultural fit:

> "I just felt my way and learned how the international system
> works. Firstly, they always look to your knowledge, your approach,
> your policy direction. Secondly, they look to your power. If you
> have the two together in the international arena, you will be suc-
> cessful […] I had been checked by them, of course, for quite
> some time because the Bank for International Settlements in Basel
> is the training centre for central bank governors […] they are
> checking you. We had a formal meeting and then an informal
> meeting over dinner. First we started with six or seven governors at
> one table and then it extended to twenty or so, all of us just

choosing a subject and discussing [it]. I was checked several times for my intervention, my approach to issues, and also my personal relations."

"Yes, I think you are constantly being tested and you will only make it further if those who are already established members – let me say some of the key members of the network – recommend you. They say, 'you can rely on him, he'll do a good job, he's reasonable, he's going to listen, and he won't abuse any rules or whatever'. I think there's something to it. But I think what they want to see is that you're constantly tested about your independence – not in material terms but in intellectual terms."

It's interesting to note that, in the second quote, the participant stresses the significance of intellectual independence. This theme is common among established members of the transnational elite, who appear to suggest that what is prized, above all other things, is the ability to think both differently and abstractly – a theme that is returned to in the next chapter. The use of the word *independence* in this context is related to the participant's willingness to detach himself from the demands of his constituents or stakeholders in order to engage in a transcendental form of discourse. This is not something that everybody feels comfortable doing but, clearly, it is a trait that members of the inner network believe they themselves exhibit. An obvious question that arises, however, is whether we should see this willingness to transcend one's constituency in the interests of reaching consensus as a positive development, or whether the people who are seen as *independent* thinkers within such contexts are, in effect, reneging on an unwritten understanding with their constituents. And, critically, whether those who engage in this kind of activity do so purely because they believe that compromise is preferable to ideological stand-off or, more worryingly, for reasons of self-gratification and personal advancement.

Conclusion

In recent years, collaboration and consensus formation has emerged as a significant policy process underpinning, as it does, our notions of the legitimate in world politics. While consensus implies shared understanding and common ground, however, it is often not the product it appears to be. Frequently presented as a natural outcome of multi-stakeholder collaboration, for instance, consensus hints at a mystical coming together of diverse – and often irreconcilable – interests. Indeed, the soothing language of consensus has largely replaced talk of zero-sum confrontations and ideological differences, promising in their place pragmatism, progress, and a hitherto elusive "third way". But scratch at the veneer of consensus and we discover the meaningful nature of its form and, crucially, the forces of power that shape it.

Notwithstanding problems of definition, the language of consensus is a pervasive feature of elite networks where, despite claims of diversity, the selection of participants and the subtle expectations of membership incline the networks towards a broad consensual understanding. On the whole, consensus formation is not the stated – or even conscious objective – of such interactions; instead, it describes the underlying momentum and overall effects of such activity. The suggestion that discreet forms of power are, at least partly, responsible for driving this process is vehemently resisted by Bilderberg organizers – who, rather than deliberately attempting to mislead, simply reinforce the point that they themselves are unconscious of such effects. Indeed, they form part of an unquestioned appreciation of the way that things are done within such settings.

While Bilderberg members were largely unconscious of the dynamics of power described in this chapter, it's important to recognize that these forces are, in fact, among the more obvious within such settings. Far more subtle and persuasive forces shape compliance within the transnational elite context. Hierarchies of influence within the elite network, and an individual desire to belong, have a considerable bearing on the nature of eventual consensus. These effects are considered in greater detail in Chapter 5: *The seductive lure of elite membership*.

5

THE SEDUCTIVE LURE OF ELITE MEMBERSHIP

Florida, July 21, 2010. Prisoner 18330-424 is released on bail by the Coleman Federal Correctional Institution after serving twenty-eight months of a six-and-a-half year sentence for mail fraud and obstruction of justice. His release, despite persistent claims of innocence and personal injury, barely seemed credible just weeks earlier. A US Supreme Court ruling had, overnight, limited the application of federal law in corruption hearings against government officials and corporate officers and deferred a decision on whether to overturn the conviction, in whole or part, to the Seventh Circuit US Court of Appeals.[1] A motion for bail was granted, pending the appeal hearing, and a $2 million bond posted by friend Roger Hertog,[2] Vice-Chair Emeritus of New York-based investment giant Alliance-Bernstein LP, President of the Hertog Foundation, trustee of neoconservative think tank the American Enterprise Institute, and a former Bilderberg attendee. The defendant was said by close sources to be "hopeful and cautiously optimistic"[3] concerning the outcome of the appeal. At the very least, legal ambiguities over the extent to which jurors in the original trial were directed to use "honest services" judgments, and the subsequent granting of conditional bail, suggested that his chances of avoiding further incarceration were good. The Appeals Court, which sat on September 29, 2010 and heard representations from both prosecution and defense, was expected to rule within weeks. If the charges were upheld, the defendant faced the possibility of a return to prison and the certainty of numerous civil suits related to his governance practices while at the helm of the world's third largest newspaper publisher, Hollinger Inc. At stake was the badly damaged reputation and personal standing of one of the previously most established, influential, and connected members of the transnational elite network: Conrad Moffat Black or, as he is otherwise known, Lord Black of Crossharbour.

According to George Tombs, one of the few biographers to have personally interviewed Conrad Black, he is:

> "a sort of bad-boy celebrity […] someone who's had tremendous power and he's lost it […] Black, Radler and the other top executives [at Hollinger] didn't understand that investors had handed over their money in order to make more money, not to gain entrée to a 'private gentleman's club'."[4]

Tom Bower, another Black biographer, cites the traumas of childhood and persistent personality traits, such as a sense of entitlement and a lack of conscience, as explanations of excessive behavior,[5] and suggests that, for Black, "buying papers meant becoming a broker of influence. He particularly enjoyed the entrée they gave him to Bilderberg."[6] Indeed, Black, has made no secret of the benefits he's enjoyed as a consequence of his media control, commenting once that:

> "the deferences and preferments that this culture bestows upon the owners of great newspapers are satisfying. I mean, I tend to think that they are slightly exaggerated at times, but as the beneficiary of that system, it would certainly be hypocrisy for me to complain about it."[7]

Moreover, in a 1990 interview with *The Jerusalem Post*, he observed that:

> "if I had invested a comparable sum in a cardboard box factory [rather than a newspaper], I wouldn't be visiting the president and the prime minister and be getting quite so respectful a welcome."[8]

But, while access to the rich and powerful might be seen as a natural by-product of media ownership and control, it seems evident that it was an increasingly important preoccupation for Conrad Black. Hal Jackman, a distinguished Canadian businessman, public servant, former Bilderberg attendee, and one of many old friends and acquaintances left aghast by Black's apparent hubris as details of his legal case emerged, commented to journalists that "[Conrad is like] a parvenu drifting away from reality. I can't understand his priorities. He does too much entertaining and not enough business"[9] – "[he] is a tragedy, so highly intelligent and so carried away with his lifestyle. It's absurd [...] there was a disconnect between his intelligence and the way he lived."[10] Black's love of entertaining was so notorious that Canadian Duff McDonald, writing for society magazine *Vanity Fair*, was moved to comment,

> "By all accounts, the Blacks are drawn to power, preferably if it can be found in the presence of cocktails and canapés. Some even say it would be a mistake to think that Conrad Black's fiercest commitment is the Conservative Party. His commitment, rather, is to the dinner party."[11]

Whatever the reality of Conrad Black's appetite for the trappings of wealth, fame, and power, and there has been enormous speculation on the subject, there can be little doubt that the allure of elite membership is something that has played a significant role in his rise to prominence and subsequent fall from grace.

Black was born into a wealthy Canadian family. His father, George Black, was the President of Canadian Breweries, the largest brewer in the world at that time. George Black owned 22 percent of Ravelston, a private company with a shareholding that controlled the Argus Corporation – a conglomerate that, in turn, owned Canadian Breweries. Despite his Ravelston shareholding, and a remarkably successful tenure, George Black was forced to stand down over an industrial dispute that was hitting profits. According to Peter C. Newman, who wrote the first Black biography, "the feeling at home was that his father was fired under unfair circumstances and that's one of the things that motivated him over the years – the desire to avenge his father."[12] In a similar, albeit more melodramatic, vein, Tom Bower argues that, deeply affected by his father's depression, bitterness, and subsequent death, Black determined to "destroy his father's tormentors"[13] and use his inheritance to gain control of Argus. Whatever Black's personal motivations, however, it seems likely that these explanations are overstated.[14] For one thing, and notwithstanding Black's personal sense of frustration at Argus Corporation's lack of direction, he remained reasonably circumspect about his father's state of mind and health during this period.[15] He also maintained good relations with a number of his father's former associates and, during a period of considerable fracture on the Argus board, remained supportive of its then President John "Bud" McDougald. For his part, McDougald, a 23 percent owner of Ravelston and a dominant member of Canada's business elite, had over many years developed a good relationship with Conrad Black and his brother. It was McDougald who, for Black's twenty-first birthday, gained him entry to the exclusive Toronto Club – one of the three oldest private gentlemen's clubs in North America and renowned for its elite membership and strict non-disclosure rules. With a long list of rejected applications from prominent Canadians, Black recalled rather nonchalantly that "I don't believe that either of us [my brother or I] had ever made out an application."[16] Black is said by Tom Bower to have "practically worshipped McDougald's mystique and power"[17] and, certainly in his formative years, there is, perhaps, some truth to this.

The first seeds of Black's interest in taking control of Argus were sown in 1975, but it wasn't until McDougald's death in 1978 that the convoluted circumstances that might make such an eventuality possible were to present themselves.[18] By this time, Black had assumed seats on the Ravelston and Argus boards, and controlled a growing portfolio of Canadian newspaper, publishing, and mining interests. Considerable intrigue, in the wake of McDougald's death, led to Black being sidelined on the executive committee, which precipitated attempts on his part to garner support for a boardroom *coup d'état*. Critically, he succeeded in agreeing terms with McDougald's wife and her sister, the widow of yet another major Ravelston shareholder, which saw them sign over voting rights to their shares – a surprising development which enabled Black to oust the recently installed executive group. Then, in circumstances that attracted both admiration and considerable criticism, he bought the shares from the two women for just $18.4 million – a decisive investment that, ultimately, led to control of a corporation controlling $4 billion worth of assets, including major

Canadian businesses such as Dominion Stores, Hollinger Mines, and Massey Ferguson. Despite Black's protestations that the women were not the innocents they purported to be,[19] his actions caused alarm in certain quarters. The fact nonetheless remained: Conrad Black was suddenly a serious presence in Canadian business circles.

Much has been made of George Black's grooming of his son Conrad for business greatness, and of Conrad Black's own natural capitalist acumen – whether it be the purchase of his first shares at the age of eight or his stealing of school examination papers and selling them to fellow students.[20] It's certainly the case that he shared his father's zealous approach to cost cutting and had developed a personal taste for restructuring. Over time, Black divested what was to become Hollinger International of many of its original Argus assets and increasingly focused the organization on a strategy of newspaper acquisition. At its peak, the Hollinger newspaper group comprised 400 publications including prestigious titles such as *The Jerusalem Post*, *The Daily Telegraph*, and the *Chicago Sun-Times*. Despite this achievement, Black drew much criticism, not simply because of his, at times, abrasive and imperious personality, but also because of what he was seen by many to represent. Staunchly conservative and, in both personal and professional terms, unapologetically self-righteous and outspoken, he found himself with plenty of enemies. A long-running spat with then Canadian premier Jean Chrétien, which eventually resulted in Black rescinding his Canadian citizenship, is just one such example.[21] Elsewhere, critics poured scorn on the nature of Black's business activity, questioning its meaningful value. The Canadian intellectual John Ralston Saul, for instance, recently went as far as to suggest that Black was not a real *capitalist* since, instead of creating wealth, he dismantled it. In a blistering attack, he argued that

> "[Conrad Black] has only created one thing – one newspaper (*National Post*) – and even that he couldn't hold on to for more than three years. Apart from that, his career has been largely about stripping corporations. Destroying them. As the most visible voice for Canadian capitalism, he has had a negative effect on how most Canadians imagine the marketplace. In fact, I can't think of anyone who has had a more negative effect on how Canadians think of the market."[22]

Many critics argued that Black's business motivations were driven less by a concern for shareholder interests, and more by personal convictions and self-aggrandizement. In a 2004 *Financial Times* article, for example, Christopher Grimes and John Lloyd observed that

> "Conrad Black's business ambitions probably always ran second to his urge to be an intellectual force of conservatism. He did not want to simply own newspapers. He wanted to use them to help to reshape the political culture of his native Canada, and to influence that of the United States, Britain and Israel […] Financially, Black was never in Murdoch's league. Temperamentally, Murdoch is a leader of the dis-establishment; scornful of titles and institutions, while Black has been famously pro-establishment. Avid for a peerage, which he finally achieved, he created a company board that included both Henry Kissinger and Richard Perle. More importantly, he was always much more overtly politically motivated than Murdoch, who has supported governments of the centre-left and the centre-right, depending on his prevailing commercial judgments."[23]

Black's newspaper interests clearly enabled him to indulge political convictions and gain access to the most elite circles. He was – and still is – a member of many exclusive and prestigious clubs and enjoys his sense of standing within them. When asked by the *London Evening Standard* whether, in light of his legal travails, he was still welcome at the Garrick Club, he rather defensively retorted "Yes, I'm a member of the Garrick, the Athenaeum, White's, The Beefsteak and, what's that other one that belongs to a duke? Pratt's, and many other clubs besides, all around the world."[24] But, with the possible exception of his seat in the House of Lords, it is Bilderberg that represents the most coveted of his elite memberships. A clue to his affinity with members of the group is provided in his autobiography, *A life in progress*:

> "Although I had first met Henry Kissinger [elsewhere], it was at Bilderberg that I got to know him and a number of our other, future, directors and advisory board members […] Not having very satisfactory recollections of school days, nor being a very enthusiastic or observant university alumnus, Bilderberg has been

the closest I have known to that sort of camaraderie [... It gave] me, and many other regular participants, a powerful and entirely agreeable sense of community with some very talented and prominent people."[25]

Thanks to introductions from prominent Canadians Don MacDonald and Anthony Griffin, steering and advisory committee members, respectively, Black attended his first conference in 1981. By the mid- to late-1980s, he was a regular presence and making a distinct impression on proceedings. As one former Bilderberg attendee of some standing reflected:

"Conrad Black used to come, and he was always very forthright and offended an awful lot of people. But he liked it very much because he was on the stage and, of course, at that time was a very powerful figure [... At Bilderberg, the debate was never heated] unless Conrad made it so."

Despite this propensity for conflict, and a bombastic personality that visibly enjoyed humiliating opponents,[26] Black could be both eloquent and charming. In time, he became a member of Bilderberg's steering committee and was considered an extremely influential and entertaining character within the group. He has his fair share of detractors but, whatever his shortcomings, Black is known as a respected historian, having produced acclaimed biographies of Quebec's Maurice Duplessis and former US President Franklin Delano Roosevelt. He is universally regarded as erudite and highly intelligent. It would be unfair to suggest that he was anything other than an obvious recipient of the group's attention. For Black, however, the lure of elite membership was irresistible, and his association with senior members of the transnational policy elite something he took very seriously. Indeed, as former *Daily Telegraph* Editor Max Hastings put it, "[Conrad is] seldom unconscious of his responsibilities as a member of the rich man's trade union."[27] He went out of his way to maintain an association with the most prominent members of the elite and appointed many of them to his corporate and advisory boards. Over the years, these were to include Henry Kissinger, Lord Carrington, Margaret Thatcher, Valéry Giscard d'Estaing, Marie-Josée Kravis, Richard Perle, Dwayne Andreas, Evelyn de Rothschild, Giovanni Agnelli, Paul

Volcker, Zbigniew Brzezinski, and William F. Buckley Jr – all, incidentally, members or attendees of Bilderberg.

What exactly Hollinger International got out of these associations is unclear, but since, according to *The New York Times*, some were paid $25,000 for simply turning up to discuss world problems once a year,[28] its clear that Black felt them to be adding value of some sort. In the following extracts, the first from Hal Jackman, the second from a media sector Bilderberg attendee, it's obvious that such appointments were seen elsewhere as "vanity" decisions on the part of Black:

> "All these fancy people, [for example] Lord Carrington and Henry Kissinger. They are interesting people but made no contribution to the company. Never did. He could have had access to these people anyway if that's what he wanted[…]good conversations."
>
> "His board had lots of Bilderbergers – he liked having these people on his board. People like Kravis, Kissinger and Perle, largely political and no experience of business. He liked to be around the political 'rock stars'."

With Black's 1992 marriage to Barbera Amiel, where, at the reception, he was seated between Margaret Thatcher and the Duchess of York,[29] his elite social network widened still further and took on a more glamorous hue. Captivating high society on both sides of the Atlantic, the Blacks were prodigious hosts and networkers whose parties were to become the stuff of legend during the 1990s. As one frequent guest put it, "I don't think you can overestimate the enormous impact they've made in London[…]the dinners, the drinks parties, the general tycoonery. I hope that people in London don't forget what a fantastic time they've had because of Conrad."[30] In a similar vein, Peter Oborne of *The Spectator* described the impact of the Blacks on the London social scene and, in particular, the curious conflation of power, glamour, and business in evidence at their parties:

> "Every year the Blacks threw two parties, one at Christmas and one summer event, at their double-fronted 11-bedroom mansion in Cottesmore Gardens. Everybody who mattered at the time went: Margaret Thatcher, Henry Kissinger, Jimmy Goldsmith, James

Hanson, Arnold Weinstock, Jacob Rothschild, royalty, the play-
wright Tom Stoppard. Some of these, injudiciously as it turned
out, agreed to join the main Hollinger board. The luckier ones –
Peter Carrington, Robert Salisbury – got away with being made
directors of *The Telegraph*. As the Tories faded out, Labour ministers started to arrive, the indefatigable Peter Mandelson, David
Blunkett and other ministers eager to ingratiate themselves with the
Tory press. Prince and Princess Michael of Kent were assiduous in
attendance. In London, the Nineties belonged to the Blacks. They
were London's most glamorous power couple."[31]

When news of trouble at Hollinger first began to emerge, Black's initial
response was characteristically defiant, but he was eventually forced to
stand down as Chief Executive Officer at the end of 2003, by which time
rumors had begun to circulate at the true state of Hollinger's finances.
Then, in August 2004, the Securities & Exchange Commission produced
its report of the investigation by the Special Committee of the Board of
Directors of Hollinger International Inc., which created major tremors
among those closely affiliated with Black. The report was unequivocal in
its condemnation of the controlling Hollinger shareholders:

> "Hollinger was systematically manipulated and used by its control-
> ling shareholders for their sole benefit, and in a manner that violated
> every concept of fiduciary duty. Not once or twice, but on dozens
> of occasions Hollinger was victimized by its controlling share-
> holders as they transferred to themselves and their affiliates more
> than $400 million in the last seven years. The aggregate cash taken
> by Hollinger's former CEO Conrad M. Black and its former COO
> F. David Radler and their associates represented 95.2 percent of
> Hollinger's entire adjusted net income during 1997–2003."[32]

Black and Radler responded immediately with denials and counter-
accusations, but it was too late. The legal process was underway and there
appeared to be compelling evidence that Black, and fellow corporate
officers, had been appropriating Hollinger monies – an accusation that
Black continues to deny. Worse still, for many of those connected with
Hollinger, Black's misfortunes were dragging other members of the

transnational elite into the legal mire. The most severely affected was Richard Perle,[33] who came in for scathing criticism and, according to one attendee at the 2004 Bilderberg conference,

> "was lamenting the legal problems he had through his association with Black".

While most of the advisors appointed by Black were subsequently cleared of any wrongdoing or dereliction of duty, Conrad Black himself was suddenly *toxic* as far as the social and political elite were concerned. Many of the Blacks' closest acquaintances moved quickly to dissociate themselves, as Hal Jackman recalls,

> "They were all about as loyal as bankers, and yet he geared his social life around these and other fancy people."[34]

Black himself, before the legal proceedings against him were concluded, reflected,

> "The pressures that it is possible for such an organization [the US government] to bring are extremely severe. They are stigmatizing, they are isolating, and they affect your life in ways that casual observers couldn't immediately imagine. It became an extremely lonely, underdog existence […] I had to endure this long period of absolute relentless vilification in the press […] about which I could do nothing. I had to endure this extraordinary cataract of defamation and the end of normal commercial relationships. And, although I'm a reasonably wealthy person […] I had to manoeuvre to make sure I didn't run out of cash. I had a reasonable rate of assets but many of those quickly developed a compromised value and it became a serious challenge. And something of a lonely challenge in that some people 'fell away', but I will say that those who my wife and I regard as friends have behaved as friends, and we're inexpressibly grateful for that."[35]

As the legal tide turned against Black, with some former Hollinger directors and advisors offered immunity in return for testimony, the media vilification intensified and, among other things, resulted in the suggestion of rather undignified expulsions from exclusive clubs.[36] While some refused to confirm or deny such rumors, Black was, and is, personally incensed by reports of this kind – the vociferousness of his sense of injustice matched only by a determination to restore his personal standing and reputation. These themes, along with a stated desire to seek retribution from those he believes to have defamed him, have been a constant feature of his robust public defense:

> "It is in fact somewhat fulfilling to find yourself set upon in this way […] It is one thing to have an active social life with interesting people – which I think I could claim to have done. It is something to build a company and hold an interesting position and execute it reasonably competently – I think I could lay claim to that. But it is a very fulfilling thing when you are entitled to a reputation, to fight to retrieve it. I can't call it a noble cause but it is a just cause."[37]

Black is determined to clear his name and resume his position at the top table. Indeed, given reports of his efforts to restore friendships with prominent members of the elite network while in prison,[38] and high-profile examples of others who have returned "celebrity-like" to elite social circles, it seems likely that Black will become a presence, once more, in polite company. Whether he can resume his position within Bilderberg, however, which has historically preferred those with tarnished reputations to avoid embarrassment and gracefully "fall on their swords," remains to be seen.[39]

What makes the Conrad Black story particularly interesting from the perspective of an understanding power in elite circles is that he is someone for whom elite membership was a right afforded at birth. He could obviously have been better placed, but it's difficult to believe that his social standing had any real bearing on his sense of security within the elite network. As Hal Jackman observes,

> "It's an odd thing to say but Conrad has all the characteristics of a parvenu. He needs to impress the people he is impressed by; everybody else can go hang. That, I think, is what has brought him down. Very odd, because, you know, he was not born above a shop."[40]

And while it's clear that Black was anything other than characteristically imperious and forthright in elite company, and would certainly have been one of those shaping opinion rather than being shaped by it, he nevertheless coveted his place in the network. Bilderberg was, and no doubt is, very important to him. He is a man who, when faced with the prospect of having to rescind his citizenship in return for membership of an elite club – the House of Lords – did so. If someone of Black's intelligence, wealth, power, and standing is unable to resist the seductive lure of elite membership, we can only guess at the influence it exerts over those not blessed with the same advantages. The fundamental question, of course, apart from why people should be so lured in the first place, is what the implications are for discourse and consensus within such environments. A possible indication is provided in an article written by Black's wife, Barbara Amiel, herself a one-time Bilderberg attendee. Entitled "Why women marry up," it's as insightful as it is succinct:

> "Power is sexy, not simply in its own right, but because it inspires self-confidence in its owner and a shiver of subservience on the part of those who approach it."[41]

Hierarchies of influence

Elite networks are frequently presented as exclusive clubs of the rich and powerful, who effortlessly intermingle, fraternize, and network with one another. And to some extent, it's clear – as described in chapter four – there are forces at play that naturally create a degree of harmony within such settings. But it is a mistake to think of elite networks as hubs of shared interest with little in the way of personal or political differences. Transnational elite networks are, after all, comprised of diverse individuals, and first appearances can be deceptive – even to those involved. Moreover, access to elite networks does not infer some kind of uniform status on all participants. Hierarchies of influence within the elite community have potentially profound implications for membership and the extent of individual receptiveness to prevailing forms of consensus.

What becomes clear when speaking with Bilderberg attendees is that, while few would openly admit it, they are acutely aware of their standing in the elite network. The first three extracts that follow are from interviews with aspiring Bilderberg participants and reveal the individual's immediate sense of their own place and importance *vis-à-vis* others in the elite community. The fourth extract is from the diaries of British politician Paddy Ashdown.

> "You look at them and you get to understand it. Who is there? Who is a 'regular' and who is there for just a year? There's no problem with that."
>
> "Well, I mean, every time a group like this convenes, you look around the room and, for a given time in the world, you can almost say, 'out of these hundred people, these ten guys are important to me'."
>
> "Is there a hierarchy? Yes, I'm at the bottom of it."
>
> "At two o'clock [I went] to Heathrow to catch a flight to Santiago de Compostela for the Bilderberg Conference – described to me as 'fifty people who run the world and twenty hangers-on'. No doubt which category I'm in!"[42]

A key factor driving individual inclination to accept invitations to parti-cipate in elite networks is an understanding of the reputational status of the community – a direct consequence of its member composition. Pro-minent individuals are not simply comparing the standing of other attendees with their own, they are subconsciously attempting to enhance or preserve their status. The most elite of networks have no problem attracting new members provided they enjoy the patronage of individuals perceived by new entrants to have a higher – or, at the very least, equal – personal standing. Of course, this simple fact is often obscured by explanations related to the value of the exercise, but it seems likely that a good pro-portion of any perceived value for new entrants is related to the benefits of enhanced association. In the following interview extracts, the first with Martin Taylor, the second with a member of various elite policy forums, it is interesting to note the ease with which elite networks attract new participants.

> "I've never needed to sell it [Bilderberg] to anybody, is all I can say. The only reason I've ever heard somebody say that they didn't want to come was that they couldn't on the dates concerned.

I mean, people are attracted, I think, by sheer curiosity at being in a group like this and hearing certain things from the horse's mouth, as it were. And I think that the personal relations that are formed there, not in the sense of some ghastly freemasonry or some sort of secret society – it is not that at all – it's just the fact that people get the chance to know each other as individuals rather than as people that they come across in their government or business careers."[43]

"Ditchley is a case in point. I don't know, you'd have to ask a number of people who go there, but they have no lack of takers. And since they take place at weekends, they presumably think it's a worthwhile use of their weekend to do that. They like meeting the other people – they find it intellectually challenging to discuss the subjects that are under discussion. They find it, I think, very welcome to do so in a way that is not on the record, which is completely private."

The benefits of network membership are explored in more detail in chapter six, on elite networks, but it is important to recognize at this stage the discreet, and highly personal, lure of elite circles to those concerned. To fraternize, or be seen to fraternize, with some of the most influential people in the world serves as an extraordinary psychological aphrodisiac. It propels the participant into the most revered of circles and, by implication, increases the reverence with which such individuals are perceived. The capacity to acclimatize quickly, coupled with the ability to network naturally rather than in a contrived and awkward manner, are critical personal qualities to possess. Entry to the most elite of these networks requires overcoming severe personal tests of nerve and self-consciousness – something that, for many, is easier said than done. In the following interview extract, for instance, a former Bilderberg attendee recalls a harrowing personal experience caused by a realization of who he was dealing with at the elite foreign policy think tank, the Council on Foreign Relations.

"Some woman came to see me, American, terribly flattering and said 'we want to invite the four ablest people under thirty-five in Europe to come and speak to us – would you do it?' I felt flattered, so I said 'yes'. And then, about a week before [I was due to speak],

I looked them up and found out they were a really terrifying, prestigious organization. The previous speakers had been the President of Turkey and the Deputy PM of India. I completely panicked and spent the whole of the next week with friends trying to think of something to say. And, boy, was I relieved when it was over [...] But I was interested in people so, when an intelligent, Ivy League-type woman working for the Council on Foreign Relations came along, I, like a complete idiot, was flattered into saying I'd do it. I've always respected them, but I've never been back, never done anything, and wasn't a member."

These reputational effects are, of course, difficult to quantify, and vary by individual attendee. It seems evident, however, that the more peripheral the participant, the more immediate the sense of fear and anxiety. As someone who was surprised to be invited to the Bilderberg conference confided,

"I was a bit freaked out. I was asked if I'd heard of Bilderberg and I said 'no'. I thought I'd heard of some slightly shady conspiracy theory stuff, but that was really hazy. So, yes, I was a little freaked out. In fact, a friend of mine called who I hadn't spoken to for about three months and said, 'how are you doing?' And I said, 'I'm freaking out, I've just been invited to Bilderberg'. And he started laughing and said that's absolutely fantastic."

These feelings of trepidation are, if anything, exacerbated by exposure to the network. Here, a number of media and academic Bilderberg attendees recollect rather isolated and intense experiences of their time at the conference.

"I didn't really contribute to any of the panels. I could have done, it wasn't a decision, I just ended up not doing it. I made a decision, which was that I was going to do everything I could there, that this is probably a once in a lifetime opportunity for me. [But] it was very hard work, there was very little downtime, in fact, there was no downtime. Every meal was with people, and they went on quite late. There was one afternoon that was supposed to be free, or you could go on this organized thing. Someone said that it's a really nice thing to do so I thought, I'll go and do it, but actually I just wanted to lie down on my bed and recover […] I didn't know a lot of these people, and it was actually very hard for me because I'm not part of their networks. I wasn't familiar with them."

"I didn't participate in the discussions. Everybody was chatty and open or, at least, they gave you the impression of being chatty and open […] but I was thinking, 'who the fuck do I talk to?' I mean it's slightly difficult to just sidle up to Kissinger at the bar."

"I settled in my room with this excitement. I wore my best suit, put on my most stylish tie, and went down. My excitement intensified when I looked around me. I was surrounded by people who almost constantly made it in newspaper and television head-lines […] I was dead tired at the end of the three days. I got out of one meeting to go into the next. I needed to participate, ask questions, and watch attentively. Everyone took the meetings ser-iously. Nobody would leave the sessions to go outside, stroll around, and have coffee."[44]

The desire to make a good impression, to be invited back, to be affirmed in some way by those we hold in high regard, might be seen to be a natural enough human response. But, within the context of the collaboration that is taking place, these personal tendencies have important implications – notably related to the unconscious absorption and dissemination of domi-nant forms of consensus. Chapter 7 considers these implications more thoroughly – at this point, it is enough to observe that the overwhelming sense of not being worthy is usually enough to ensure that peripheral members are either not heard, or more pertinently, are heard saying the right things. In this interview extract, a one-time participant describes how feelings of alienation were reinforced at the conference:

"I got to talk to people I wouldn't have had access to normally, or rarely at least. [I remember] a guy said to me 'I wouldn't talk to you normally'. As I say, it was quite difficult for me because everyone was of a quite high status. It's difficult when you go up to people and say 'what do you do?', and they respond 'I'm the Queen of the Netherlands' […] it can be pretty hard work."

Even for more prominent individuals, invited into networks for the first time, the personal demands of socializing and networking are not easy to deal with. In the three extracts that follow from interviews with an international banker, a respected newspaper editor, and a policy expert, there is acknowledgement, sometimes defensive, of a personal inability to perform well in such contexts.

> "Intervening in debates and talking, I'm not good at that [...] I don't do that. And I doubt whether I talked enough there. I doubt whether I strutted my stuff, such as it was, so I guess they didn't invite me back because I didn't contribute very much [...] I'm not very 'clubbable', I suppose, I wasn't much good from their point of view [...] I do remember the number of recently retired prime ministers and presidents seriously impressed me, and also made me feel quite shy. Lloyd Bentsen, for instance, who had been US Treasury Secretary [...] I remember thinking 'shit, this man in the cowboy boots is the US Treasury Secretary'."
>
> "It wasn't a world I enjoyed, and I didn't go out of my way to do it [...] And since then, I haven't sought it and they haven't sought me out."
>
> "Once I'd been there, quite frankly, I thought it wasn't what I thought it was going to be. I wouldn't be concerned if I was never invited again. Of course, there's a higher concentration of important, influential people than there might otherwise be, but I've met these people in many other forums and events [...] I personally didn't get much out of it, but I'm sure others did. I'm not good at networking."

It is also evident that not all business entrants to the network feel as confident as each other discussing political issues. Some, despite being attracted to the network, are "star-struck" in the presence of revered politicians, and feel that they have little to add to the discussion. Others simply don't have the degree of interest in the subjects under discussion that would enable them to feel comfortable interjecting. Indeed, political attendees are often perceived by their business counterparts to hold an advantage – related to both the subject of discussions and the skills required to hold court in such settings. Here, three Bilderberg financiers and industrialists reflect on the personal demands of elite membership and the importance of transcending parochial interests in order to engage with macro-political discussions.

> "I do think an awful lot of the people who make it in these competitive public life things are very […] they're actors, and they need stripes on their shoulders, they want to be seen in places and have ticks in the box. We all want a bit of that. I'm not very strong on that. I've got other vanities and weaknesses, but I think being seen in those circles [is not necessarily one of them]. I don't know, why do politicians become politicians? They like the buzz of being in Whitehall, the feeling of feeling close to the centre of things, it's part of all that […] So I think the political classes [have a natural advantage in these networks]. I mean, take Peter Mandelson, he always goes to these things and he's brilliant at them. He's absolutely spectacularly good. Now why would he carry on going? I guess he gets stuff out of it. Yes, you get an opportunity to relax with people who you [wouldn't] normally. And you can talk at great length and talk seriously […] backstage gossip. Well, that's not me because I don't do it for a living. I'm not in politics for a living. For me, I get educated. That's probably a good thing really, it's probably a very good idea for me to have some idea as to what the guy responsible for world trade is thinking. And Pascale Lamy always used to come."

> "There are people who are less interested – either they don't have the academic background or they don't feel comfortable in this kind of thing. It's quite an intellectual discussion that you have. Everybody tries to be as intelligent and as well informed as possible, you know, it's obvious. And you get into this kind of mood where you ask questions that you wouldn't normally do in business circles. And some people find that this is all nice words, but there is no action. Or they don't feel comfortable in these kinds of gatherings. But the primary thing is that you have to be open to many of these issues. If you are a businessman, running a big company in Texas or wherever, are you really interested in talking about the Palestinian–Israeli conflict? Many years ago we had a lot of discussion between the Greeks and Turks about Cyprus. Now, how was

this relevant to many of us? They talk now about Georgia and Russia, and some people say, well, you know, I'll leave that to the politicians."

"There are people who are not interested in it – it's as simple as that. Who ask themselves, is there any benefit, any added value, for me? And maybe come to the conclusion it's not. On the other hand, I must say, if you [do] become part of it, it makes you much better informed and it's a very enriching experience."

Despite these challenges, it's clear that aspirant members of the elite network go to some lengths to be fully accepted. This process takes time – often several years – and, for some who appear to have made it, it's not entirely clear whether they feel themselves to be comfortable in their seats. As the interviews for this book unfolded, it became obvious that the more established the member of Bilderberg, the more comfortable they were discussing the subject. Other members of the network – irrespective of the number of years they had been in attendance – were often coy and, at times, defensive on the subject. Indeed, these responses became a reliable indicator of the standing of the participant in the network. In the following extract, it is interesting to note how the participant became nervous mid-way through his sentence. First, and despite several years of attendance, he states that he is not a full member of Bilderberg. Second, in an attempt to check himself and protect against the accusation that he is over-sharing details of the group, he tries to broaden the discussion away from the subject. This evasiveness demonstrates the insecurity of some participants and their desire to not be seen breaking rules.

"One thing I want to state is that I have participated in Bilderberg a number of times. I am not a full member of Bilderberg. I would be happy to just cross out Bilderberg from this […] basically, I just used Bilderberg as an example. I've been to other forums as well."

Other established members of the group were reluctant to be drawn on the subject of how new attendees ingratiated themselves with more powerful members of the network, but, despite themselves, provided some insights into what is required. Here, two regular Bilderberg attendees, one of whom is now certainly a full member, reflect on the personal requirements of membership. The first highlights the initial significance of role-playing; the second emphasizes the importance of not questioning the underlying philosophy or purpose of the group.

> "Well I don't want to go that deep into [the] psychology [of why people do the things that they do]. I think you just get accepted after two or three years because you are part of the group, and each time so many are new. Actually, it doesn't take a lot of time to become one of the senior people there […]. But I don't think you have to […] it's not that a young man has to go through on their knees to be accepted; no, no, you are immediately part of the group. I'm just saying before you really start, well [you're] playing a certain role and you're part of the integration elements. It probably takes some years, there's no doubt about that."
>
> "Nobody is going to change my way of thinking, my approach, [or] my wishes. I learned lots of things. Maybe there are some effects of that but, for my part, I got lots of benefits: I learned lots of things; I met several people; and established good relations. It's an opportunity […] It's a golden opportunity. Mark [me], if you say this is the Bilderberg meeting and there are some question marks in your mind, and you approach the meeting in that way, it's quite different. But I didn't do that."

Given the general defensiveness of interviewees on this subject, it seems reasonable to suggest that the line of questioning was perceived as threatening in some way. Participants are clearly reluctant to concede that they've ingratiated themselves, or had their views or opinions compromised by efforts to gain favor. But, as subtle as these processes no doubt are, it seems evident that this is precisely what is occurring. To admit to compromising oneself in return for membership would be embarrassing and possibly overstating the extent of the compromises that such members feel themselves to have made. Elite participants see these processes as part and parcel of everyday social interaction and, for the most part, do not perceive any political significance to their actions. Similarly, organizers seem largely unaware of these mechanisms of compliance at work within the network, but this should not detract from their very real existence. They may be unconscious, but their effects are by no means random.

Elitism and the elite network

Unsurprisingly, perhaps, elitist attitudes and behavior are an integral part of the functioning of elite networks. The most obvious manifestations of these elitist tendencies relate to the selection and acceptance judgments made by members and invitees. In the following extracts, two influential elite participants emphasize the importance of "quality" to such considerations – an overtly elitist concept when one considers its application to individuals.

> "I think, probably, I may be being cynical in my premise but they all got something, [or should I say] get something out of it. But you need high-quality people."
> "But it was a different sort of person [at Bilderberg], I mean, there were the 'Nods' – David Rockefeller, Henry Kissinger, Agnelli [and] those sorts of people – smart Europeans and top people […] Oh yes, the 'Nods' like the 'Nods' […] they wouldn't come if they thought the people there were not comparable to them, if you see what I mean. So, you had to keep up the quality, quality in that sense, of people who came, otherwise it wouldn't have worked at all […] Is that elitism? I don't know what elitism means […] I think people felt it was a compliment to be asked. You were joining a rather superior group of people and, I suppose, in that sense it was elitist. But they were rather superior people."

A common understanding among members of the elite is that they are, for the most part, invited into the network because of who, or what, they represent. It is their position of responsibility – or *superiority* – that marks them out as potential participant material. An invitation to join the most elite of networks is a reflection and affirmation of one's standing in this regard. In the four extracts that follow, with a variety of business, political, and media representatives, it's clear that importance, prominence, responsibility, and influence are seen as critical factors determining individual attractiveness to the elite network.

> "I'm not terribly sure whether it's elite power or statutory power, because the people who are there, in groups like Bilderberg and

the World Economic Forum, are not invited because they're Tom, Dick, Harry, or Ahmed. They're invited because of what they represent."

"There is a bit of flattery, though, isn't there? If you're asked to join, I mean, if you think about the people concerned, who go to these things, they're all quite important – particularly in the political and industrial/financial field. You're flattered if you're asked."

"I was a successful entrepreneur. I had my own successful businesses and I was doing a lot else besides […] I was very famous, and everyone read about me. I was the 'pick of the month' […] and, when Mrs Thatcher came to power, she held a party and there I was with a small group of other entrepreneurs, various permanent secretaries, and the chairmen of numerous nationalized industries, and that was it. It was just the kind of thing that happened to me then. That was my moment."

"[Bilderberg] had a motive in setting this up and supporting it, and this affected things. On the selection of people, it seemed to me, on the occasions I went, that they liked to select people who were in some way prominent."

Receiving an invitation to join one of the more esteemed gatherings is therefore both flattering and humbling: flattering in the sense that one is clearly recognized as a successful and pre-eminent presence within a particular domain; and humbling because one gains access to a higher-order level of influence within which one must, once again, seek to establish credibility. This is a critical consideration because, while the position of influence one occupies may be enough to warrant an invitation, to be welcomed back year after year requires establishing one's personal credentials with established members of the network. This is, in some senses, a test of how one responds to the challenge of being oneself in such settings, rather than the representative of an organization or constituency. Failing to recognize this and, importantly, failing to demonstrate a degree of openness and free thinking in one's interactions is a chief reason cited by members for exclusion from the network. Here, three well established Bilderberg attendees, including two steering committee participants, emphasize the significance of adding value to the network – a value specifically related to one's ability to think transcendentally beyond stated facts and positions.

"In that kind of gathering, you cannot sit on the fence or just stay in line; you have to say something. This something should be a contribution of new ideas or new dimensions that will give other people, the audience, something. Otherwise, going there, having lunch, dinner, sitting around, listening and saying things like 'it's been lovely, what a lovely view'. It doesn't work. You have to be active in that sense."

"Well, it's clear, if you're not invited again there are a few things to consider: did you add value, and did people feel that you were engaged? If you spend three days [there] and never open your mouth at the conference or in the evening, at dinners or lunches, if you sit somewhere apart, which happens, you know, then people say 'he's not a very interesting guy'. This, in these circles, is what counts. It's a little bit like university or school. It's about being an interesting discussion partner. It's not whether you're important or rich. It's a question of whether you are attractive and whether it's interesting to talk to you. If I were to boil it down to one thing, I would say it's the intellectual curiosity which is the most important thing. You must be intellectually curious and you must respond to the intellectual curiosity of others. You must at least have some kind of fresh view or your own opinion. If you quote all the time from CNN or comment constantly on what the FT is writing, people are likely to say 'well, we don't need him, he's not adding any creativity, anything new, no dynamism, nothing that makes him an attractive discussion partner'."

"I expressed myself, I spoke, and I asked questions – not only in the formal sessions, but the informal ones. It was a channel for increasing the credibility of yourself, your institution, and your country [...]. If you were not a devoted participant, that is, a participant who opens their mouth and asks, hopefully, good questions or provides good answers, or whatever, and participates in the debates in sessions but also out of session, maybe over dinner, they would say, 'he's a very dull person, obviously very little to say. We don't want to see him again'."

In a similar vein, the journalist and writer Jon Ronson, who interviewed a number of Bilderberg organizers, recounted the following anonymous account[45] – made by a former steering committee member – of Margaret Thatcher's introduction to the group in 1975:

> "The invited guests must sing for their supper. They can't just sit there like church mice. They are there to speak. I remember when I invited Margaret Thatcher back in '75. She wasn't worldly. Well, she sat there for the first two days and didn't say a thing. People started grumbling. A senator came up to me on the Friday night, Senator Mathias of Maryland. He said, 'This lady you invited, she hasn't said a word. You really ought to say something to her.' So I had a quiet word with her at dinner. She was embarrassed. Well, she obviously thought about it overnight, because the next day she suddenly stood up and launched into a three-minute Thatcher special. I can't remember the topic, but you can imagine. The room was stunned. Here's something for your conspiracy theorists. As a result of that speech, David Rockefeller and Henry Kissinger and the other Americans fell in love with her. They brought her over to America, took her around in limousines, and introduced her to everyone."

The expectation that aspiring members of the network should somehow impress from the outset is, perhaps, a little unrealistic for the vast majority of first-time attendees – not least because many of them are busy trying to ingratiate themselves with members of the network by being anything other than free-thinking. Moreover, there is another problem with the suggestion that prospective members are being vetted according to the demands outlined above, and this relates to those who do the vetting. To highlight certain qualities in this way is to suggest that they are not only of value to the network, but are very much in evidence among the more established members of the group. In short, this is how established members of the network view themselves. Irrespective of whether it is free thinking or openness that is being valued, what established members of the network are unconsciously doing is selecting people they consider to be like themselves. This is an established, albeit unconscious, exercise in social acceptance, and has profound implications for debate and consensus in such settings.

One aspect of this exercise that requires some mention is the pervasive element of patricianism to elite activity. One's upbringing and a perceived degree of refinement, learning, manners and, where possible, nobility are always valued commodities within such settings. Of course, not all Bilderberg steering committee members represent nobility and, it must be stated, there is no contradiction between patricianism and a commitment to public service, but certain attributes are definitely considered advantageous to network membership. Here, Conrad Black describes the qualities of another Bilderberg attendee – Andrew Knight – and, in so doing, reveals his rather privileged sense of Knight's disadvantages:

> "Andrew Knight, an ever youthful and attractive-looking man, enjoyed a huge prestige as editor of *The Economist* […] He was almost universally respected and very influential, but he had a modest salary and no accumulated means."[46]

This could, of course, be just a characteristically pompous observation on the part of Black, but it was clear in the interviews conducted for this book that elitist and, for want of a better word, rather patronizing attitudes were in evidence – not from all participants, but certainly among a good proportion – and most especially with those positioned towards the center of the network. In the following three interview extracts, for instance – the first with the organizer of numerous elite gatherings, the second with Viscount Davignon, and the third with another Bilderberg steering committee member – a number of observations can be made. A commitment to public service is still considered, in patrician circles, an honorable pursuit and continues to color the composition of practically all policy elites. It should not be entirely surprising, therefore, to find elitist thinking, behavior, and structures at work within such communities: note, for instance, the appeal of patricianism to the first interviewee. Similarly, Étienne Davignon sees those who resist globalization as failing to grasp the bigger picture and lacking the capacity for understanding of the more *enlightened* members of the internationalist community (whose responsibility is to better explain its requirement). And finally, the rather sage-like comments of the third interviewee reflect the conservative outlook of those to be found at the center of the network, where there is suspicion of characteristics such as haste, ambition, and single-mindedness.

"I definitely have 'pure and ethical' writ large throughout my life. I definitely had views about trying to make the world a better place for the majority, even if I'm just 'pissing in the wind' – only making a slight dent. So, patrician, I smile, I quite like the idea of being a patrician."

"[To believe that we are a small group of 'internationalists' beset by those who can't see the bigger picture] would be very vain and arrogant. If they can't see the bigger picture, it's because you've done a pretty poor job of explaining why it's important and why it's significant for their daily life, for development, for economic growth. To blame people who don't understand, you first have to blame people who can't explain."

"The older you get, the more developed your capacity to detect very special deformations in another person's personality. Of course, this is true. We all act and react differently, and in the world of business, as much as in politics, there are people who think they cannot fail, who think they know it all, who've seen it all and who are what I call 'advice-resistant'. And they very often fail miserably in the end. There are others who soak up everything like a sponge and try to digest it, and probably come to better decisions. There may be situations where this 'seen it all' type may do better for short periods because they just do their thing, but that will not carry them through a longer period of time."

Most significant of all, however, there is an implicit understanding that elites are a natural and, for the most part, desirable response to the complexity of contemporary societal and political challenges. As the following Bilderberg attendee put it:

"As long as people get there because they're intelligent, well read, well informed, sensitive, etc. [it's fine with me]. I think the world has always been ruled by elites, but the question is whether the elites are well qualified."

Throughout the interviews conducted for this book, there was very little questioning of the legitimacy of elite structures and power in contemporary policy formation. Instead, there was acknowledgment of the inadequacies of existing structures and an unspoken understanding that elites have always been responsible, in one way or another, for shaping our appreciation and experience of the world – and, moreover, that they always would be. To that end, there is no real questioning of whether elites are legitimate or good – they are simply a fact of life. The more pertinent question for elite participants, or those who think about such things, is whether the elites that we have are the most appropriate.

Conclusion

The idea that elite forums and networks are, in some way, permeable and meritocratic clubs of free thinking simply does not stand up to close scrutiny. Notwithstanding the good intentions of organizers, and a highly intelligent member composition, elite policy networks are structurally biased at source and, consciously or otherwise, have the effect of amplifying their biases.

While it's not possible to state with any degree of certainty whether the bias is the product of conscious intent on the part of organizers, or whether it is a remnant of earlier objectives and structures, it seems reasonable to summarize that it has become a largely unconscious driver of consensus. Certainly the compliance of new entrants to the network is the product of complex processes that unconsciously result in adapted preferences and beliefs – indeed, new members are reluctant to concede that their preferences have altered at all despite, as will be seen later in the book, recognizing the value of the information and learning available in such settings.

Establishing oneself when invited into elite circles becomes an important preoccupation for aspiring participants although, admittedly, this concern varies by individuals, and tends to be more acute the more peripheral one is in relation to the core of the network. It is a remarkably personal motivation for those concerned and, within the context of groups like Bilderberg, is inextricably linked to one's own sense of worthiness and enlightenment. To be rejected, no matter how seemingly unconcerned the individual, is a personal slight implying social or intellectual failure at the very highest of tables. The rejection is, of course, presented by elite networks as a desire for "new blood," fresh thinking, and general dynamism, but ultimately it is a reflection of the networks' belief that the entrant did not fit in or add value. The frequent characterization of such people as "dull" is, in many ways, the ultimate elitist dismissal.

Not all elite policy networks are consciously designed as private clubs of tightly knit individuals. Bilderberg, in particular, goes to some lengths to turn over its attendance. But such dynamism really takes place only at the periphery of the network; over time, the more permanent members, its advisory group and steering committee members, can be seen to have formed a "club" of sorts – a club that, consciously or otherwise, influences the collective perception of common sense and enlightened thinking within the group. For those entering the network, this thinking is the pretext for ingratiating oneself and establishing network membership. In a bizarre sense, it has become the mechanism of its own unconscious dissemination.

6

ELITE NETWORKS IN WORLD AFFAIRS

Sun Valley, Idaho, July 8, 2010. Eric Schmidt, Chairman and Chief Executive Officer, Google Inc., member of President Obama's Council of Advisors on Science and Technology, Board Chairman of the New America Foundation,[1] member of the Council on Foreign Relations, and notable Bilderberg attendee of recent years, informs members of the press that Google intends to resolve its ongoing privacy and censorship disputes with the Chinese government. Moreover, it expects to have its critical operating license for the country renewed.[2] The comments were made to a select group of reporters at a private briefing session during the exclusive Allen & Co. conference – an annual gathering of the world's media, communications, and technology elite – and provided a welcome opportunity for journalists to report something of substance from the event. Consistent with its carefully cultivated aura of mystique, and the time-honored protocol of most elite networks, Allen & Co. participants are broadly discouraged from fraternizing with members of the press. For their part, journalists content themselves by observing from the sidelines, exchanging pleasantries with mogul participants, and reporting conference trivia of one kind or another. As the *Los Angeles Times* reported:

> "once again the industry's top executives are gathering in Sun Valley, Idaho for investment bank Allen & Co.'s 28th annual

gathering of the media elite […] Hiding in the bushes hoping to break some news or at least score some gossip will be a handful of reporters including the folks from CNBC. For one week, media executives get to see what life is like for Brad Pitt and Angelina Jolie. Instead of being asked if they are having another baby or if their marriage is on the rocks though, they get asked if they're doing any deals. The executives chuckle and walk on since Allen & Co., while loving all the attention their little shindig gets, discourages attendees from mingling with the press. In fact, last year they even made the bar at the resort where the conference is held off limits to reporters […] That's what life is like for the press at Sun Valley. They see someone, write where they are going, and then try to figure out what they might be talking about […] A highlight of last year was Universal Pictures chief Ron Meyer accidentally driving off in BET founder Bob Johnson's rental car. Yes, lots of deals have been born out of the conference including the marriage of Comcast and General Electric Co.'s NBC Universal. However, that wasn't learned until after the fact, which no doubt left the media wondering how they missed the moment."[3]

Indeed, so unequivocal is the insistence on non-disclosure for participants that newcomers to the event, desperate to ingratiate themselves and be welcomed into its elite fraternity, see it as an explicit condition of entry. As an acquaintance of one of the authors, approached to comment anonymously on his recent perspectives of the event, rather sheepishly responded,

> "Listen, on the Allen Conference, part of the deal is that we're really not allowed to discuss anything about the conference. So […] I'm really sorry that I can't be more helpful. Maybe I'll get invited to another one of these conferences that qualifies."

On closer inspection, however, the non-disclosure rule is somewhat difficult to understand when one considers the nature of the conference itself. It is, to all intents and purposes, an industry event, albeit one attended by its most senior representatives. If we accept as a starting point that those in attendance are reluctant to gift competitive advantage to their rivals, and that most of the corporations represented have share-holders to consider, it's reasonable to question just how significant any exchange of information is at the event. Notwithstanding the preference of prominent individuals to avoid embarrassing revelations related to their bar-room antics or "off-the-cuff" remarks, and the desire of organizers to create an informal and collegiate atmosphere, the rule almost certainly has more to do with reinforcing a sense of club-like exclusivity than any practical attempt to control sensitive information flows. Indeed, the private exchange of sensitive information, were it to occur, might lead to accusations of insider trading – something corporate executives are, for obvious reasons, keen to avoid. And the suggestion that the non-disclosure rule allows participants to fraternize freely, avoiding unnecessary speculation about their activities, is clearly nonsense given that those most immediately affected are present at the event. As a mechanism for facilitating free expression, therefore, its benefits are exaggerated and, possibly, illusory; but as a device for fostering a sense of cohesiveness among participants, its effects should not be underestimated.

The Allen & Co. conference has been in existence for over twenty-five years and, with the powerful convergence of once-distinct industries, has evolved into the most significant business elite conference of its kind in the world. This is, in part, a reflection of the contemporary economic and political significance of its attendees – owners and executives whose corporations exercise considerable influence over world technological, economic, cultural, and political development. Of course, business lobbying is nothing new, and a number of the Allen & Co. participants are members of more formal elite advocacy groups such TechNet,[4] the Business Roundtable[5] and the International Business Council of the World Economic Forum;[6] but it is the transnational, and arguably transcendental, nature of Allen & Co. discourse that distinguishes it from the more deliberate objectives of lobbying. Indeed, Allen & Co. organizers, like those of Bilderberg, would no doubt argue that there is no specific objective to the event other than providing a forum for the exchange of views on salient business issues of the day. And with a media focus on deal-making – which, it's important to state, doesn't require an event like Allen & Co. – one could be forgiven for not seeing the inherently political consequences of such activity. Whether intended or not, however, the global conflation of technological, social, economic, and political development means that the consensus created and perpetuated within elite networks like Allen & Co. has increasingly profound implications for all of us.

As if to emphasize this point, the conference is regularly attended by prominent cultural and political figures, and boasts many attendees with membership of more policy-oriented transnational elite networks. The interconnectedness of these transnational networks, via their most established and influential members, explains, at least in part, the development of common narratives within the elite community. Take, for instance, the emergence of *global society* rhetoric in recent years and its legitimizing function within the self-consciously elitist realms of the transnational network. In the first of the two extracts that follow, the World Economic Forum describes its *not-for-profit* commitment to the "global public interest"; in the second, the TED Foundation – which hosts enjoyable, stimulating, and somewhat indulgent elite events – explains why its important for the "global community of knowledge-seekers" that only "exceptional" people should be allowed to be present at their *non-profit* conferences:

> "The World Economic Forum is an independent, international organization incorporated as a Swiss not-for-profit foundation. We are striving towards a world-class corporate governance system where values are as important a basis as rules. Our motto is 'entrepreneurship in the global public interest'. We believe that economic progress without social development is not sustainable, while social development without economic progress is not feasible. Our vision for the World Economic Forum is threefold. It aims to be: the foremost organization which builds and energizes leading global communities; the creative force shaping global, regional and industry strategies; the catalyst of choice for its communities when undertaking global initiatives to improve the state of the world."[7]

> "It's certainly true that the majority of those attending the annual TED conference have been extremely successful in some field or other, and we wouldn't want it any other way. But financial success (which is what 'elitism' sometimes implies) is not the key measure. TED attendees include thought leaders and innovators from a broad range of endeavor: technology, entertainment, design, science, business, global issues, philanthropy and the arts. Because

of their recognized achievements, most of these people can afford the standard membership fee, and understand that the cost helps to support TED's many initiatives [...] In the past few years we've taken several steps to further diversify the audience [...] Of course, we're still seeking to ensure that everyone who comes to TED is exceptional in some way. Without an amazing audience, we couldn't attract amazing speakers. Our speakers aren't paid [...] they attend because of the audience [...] Indeed, the whole mission of the nonprofit foundation that owns TED is to leverage the power of good ideas and let them spread as widely and effectively as possible. TEDTalks have been viewed 300 million times by people around the world (as of July 2010). In our minds, that is the real TED audience. A global community of knowledge-seekers."[8]

The legitimizing presence of *global society* rhetoric is also very much in evidence among transnational corporations, and is particularly prevalent in the communications, technology, and media sectors – demonstrating a subtle consensus over its desirability, and underscored, no doubt, by the role they have played in forging such an eventuality. It should come as no surprise to discover an unbridled enthusiasm concerning the promise of communications technology among members of its elite community. Communications technology is, by its very nature, highly disruptive. It has facilitated and accelerated the most disruptive social and political movement of the past fifty years – economic globalization. No great respecter of existing structures – be they social, cultural, economic, or political – communications technology has, with its rapid and anarchic development, evolved into the single most important instrument of contemporary globalization effects. But it is no longer just shaping and fulfilling the requirement of needs determined elsewhere; it has become a powerful driver of its own globalization requirement. And since this requirement necessitates cultural and political change, the substance of global society rhetoric espoused by its transnational corporations and executives is of increasing relevance and interest.

In January 2010, Google Inc. stoked political tensions between the United States and China, and staggered the investment community by announcing that, in light of cyber-attacks on its server infrastructure that had originated in China – specifically, attempts to access the Gmail accounts of Chinese human rights activists – it was no longer prepared to censor search functionality in the country.[9] Since establishing its Chinese search business in 2006, Google had consistently struggled to reconcile itself to the government's censorship demands.[10] And its founders and executives were clearly wounded by ongoing criticisms that it had compromised its integrity, and a more general code of conduct to "do no evil," by entering into a written agreement with the Chinese government to filter out banned topics from its local service. Its provocative statement, therefore, was more than just corporate posturing – it reflected a deep-seated anxiety related to compromised principles and, specifically, the democratic principle of free speech. David Drummond, Senior Vice President, Corporate Development and Chief Legal Officer at Google, made clear that it was prepared, if necessary, to abandon its Chinese business rather than continue to compromise over the issue:

> "We launched Google.cn in January 2006 in the belief that the benefits of increased access to information for people in China and a more open Internet outweighed our discomfort in agreeing to censor some results. At the time we made clear that 'we will carefully monitor conditions in China, including new laws and other restrictions on our services. If we determine that we are unable to achieve the objectives outlined we will not hesitate to reconsider our approach to China.' These attacks and the surveillance they have uncovered – combined with the attempts over the past year to further limit free speech on the web – have led us to conclude that we should review the feasibility of our business operations in China. We have decided we are no longer willing to continue censoring our results on Google.cn, and so over the next few weeks we will be discussing with the Chinese government the basis on which we could operate an unfiltered search engine within the law, if at all. We recognize that this may well mean having to shut down Google.cn, and potentially our offices in China."[11]

Human rights activists and free speech advocates heaped praise on Google over a stance that had clearly embarrassed and angered the Chinese government. Investors were more luke warm in their appreciation of the move, simultaneously recognizing the lack of immediate damage to

Google's international revenues, and identifying the longer-term business implications of not being present in the world's most internet-connected market. Elsewhere, Google's announcement, set against a backdrop of worsening political relations between the United States and China – related primarily to currency and balance-of-trade issues – was a timely political gift for the US government, which was quick to express support for the company. Speaking on the subject of internet freedom just days after the announcement, US Secretary of State Hillary Clinton proclaimed that:

> "New technologies do not take sides in the struggle for freedom and progress, but the United States does [...] We need to synchronize our technological progress with our principles [...] Increasingly, U.S. companies are making the issue of internet and information freedom a greater consideration in their business decisions. I hope that their competitors and foreign governments will pay close attention to this trend. The most recent situation involving Google has attracted a great deal of interest [...] The internet has already been a source of tremendous progress in China, and it is fabulous. There are so many people in China now online. But countries that restrict free access to information or violate the basic rights of internet users risk walling themselves off from the progress of the next century. Now, the United States and China have different views on this issue, and we intend to address those differences candidly and consistently in the context of our positive, cooperative, and comprehensive relationship [...] This issue isn't just about information freedom; it is about what kind of world we want and what kind of world we will inhabit. It's about whether we live on a planet with one internet, one global community, and a common body of knowledge that benefits and unites us all, or a fragmented planet in which access to information and opportunity is dependent on where you live and the whims of censors. Information freedom supports the peace and security that provides a foundation for global progress. Historically, asymmetrical access to information is one of the leading causes of interstate conflict [...] it's critical that people on both sides of the problem have access to the same set of facts and opinions."[12]

The Chinese government's position, however, was unequivocal. Google was reneging on a written promise and behaving in a way that it believed to be "totally wrong."[13] The state-controlled Xinhua news agency, quoting an unnamed official within the State Council Information Office, relayed the view that "Google has violated [the] written promise it made when entering the Chinese market by stopping filtering its searching service and blaming China in insinuation for alleged hacker attacks."[14] It made clear that any move on the part of Google to offer an uncensored Chinese search service would not be tolerated – the company would "pay the consequences"[15] for any transgressions. Furthermore, it attacked Google for its "intricate ties" with the US government and took a side-swipe at the company's cooperation with US intelligence agencies.[16] As the stand-off intensified, it was clear that any attempt by Google to maintain an illegal uncensored service would, under the circumstances, be extremely inadvisable. In an attempt to circumvent the restrictions, Google took the decision in March 2010 to direct its Chinese search queries through its uncensored Hong Kong-based servers – a decision that further angered Chinese officials. In another statement from Google, its spokesperson David Drummond explained the move:

> "Figuring out how to make good on our promise to stop censoring search on Google.cn has been hard. We want as many people in the world as possible to have access to our services, including users in mainland China, yet the Chinese government has been crystal clear throughout our discussions that self-censorship is a non-negotiable legal requirement. We believe this new approach of providing uncensored search in simplified Chinese from Google.com.hk is a sensible solution to the challenges we've faced – it's entirely legal and will meaningfully increase access to information for people in China. We very much hope that the Chinese government respects our decision, though we are well aware that it could at any time block access to our services."[17]

Demonstrating, perhaps, the rather transitory and expedient nature of political indignation, the US administration was said to be dismayed at the inability of Google and the Chinese authorities to come to an agreement,[18] although it's unclear whether the dismay was aimed at Chinese insistence on censorship, or Google's apparent escalation of the stand-off. In a statement, National Security Council spokesperson Mike Hammer confirmed that the White House was informed of the company's decision concerning Hong Kong before the announcement was made.[19] Appearing to put some distance between the administration and Google, he stressed that bilateral ties between the countries were "mature enough to sustain differences" and that Google's actions were, ultimately, motivated by its own interests.[20] Similarly, the Chinese authorities began to play down the significance of the dispute. In a press briefing, Qin Gang, a spokesman for the Chinese Foreign Ministry, argued that Google's move would be dealt with "according to the law" and that it represented an isolated act by a commercial operation. It would not, he said, affect China–US ties "unless politicized" by others.[21] At this point, it appeared that the Google situation had, in effect, become something of an irritation for both governments.

In the days and weeks before the expiration of Google's license in China, tensions were allowed to diffuse sufficiently for renewal of the license to be the least damaging outcome for all concerned. Sensitive searches made by mainland Chinese visitors to the Hong Kong-based Google servers were effectively blocked by the government and, in the days before the license renewal, Google appeased the authorities by ending the automatic redirection of Chinese traffic to its Hong Kong-based website. Instead, its homepage featured a link, for those who wished to use it, to the Hong Kong servers.

Since the end of 2009, Google has seen its share of the Chinese search market fall from 35.6 to 21.6 percent[22] and it currently runs a distant second place to dominant local search business Baidu. Despite this, and the possibility of punitive market conditions in the years ahead, Google executives continue to publicly question the long-term viability of Chinese censorship. At a November 2010 meeting of the Council on Foreign Relations, a bastion of the US foreign policy establishment, Google's Chairman and CEO Eric Schmidt opined that China's attempt to control internet usage would ultimately fail as ever more Chinese people went online and found expression:

> "Ultimately, the people will win over the government. The yearning is so strong. [...] China heavily invests in policing the

web, using a large organization of regulators estimated between 30,000 to 50,000 people […] The question is at what point will there be so many Chinese people online that such mechanisms break down in terms of censorship and so forth? […] If you think about the scale, they've got a billion phones that are trying to express themselves. It will be difficult in my view to completely keep up with that."[23]

As the Google/China conflict played out during the course of 2010, it became increasingly difficult to understand, notwithstanding the US administration's claim that Google was acting in its own interests, what possible commercial motivation the company could have had for its stance. Cynics might suggest, of course, that the company looked to gain materially through the enhanced reputation of its brand, but the risks associated with the move make it difficult to see this as anything other than a happy consequence of what must have been, despite all suggestions to the contrary, a genuinely principled position. Google's executives were undoubtedly aware, from the outset, of the likely commercial repercussions of their actions. And, certainly, if we take the muted response of its competitors, and other US corporations active in China, as an indicator of such things, there was, and is, a conspicuous absence of corporate criticism of the Chinese authorities. Google's actions were not driven by anything resembling an immediate business consideration; what they represented, in fact, was a remarkable blurring of the lines in contemporary world politics.

The political power of transnational corporations has always been understood in terms of economic self-interest. And there are many examples of how this self-interest is shaping the world in which we live. Individual governments, for their part, have long championed their business interests overseas – to the extent that it's sometimes difficult to understand what other motivation there is for foreign policy. But Google's stand-off with the Chinese government represents something quite different. It's clear that the US administration was aware of, and supported, the initial action taken by the company. Aside from the benefit of forcing the Chinese into a defensive position over the breached security of US business interests, the administration was no doubt interested to see where Google's actions might lead. In particular, with US interests reporting a harshening of environmental conditions in China, it provided an opportunity to see how the authorities dealt with full-frontal resistance from powerful transnational business interests. In the course of subsequent bilateral discussions with the Chinese, however, it seems the administration concluded that wider US interests were best served by encouraging an end to the stand-off. Google, having threatened to pull out of China over the dispute, in the event opted for a quieter resolution. Whether this decision was the product of second thoughts and consideration of their other Chinese businesses, the fact that they were left isolated over their actions, a concern for Chinese employees, pressure from shareholders or, more interestingly, administration influence, is impossible to know with any certainty, but it seems highly unlikely that it was a decision taken without consideration of interests beyond its own.

Google's stand against the Chinese government may, ultimately, prove to have been little more than an expression of the will of its founders, but it has forced us to rethink the strategic alignment of corporate and governmental agendas in international relations. It highlights the proximity and interdependence of corporate and political decision making and, crucially, the networked values and motivations that underpin it. And, while many will applaud the courage and conviction of Google for taking seriously what it sees as its corporate responsibility and brand values, others may see its moralizing, liberal internationalist stance as representative of something quite new in international politics: the corporation as a proxy for the wider economic and political interests of its government.[24]

Elite networks and global coordination

The idea that informal elite networks are a force for good in world politics is an accepted truism of the elite community, with many members failing to see any downside to participation. The conscious rationale for the transnational network, which historically has been related to security relationships, has evolved, over time, into one of communication within the context of a rapidly expanding global economic framework. Of particular interest is the explicit interrelationship of business and political interests within this emerging global reality. In the following interview extracts, two established Bilderberg attendees cite the role of business in the expansion of the transnational network and point to market forces as a critical determinant. The third extract, from an interview with a steering committee member, is of particular interest because it hints at conscious efforts, among established members of transnational elite, to create linkages between disparate clusters of transnational network activity. Crucially, it points to the identification of individual networkers capable of bridging divides between these clusters.

> "The way I see it is more as an adaptation to new economic realities. It has always been the case that, when the world becomes wider, companies try to become wider. So now we have China and India rapidly becoming actors."
>
> "I think [these networks] have created new linkages and new ties for foreign investment into Turkey. [Take the business councils, where there is] some business development and discussion of trade issues with [the] Eastern countries or caucuses – Russia, Kazakhstan, and all those – it all turns into a business development function where leaders from both governments come together with their own business communities and try to match projects and investors together. So that influences foreign policy in some respects, I would say."
>
> "These networks are also active in Asia, maybe not so visible and known to us, but they do exist. A typical 'networker' there for the last thirty years has been Lee Kuan Yew,[25] who is extremely well connected in the Asian world. He has the trust of people who are certainly very different – let's say the Chinese. The old, and now the new, Chinese leadership certainly have very different views on how to run their country, but they trust him. He is extremely well connected with some of the Muslim leaders of the region, and all this he makes very good use of. Now the important issue for us is, here we have another regional level: how do we connect our transatlantic network into that Asian or South East Asian network? To interconnect these different patches on the globe is a very important issue."

While there may be a conscious desire on the part of organizers to establish connections between regional elite networks, it seems clear that other, more discreet, globalization effects are driving overall participation in this kind of activity. Here, an established member of Bilderberg describes his experience of another, more "enterprising" elite network; in the second interview extract, a Turkish Bilderberg delegate describes how even the reluctant Islamic elite of the country has come to recognize the value of participation.

> "I was involved in one of these things in Portugal called Da Arrabida, which is tiny; it's very, very, small [...] thirty people, in this wonderful monastery on the coast south of Lisbon. But they were much more enterprising: they had the Poles; the Russians, Gidar from Russia come along; they invited the Indians; and all the rest of it."
>
> "It's a very small community in Turkey, certain people are part and parcel of transatlantic networks and some are becoming involved in Far Eastern networks. Traditionally these people were raised in good schools – the secular elite – but the new Islamic elite is becoming active in this regard whether they believe in it or not."

The value of informal elite networks is therefore related to their ability to enable narratives that may create the conditions for political and economic rapprochement. Without this informal activity, the more postured narratives of international engagement would likely result in protectionism and conflict. The strengthening of global economic dependencies is, of course, the liberal international pretext for greater harmony between states. Where formal political differences appear irreconcilable, elite transnational networks facilitate a consensual narrative based on shared interests. The establishment of this narrative is the precursor to the strengthening of structural economic ties, which, in turn, create the conditions for a more aligned political engagement. Here, an industrialist on the Bilderberg steering committee explains the value of "unofficial exchanges," while in the second extract, political commentator Will Hutton describes the significance of informal networks in contemporary world politics.

> "Is it indispensable? My clear answer is it is absolutely indispensable. I think people would live in a different world if there were no exchanges, unofficial exchanges, of views. I very strongly believe

this […] I know from business that some of the most serious and most important decisions being made were made after a very private, unofficial discussion – and no [formal] meetings."

"It's very striking in the America–Chinese relationship that the Americans have a number of informal contacts with the Chinese as well as the formal ones [where they're] staring each other down in a rather hostile and frosty way. But the informal networks work very well. I think there's no question that it's the informal networks that have persuaded the Chinese they've got to act in getting the North Koreans to abandon their nuclear weapons program. That is the upside of it, but how that conversation took place, what *quid pro quo* the Americans have offered for it, we will never know. This is the way the current world 'wags'."

The existence of a parallel track of elite discourse, running alongside the more public political narrative, is therefore viewed as a perfectly acceptable and desirable response to the challenges of international governance. And, given the critical globalizing role of transnational corporations and international finance, the incorporation of such interests is seen as a natural and necessary development. The degree of non-political participation has, in the case of Bilderberg, increased over time, reflecting, no doubt, the shifting preoccupations and relevance of its attendees to the globalization, rather than the Cold War, debate. It is tempting to suggest, as some have, that elite transnational policy networks were formed, and are run, by the interests of global capital explicitly for the purpose of promoting such interests.[26] And, if we take a historical perspective, one can see how such a conclusion might be reached. At the level of participation, however, the conscious intent of such activity, and its overall effects, are not necessarily the same. Likewise, the stereotyping of participant motivations is, in many ways, an extension of the tendency to see individuals as conforming to some kind of predestined historical or economic role. Journalist and author Jon Ronson, for instance, who followed the Bilderberg group for research he was conducting on the conspiracy theory community, was invited to a conference by Bilderberg organizers – presumably with the intention of demystifying certain aspects of the network's activities. He described the relationship between conference organizers and emergent political attendees in this way:[27]

> "They'll get an up-and-coming politician who they think may be president or prime minister one day, and as globalist industrialist leaders who believe that politics shouldn't be in the hands of politicians, they try and influence them with wise words in the corridors outside sessions."

The problem with his account is that, while there may be a degree of truth to the characterization of network members as "globalist industrialist leaders," it is overly simplistic in its appreciation of the distinction between business and political interests. Set against a backdrop of globalization, business and political interests are interrelated and hugely interdependent. In fact, the emergence of elite policy networks, a feature of practically all policy domains, can be seen to be a reflection of ever closer alignment and coordination between these interests. They may be insidious, and might favor certain interests over others, but they have become an essential and embedded feature of contemporary world politics. In the words of Will Hutton:

> "Where does one begin? Very few legislative decisions in the US get taken without enormous shaping by corporations. Large parts of the US tax code, some of the deregulation […] in Britain the restructuring of the NHS on market principles very much shaped by informal networks. You've seen in Germany the abuses of co-decision-making in VW where money's been changing hands to get the kinds of deals which are wanted. Almost nothing in China moves without the say-so of the Communist Party and palms being greased. It's almost dignified the Guānxi network. Maybe we in the West need to see these informal networks not being the past but the future. I think it's very difficult to think of any decision which hasn't been influenced by the kind of power networks we've been discussing."

In short, elite policy networks should not be seen as distinct from the policymaking machinery; they are a fundamental part of it. And, as the spread of neoliberal orthodoxy has blurred the political distinction between public and private, the emergence of elite policy networks can be seen to have blurred the policymaking distinction between formal and informal.

The media and elite networks

One facet of elite networks that receives a great deal of attention is their apparent lack of transparency and frequent insistence on non-disclosure. In the case of Bilderberg, for instance, the conspicuous absence of coverage of the event has raised suspicions that the media is somehow complicit in the activities of the group – not least because of the active participation of media executives and selected journalists. Indeed, the involvement of the media is seen by some as evidence of a conscious and deliberate conspiracy perpetrated by the global power elite.[28] Our own research suggests that such claims are significantly overstated, but the presence of the media within such networks – and the more general culture of co-dependency that exists between media and policy elites – does have obvious implications for the acceptance and dissemination of elite consensus. The reason that this is disputed by elite participants, and media participants in particular, is that they refuse to acknowledge the hidden and unconscious mechanisms of compliance at work within such networks. Take, for instance, the rationale for confidentiality that exists within the elite community: a rationale that emphasizes the importance of enabling a full and frank exchange of views. Media discretion is seen by organizers and attendees alike as being a natural consequence of the underlying requirement for free expression. In the following extracts from interviews with two steering committee members (the first Dennis Healey) and a media executive, it's clear that this need is well understood among participants.

> "You can't get people to talk openly to one another, especially in front of political opponents in their own country, if they're going to be quoted. Because people will only talk freely if they know they're not going to be quoted and distorted by prurient, ambitious, journalists."[29]
>
> "I think the confidentiality of this meeting is another big advantage Bilderberg has. There was one journalist – British – who liked to write about it – he has never been back. Because people said, you know, he's using that for information-gathering and then he's writing about it. You cannot do that, and I think that's true for others."
>
> "The reason for the confidentiality of the meetings is that attendees can reveal their views without constraints. So that they

do not bite their tongues, worrying 'how will the media reflect what I say?'."

The assurance of media silence and, more importantly, the agreement of attendees to refrain from media-related activity at the event, is seen as critical to the effective management of such groups. Here, Martin Taylor describes the challenge of constraining participants on this issue:

> "I don't think it's true to say that we want to keep it out [of the media]; we've never wanted to get it in. We don't encourage people to go to the mainstream press because we don't encourage, you know, idle speculation about what we do. We forbid individual attendees to give meetings at our concerts, and we do that not because we're secrecy-led, but because we want to control the politicians who come. If we let them, they would all give press conferences on television all day. They're insane."[30]

It's important to state at this point that discretion and non-disclosure are more fundamental to elite networks than they first appear. They represent deeply embedded norms of acceptable personal and professional conduct within such settings. To disclose information is to breach the trust of the network and display a lack of personal integrity. Transgressions of this kind are rarely forgiven and the participant is usually expelled from the group. The fear of expulsion is especially palpable among those who are not yet established members of the network and, it's important to note, this group includes ambitious journalists. As one influential reporter, realizing he'd shared rather more information that he felt comfortable with, pointedly remarked:

> "Don't stitch me up. I want to be invited back."

The attraction of participation to media representatives, even if they're constrained from reporting directly what they've heard, should not be underestimated. To be granted access to such a group, to hear first-hand what such people are thinking before it is publicly articulated, is of enormous contextual value to journalists, as the following extracts, from interviews with three media participants, make clear.

"From a media perspective, they sometimes have considerable value as a source of information, a source of stories. I preferred, when I was editing [a prominent national newspaper], to spend time in mixed groups such as Ambassadorial dinner parties or something like that. Obviously the Ambassador has a reason for inviting the guests that he does invite and, no doubt, he hopes that most of them are fairly friendly to his nation but, on the other hand, good Ambassadors are also very interested in getting to know what different currents of opinion are, so the groups they invite are likely to have varied views."

"For me, they were unique occasions; I've never had the opportunity for such sustained exposure. It's invaluable to my work. I can't imagine why a journalist would not want to be involved […] because my job is to be in the know, to be informed."

"I've gone to meetings of this kind because, as a journalist, it's useful for me to know what people think. It clarifies. It's my job to know what people think and then discuss these arguments in public and bring them out. The Trilateral Commission is similar, all these sort of groupings are similar. If you can talk to people informally rather than just read the press releases or see them delivering speeches, talk about what the problems are, the way they see them, you find that you learn a great deal about these perceptions and what's driving policy. And that makes it easier to write better about them. Ultimately, a columnist's job is to clarify issues, and it's far easier to do if you have some idea what's actually going on."

The access and insights provided by participation in elite policy networks are, clearly, therefore, of great importance to the select group of journalists lucky enough to find themselves invited. It also goes without saying that the reputational career benefits that come from being perceived to have elite contacts of this kind are not insignificant for journalists. What is less obvious, although the first interview extract alluded to it, is what value the elite host gets from the presence of the media. There must, after all, be some reason for inviting members of the press into these elite networks. When the question of why they were invited was put to the Bilderberg Chairman, Viscount Davignon, his response was curious to say the least:

> "they [the media] give us a good feel. It's not that we want them to write [things] but we need to not be disconnected with what is the state of opinion. And media people are the best people to give us that."

If we are to accept this response at face value, journalists are invited along on the pretext of providing some kind of reference for the discussions that take place. It's not clear, however, whether the "state of opinion" that's being referenced is that of expert commentators, the people they speak with, or, in some sense, that of the public. Of course, given the relationship between the media agenda, the policy agenda, and the public agenda, perhaps it's all of the above. Whatever the case, Davignon appears to be hinting at the role of the media in providing a feel for the context against which emergent narratives must be evaluated or framed. One can see how this might work, but it overlooks the bias of the journalists involved and their relationship to the policy elite. To be selected in the first instance, a journalist must be perceived by a steering committee member to be somehow enlightened and influential. For reasons explained previously, the biases of the group come into play in selection and are reinforced when invitees, consciously or otherwise, attempt to ingratiate themselves with existing network members. If, as Viscount Davignon suggests, the "state of opinion" is being sought, and we accept that this opinion is, to some extent, shaped by privileged access to the thinking of elite participants, it seems reasonable to question its validity as a source of objective insight. After all, it is partly a reflection of the prevailing consensus of the network.

As if to emphasize the discreet and seductive influence of elite consensus on journalist participants, an article written for *Hürriyet Daily News and Economic Review* (formerly *Turkish Daily News*) by political commentator Mehmet Ali Birand recounts, with unbridled enthusiasm, his experiences as a first-time attendee at the Bilderberg conference:[31]

> "I got to 'breathe the air'. I learned a lot. I would like to give a couple of examples: We started with the developments in Iraq and went on to discuss China's place in the world. Would it be a single-polar world or a multi-polar one? How Iran's nuclear power would affect all of us was discussed in detail. Concerns on the issue

were conveyed. The developments in the United States, what the elections would bring, and how the public opinion in the United States was progressing was deliberated. The most important issues facing the world, from energy policies to expansion in the communication technologies, were reviewed. At the end of the three days, we have learned and discussed the world's most prominent problems with the world's experts."

Going to some lengths to dispel conspiracy theories about the group's activities, Birand unwittingly affirms the existence of a more discreet form of influence. He talks of "breathing the air," as if it were otherwise beyond reach, and the great learning he took away from the event. It doesn't occur to him, for one moment, that the consensuses formed in networks such as this are anything other than the most informed and accurate. And it's difficult to believe that they have not influenced his interpretation and reporting of world events in the months and years that followed. A fundamental question, therefore, relates to the directional flow of the "state of opinion." For the most part, media participants are quick to rebuff the suggestion that they are somehow influenced in their thinking, but acknowledge that it can, and does, happen. Here, two influential media representatives reflect on their own attempts to remain circumspect in the face of policy elite consensus.

> "I tend to react against this kind of consensus […] I'm suspicious of them and like to form my own views without a degree of commitment towards them. [But], yes, I do think they exist and that they have some influence upon people […] I don't think journalists consciously take these decisions so much as being influenced by the same things [… but, on the suggestion that the media and policy elites are homogeneous,] I think there's a good deal of truth in that. I mean, for instance, on economic policy, journalists tend to have a basic underlying, open market, analysis. They're free traders and they believe the system works because markets work."
>
> "No, [they don't influence me] because all my life I've been my own man. I hate to repeat other peoples' ideas. I try to seek out my own mind. Even if they had such an idea in the back of their

minds, it wouldn't do too much to me because I love to play my own game and speak my own mind rather than being told [what to think […]. But, of course, if it's snowing outside you cannot have summer inside; there is an enormous interaction in the way of thinking."

Another media participant, who acknowledged the role of younger journalists in bringing fresh perspectives to the network, suggested that they tended to be invited instead of older journalists because they were easier to manipulate:

"I'm very old, obviously, and they tend to keep the old hacks at bay. They're bringing in new people to refresh old ideas and to pass on some of the messages they want to pass on to the outside world by using them as their messengers."

In all of this, it's tempting to jump to the conclusion that the presence of media participants is about anything other than co-opting opinion-formers into the process of elite consensus formation and dissemination – even if the process is more unconscious than it first appears. At the same time, we must move beyond the idea that media interests are directed in some tangible way to fulfill their destiny as servants of globalizing interests. Certain media participants, along with a number of prominent intellectuals and policy institute representatives, have become an integral part of the collective's consensus formation activity – they are not simply an adjunct to it. It is impossible, of course, to discount entirely the possibility of conscious co-optation, but the research conducted for this book suggests, in the contemporary setting at least, that more unconsciously deterministic forces are at play, driving the convergence of media and policy elite interests.

It's important to state, however, that this doesn't make the effects of such a relationship any the less significant. When one considers, for instance, the longstanding relationship between Bilderberg and the senior editorial team of *The Economist*, which has the stated purpose of "[taking] part in a severe contest between intelligence, which presses forward, and an unworthy, timid ignorance obstructing our progress,"[32] one can understand how the line between analysis and advocacy might become blurred. Frequently called upon to chair panels and act as rapporteurs at Bilderberg events, members of its respected editorial team benefit from unfettered access and make no secret of the free trade/free markets stance of their publication. *The Economist* isn't, of course, the mouthpiece for Bilderberg — in fact, no such thing exists. It is, all the same, remarkably close to the emergent currents of opinion within this influential group — indeed, it is instrumental in facilitating their emergence. It is uniquely placed to reference its informed editorial against the prevailing consensus and logic of the transnational elite network — one might argue that this is what makes it informed in the first place. And, given that it has been doing it for so long, it seems reasonable to suggest that its editorial participants are no longer, in any meaningful sense, distinguishable from the policy network itself.

Acting in the shadows

An important aspect of the wall of media silence that is characteristic of so many elite networks is the sense of detachment it can reinforce. This detachment is particularly evident at the most exclusive of events, where security measures help to insulate participants from the outside world, and it has consequences for the atmosphere within which interactions take place. In the following extract, for instance, a first-time Bilderberg attendee describes the open and individualized consequences of detachment at the conference:

> "It felt quite isolated from the rest of the world. I suppose, from a security viewpoint, you're cut off and there is an implicit celebration of that. You can talk about whatever you want to talk about — it's very comfortable, very nice […]. There weren't huddles of advisors, or things like that, for the politicians — and even for the heads of the companies. I would imagine it's rare to be there without somebody else. So the individualized aspects […] I imagine it's a useful place to talk about big issues [and] they can rarely do that. And it is a fairly useful way for them to individually network with each other, to talk, and to do whatever they want to do with those networks. Maybe build up things for the future […] I asked people what they got out of it and, you know, you get very

anodyne answers. They get networks out of it, they get contacts. The coffee breaks were very important to them, it struck me; that's probably almost the reason for being there. I'm sure they got a lot out of it – the abstract chance to discuss world issues is quite rare without the constraints of being free to say what you want to say."

These sentiments are shared by more established members of the network. In the following interview extracts, the first from Viscount Davignon, the second from Martin Taylor,[33] and the third from another member of the steering committee, the lack of posturing and role playing, and the more personal nature of interactions, within such settings is emphasized.

"The interesting thing is not why they come, but why they come back. The first time around, why not? It's not an expensive exercise, it's not Davos. They come back because there is no exposure, there are no big statements, and nobody can run around and posture. That's why it's still running after all these years."

"It's a private organization and we live in an age that can't distinguish privacy from secrecy. Privacy is then seen as secrecy, and secrecy is seen as sinister by definition […]. People who are there, and [who] talk privately over dinner, deserve to have their confidences respected. For me, the value has been [in] building a group of friends, a network if you like, people I've come to know and who have come to know me."

"At least you get to talk about things openly. It's always friendly – it's not aggressive. In political circles, at official conferences, you have to play a role because you are the representative of Britain, Germany, France, or wherever; but here you can be critical, self-critical, and you can try to find new ways. There's normally no leaks, no coverage, which is very good. The confidentiality of this meeting is a big advantage."

The detachment and relative intimacy of these elite gatherings is significant for another reason: it has the effect of reinforcing the sense of inclusion and exclusion for established and peripheral members of the network. Attendees are welcomed into a world in which they can, in principle at least, speak freely and in confidence to other members of the network. They experience a degree of access and frankness that is stripped bare of its veneer and many layers of formality. For new entrants, this aspect of elite membership can be both exciting and intimidating. And, even for more established members, the spectacle of heated debates between prominent individuals, the realization that nobody is really in control of world events, and the insight that one gains into the person-alities of world business and political leaders, always has the capacity to surprise and reward. Here, five established Bilderberg attendees reflect on the uniqueness of its transnational elite gatherings.

> "All that stuff goes on. I quite enjoyed it really. I mean it was quite amusing and interesting being with all these powerful people because some of them were powerful and amusing and others were very deeply un-amusing and awful – but still powerful. I remem-ber Vernon Jordan, a very powerful man in the democratic world, I forget where we were [… but] he came up to me and said, 'Meet the next President of the United States' and introduced me to Clinton. Well, I'd never heard of Clinton, it was well before he ran for President [… but] I thought 'Vernon Jordan's a wise old man, I'll keep my eye on him'. And it was interesting because Clinton was obviously quite something – as, indeed, he proved to be."

> "So you get into all these kinds of conflicting views and feuds but, the more you get into the debates, the more you find out that the politicians who started all this were not prepared at all. And they don't know what to do now either. This is the kind of learning and sharing that you get into."

> "I always find it interesting to hear different aspects in small circles. I mean, Condi Rice talks about Iraq and then Dick Holbrooke comes – so, you know, it's completely different. To hear different stories with different views makes you richer."

> "One of the reasons [Bilderberg was interesting] is that the sub-jects were not only economics; they were different. For example, [take] the 'green revolution'. The President of the Green Party and three or four professors from the University of California came along, and discussed genetically modified food. Plus there were lots of so-called prominent members: Hillary Clinton, on one hand,

who I saw several times,[34] or Rockefeller. It was a very good platform for me: first of all to learn something and then [to] establish good relations. Also, they want to establish a good relationship, it's a two-way street, no question about that. And you get a different kind of atmosphere [...] I expressed myself, I spoke, and I asked questions – not only in the formal sessions, but the informal ones. It was a channel for increasing the credibility of yourself, your institution, and your country."

"[On a debate related to oil and energy], Lord Brown and Jeroen van der Veer could never have been that open in public. On the European economy, Trichet was absolutely scathing about European structural rigidity. Now he could never have been so open in front of the media or his own constituents. Seeing Ackermann and Schrempp at loggerheads over 'off-shoring' was also very revealing."

The seductive appeal of "breathing the air," therefore, should not be underestimated. The congeniality and openness of the network reinforces its sense of club-like exclusivity and attracts those for whom exclusivity is important. To be privy to the open and frank exchanges, to be an accepted member of the most elite circles, to enjoy the perceived benefits of membership, are important preoccupations for many new entrants. These perceptions may be exaggerated in the minds of some participants, but there are clearly material benefits to be gained from membership of the group. Here, for instance, an industrialist steering committee member describes the networking and reputational benefits of his Bilderberg association:

"I think, first and foremost, it's a form of self-enrichment: you know more people; you have more people to pick opinions from; you get to know some people better than others and may wish to engage them in some form. So, for instance, if you are on the board of a French company, you can say, 'why not choose someone from Britain for our board? It's high time we did so with all the business we have there'. And they say, 'yes, but we don't know anyone'; so you suggest someone, or two or three [people], which means, in turn, that you meet more often with these people, and on it goes […] And this very often leads to something that I've always regarded as a special phenomenon: someone approaches you and says, 'I've heard from [someone], who knows you from the Bilderberg meeting, that you're willing to do this or that, or that you're interested in this and that. How about that? Could we talk about it? Or, would you like to join our board?' I've never met this guy before, but it comes through some kind of network."

In many ways, of course, membership of the most elite networks is conditional on one's existing network of contacts, as well as the extent and nature of one's personal relationships. During the research conducted for this book, the relationships and personal networks of Bilderberg members were occasionally mentioned by interviewees. While most of this information is in the public domain, some more obscure material has, by its nature, been difficult to verify. It's possible that the informality of contact has escaped the attention of journalists or, indeed, that the information is inaccurate. Either way, there is a perception and acknowledgement that certain members of the network are historically connected by more than a common interest in world affairs. It points to the existence of an "old-boy network" within Bilderberg – a subject that is returned to in the next section of this chapter.

The fact that many new entrants to Bilderberg are influential in their own right, and have extensive personal networks, means that the benefits of access are of more importance to those at the periphery of the network – those who would otherwise not have it. Indeed, for established members of the elite network, the idea that they need access, or need to be present at such events to gain access, is laughable. In the following interview extracts, the first from Viscount Davignon, the second from an influential media participant, access is seen as a by-product of the perceived importance of what one does, what one represents, and, of course, who one is. The elite network might facilitate more convivial introductions, but they are, for the most part, unnecessary for the cultivation of professional contacts.

"[As for the idea that connections might open doors] I don't think so. I really believe that if someone is important, doors will open. If somebody needs support, he will get it or he won't get it. The fact that he knows somebody can help him here and there but it is only 10 percent of the 100 percent."

"I think some people attach great importance to them, which I never have, partly as a way of making contacts. I haven't ever found that that was really necessary. I mean, if you hold a position where you ought to have access, you have access. If you don't hold such a position at that point, then people may give you time, for old times' sake, or whatever, but you don't have a position of influence from which to argue your case – and they have, therefore, no particular reason to be influenced by what you have to say. So I don't believe that access arises out of having been there."

This does, of course, raise an important question: why do the more central members of the network – by definition its most well connected individuals – attend these elite gatherings? After all, they're present in a private capacity rather than as formal representatives of their governments or organizations and they are certainly not compelled or obliged to attend. The investment of time and energy is not inconsiderable for otherwise busy people, and yet they volunteer themselves and appear to enjoy activity of this kind. While some see this as evidence of complicity in some kind of conspiracy, the real answer to the question of why the more established members of the network take part is rather more prosaic. A clue is provided in the choices that are made concerning which events or networks to participate in, because such individuals clearly can't take part in everything they're invited to. In the following extract, a seasoned policymaker provides a sense of the time pressures and demands that people in positions of influence experience, and hints at a general disinclination to be involved in additional activity:

"When you are in the middle of a big policymaking machine – the British government, the European Union, the United Nations – whatever it is, and you're working full time, you have enormous quantities of information flowing towards you from intelligence, from overt sources, from the public domain, everything, and you're grossly overworked. If you're reasonably successful, you are grossly overworked and you have very little time. Regrettably, in my view, people in that position, working full-time jobs, tend to be fairly dismissive of all the penumbra of civil society activity and networks and so on. They just don't have time to do it all, they're exhausted. They have a family life and they don't want to lose all their weekends, so their involvement in these things is not that great."

It's important to state, therefore, that a decision to attend a network event over a period of days requires a personal desire to take part. And while practical decisions, such as geographical location and the relevance of the gathering, might affect one's choice to be involved, it is personal motivation that underpins the decision. In the first of two extracts that follow, a steering committee member highlights some of the more practical considerations for attendees, but identifies the amount of effort that is required to establish oneself in the network. For some, especially those not comfortable networking, or those towards the ends of their career, the thought of having to spend at least two to three years ingratiating oneself is not a compelling one. It is, nevertheless, a decision that many will take if the network is considered attractive enough. In the second extract, it is particularly interesting to note the dismissive nature of the criticism leveled at anything other than the most elite networks. Since the prominence of participants, and the perceived exclusivity of the event, are intimately related to the perception of its quality, it's fair to say that the decision to attend is taken, at least in part, out of a sense of seeing oneself in good company.

"There are always people who say this is the best one, I like to go here more than there. And, also, it's true that some people prefer European gatherings, some industry gatherings, and others more global. So there's a bit of a difference [… and, of course] not everyone is interested in this kind of broader discussion. It's really not only skills, it's also whether you like it or not. And, of course, if you don't do it, that's another thing. I mean, I got into these circles fairly early because I became CEO here, and then you grow a little older with all the others. If you become CEO at the age of, I don't know, 57 or so, and then you get involved and don't know anyone, and it takes some time to get to be an accepted member of these circles. Maybe you say to yourself 'I don't want to do this,

I'm not the right person'. And, for politicians, very often language skills, you have to speak English otherwise it is difficult."

"When one is talking about transnational things, the Bilderberg was the one; that was a very good example. The other one was the Trilateral Commission, but that's much more formal. I have my doubts about some of these organizations. I think the Bilderberg one was successful in the way that I've described, I don't think all of them are. People spend an awful lot of time going around to these conferences and listening to other people. I think they're a waste of time, a lot of them."

What these comments demonstrate is the significance of personal interest and motivation to the attendance and functioning of elite networks – even among their most established members. This is not to say that an interest in public policy, civic-mindedness, or even a sense of calling, are unimportant – simply that there are a variety of more immediate personal and professional considerations motivating participation. The suggestion, therefore, that the transnational elite network is a consciously organized and directed instrument of globalization is questionable. It's not that elite participants deny the possible effects of such networks; simply that their appreciation of why they themselves take part is not couched in terms of such overarching objectives. As one elder statesman rather disbelievingly asked:

"Do you think there's all that sort of talk around the world, people picking up telephones and all that [... organizing globalization] being neoliberals? Do you really think they do?"

The more pertinent question, then, is not whether members of the trans-national elite are busy fulfilling their globalizing function, but whether they're aware that they are. Indeed, one of the surprising features of elite network activity is just how little thought is given by participants to what is taking place. In the interview extracts that follow, two Bilderberg steering committee members reflect on the purpose of their own participation.

"You never think about it really, I've never done so. It's been an important part of my life, but unintentionally. You don't do these

things because you want to be in a network, and you're not aware
that you'll be entering one, or whatever, but you may end up
being a part of it."

"Well, it's an interesting question. I'm [on the organizing committee of another prestigious elite transnational forum] and we've
only just had the discussion […] what is the value for members
and participants, and what is the value for society at large?"

Whatever the reasons for the lack of inquiry, it's clear that participants
feel themselves very much drawn to such activity. It is almost as if the
benefits of elite membership are self-evident, and that to be involved is a
natural extension of what it is to be a person of influence. Indeed, participation
in elite networks reinforces the perception of influence and, ultimately,
defines one as a member of the elite. This process, while largely unconscious, has implications for consensus within such settings, since participants
are identified, and identify themselves, as having the characteristics and
worldviews appropriate to membership. The subtle impressions of prevailing consensus within elite networks define what constitutes elite
"thinking" for existing participants and new entrants to the network. To
think otherwise is, to some extent, a mark of one's unsuitability to elite
membership.

The "old-boy" network

A frequent justification for transnational elite groups is that they are
dynamic networks rather than exclusive members' clubs – the latter being
more concerned with friendship and mutual assistance. Given the massive
increase in corporate board interlocks, and the cross-membership of lit-
erally hundreds of policy institutes, forums, councils, institutions, and
networks, an interesting question concerns the actual extent and dynamism
of transnational elite membership.

There are, of course, significant problems defining what constitutes the
transnational elite, because it has no obvious beginning or end. Some
have suggested that the transnational power elite runs into several thousand individuals, while others suggest a much smaller number.[35] The
problem is that these estimates are highly subjective and based on definitions of power and influence that are, at best, questionable. Our own

evidence is reputational in nature, based as it is on the subjective accounts of interview participants, and is unlikely to satisfy those looking for more substantive evidence. Nevertheless, when discussing those with mean-ingful influence, members of the most exclusive networks believe the transnational elite policy community to be reasonably familiar – and made up of no more than a few hundred individuals. This judgment may, of course, be relative in nature. If we'd asked members of elite networks that were not necessarily as exclusive as Bilderberg, we would likely have encountered a larger estimate. It could be argued, of course, that those within the most elite of networks have a greater appreciation of what constitutes influence and power in world affairs. If so, the anecdotal estimate of a few hundred individuals might be seen to be more insightful than estimates that rely on alternative definitions of power and influence.

What we can say with some certainty, however, is that there is a per-ception among Bilderberg participants that, very often, the same people are active in different contexts. Here, two extremely active elite "net-workers" talk about meeting the same people, over and over again, at different elite events.

> "The funny thing is, of course, that unfortunately we're not talking about a huge group of people. It's sort of an 'old-boy' network; you bump into each other every time. Not all of them, of course, but I have different levels, different types of international connections."
>
> "The Trilateral Commission is very much the same, the Eur-opean Roundtable,[36] there are so many. I mean, there was this 'Club of Three'[37] in which I participated many times, but even-tually I said to the organizer, 'it's too much'. I suddenly realized I was meeting people there who I'd met on other occasions, and so I told the organizer, 'it doesn't make sense for me to continue here. I'm not able to add any new input. Why don't you take somebody from the younger generation?'"

The overlapping membership of different networks, and the sheer volume of groups performing similar functions, has led to some calls for rationalization. But there is resistance to such demands, as the following extract, from a Bilderberg steering committee member, points out:

"You could merge many of them. They all have their history, they all have their pride, their tradition, their 'people who care'; you could easily say, 'why not merge things – it would be far more efficient?' And this question always comes up, to be honest. I mean, every time, someone says 'we will consider that' when we talk about succession planning [but] it's very often, you know, the people who are involved. It never quite works primarily because of tradition."

The tradition referred to here has less to do with the preservation of institutional identity than the inclinations of long-standing members in the groups concerned. Many are reluctant to accept rationalization for fear, perhaps, that they'll find themselves no longer participating. It's worth stating that, notwithstanding the unconcerned air affected by some network organizers, elite associations and networks are extremely important to their long-standing members. They not only derive some of their identity from such associations, but are also able to remain connected with policy issues when, otherwise, they might be cut off from such activity. This desire to remain *in situ* has led to accusations that many elite groups, including Bilderberg, are controlled by elderly, and in some cases geriatric, members of the elite network. Here, a member and attendee of various elite forums describes the motivation of some people to remain involved and, importantly, the impact of this on the overall dynamism of the network:

"When you retire from full-time work, you take up a lot of part-time jobs which still keep you – because you want to [be] – involved in international developments and so on. Then all these meetings become your lifeblood because this is how you keep in touch with people who have full-time jobs, with other people like yourselves, with the literature – because you're not receiving all that information any more. So it becomes your lifeblood, which is one of the reasons people who have retired go to these things so regularly [… Bilderberg?] I'm not sure how up to date it's kept, as I say, I think it's a bit on the geriatric side because it has a membership. That is to say, people who go every year from certain countries. And that means that it's very static – it's the same people who go year after year. It's a little bit the same with the Wehrkundetagung in Munich – the big security forum – which also has a certain sense in which it is rather static."

In the case of Bilderberg, the presence of elderly statesmen, financiers, and industrialists has undoubtedly lent cachet to the network and is part of its appeal to potential entrants. It is also, for this reason, a factor in the shaping of consensus within the group. In the following extract, an attendee of multiple Bilderberg conferences describes how its European consensus was clearly associated with its longest-serving, and somewhat iconic, figures:

"I think there probably is an inner group who probably do want to support the ever closer union of Europe, for instance, and they have been there since the beginning, whenever that was. Certainly from before the first time I went, anyway. On the occasions that I went, Dr Agnelli was, it seemed to me, the key figure in some way; the figure to whom other people were paying attention and deferring. And the second time, there was also the Queen of the Netherlands, who obviously played an important role and is a European federalist. But how that inner group works, I don't know, but it had a motive in setting this up and supporting it, and this affected [things]."

Longevity of membership, therefore, is clearly associated with perceived influence within the elite network. The more select and exclusive the network, the more reluctant its established members are to leave. This does lend a static quality to the more elite of networks and, over time, contributes to a more club-like atmosphere. Here, a member of various elite groups describes the attraction of smaller networks and the tendency of their members to remain in place:

"There is a French–German get-together that takes place at the highest levels. Actually I wouldn't say it's about levels, it's more about size. For instance, Davos is very big, but there is a group which is called the International Business Council – about a hundred CEOs of the largest companies meeting together, sometimes

under the umbrella of Davos. It meets twice a year and normally it
has about 50 percent participation – so only fifty people, but they
are top-level, CEO, representatives of the largest global corporations.
It's a bit more difficult maybe to get the [politicians together],
although even there, with politicians, you have top people in
smaller circles. It's very much tradition. If you started as a young
leader in one of these circles, you normally stay. There's another
one, the 'Group of Thirty',[38] for instance, and you are asked to
join and then people stay until they die."

This feature of elite membership is frequently seen as dysfunctional by
members of the network, but it nonetheless persists. In the two Bilderberg
interview extracts that follow, the first from a retired statesman, the
second from a prominent industrialist member of the group, it's interesting
to note the apparent contempt that both share for aspects of this
arrangement.

"I think it's a mistake for people who have been things to hang on
and go on speaking and boring everyone to tears with what they're
saying. I think it's much better that you shut up, go there and listen
to the others – and think how awful they are of course – but not to
go on taking a part. I think it's a mistake."

"Not everybody thinks the composition of these groups is ideal.
Those who are interested in attending these meetings are very
often 'has-beens'. I mean, Bilderberg has a lot of people, I don't
want to mention names but we all know them, the famous eighty-
to eighty-five-year-old politicians. Well, Davos does not invite
them. At Davos, when you're retired, you're retired. Which is not
a bad thing, because then you get the young people moving up
as well."

There is, implicit within this criticism, a feeling that long-standing
members of the network should "let go" and allow the scope for new
influences and fresh currents of opinion. The conservative tendency of
established networks towards the application of existing paradigms is seen
as a significant factor, therefore, in tempering and moderating the influence of new, emergent forms of consensus. The reasons for this are seen

as natural enough, but the pace of change clearly frustrates certain members of the network. It might also explain, given the development of communications technology and 24/7 media coverage, the emergence of more dynamic, fluid, and direct forms of elite network activity.

Conclusion

An appreciation of transnational elite networks is critical to an understanding of contemporary geopolitical activity. While many elite policy networks tend to be preoccupied with national issues, and many transnational elite networks are regional rather than truly trans-world in nature, there is a conscious desire to create understanding and linkages between once-disparate networks. Indeed, the networking activity of a relatively small group of prominent individuals is creating goodwill and linkages between once-disparate hubs of activity. The pattern of such networking is undoubtedly driven by the demands of a global economic imperative, but this is seen as creating the grounds for political, as well as economic, rapprochement. Fundamentally, elite transnational networks facilitate the alignment of interests in world affairs — although participants are frequently unconscious of their part in such a process. For members of elite networks, personal interest — however defined — is as critical to an understanding of motivation as any sense of global civic-mindedness.

The presence of media participants in transnational elite networks is especially interesting because it demonstrates the degree of interdependency that exists between the transnational policy and media elites. And, while it's impossible to state with certainty that media interests are not consciously co-opted into such networks for the express purpose of disseminating explicit messages, we suggest that the reality is rather more nuanced than it first appears. Media participants are an integral part of the consensus-formation process within such networks, to the extent that it's difficult to know where the interests of one begin and those of the other end. And mechanisms of compliance within the elite setting, such as the requirement for non-disclosure, reinforce the complex interrelatedness of the parties concerned. Specifically, they have the effect of establishing a subtle sense of inclusion and exclusion for those entering the network.

Elite networks exhibit a high degree of interlocking, which means that the overall number of participants is less than it might first appear — the anecdotal evidence of the Bilderberg attendees interviewed for this book suggests a transnational policy community comprised of no more than a few hundred individuals. The extended transnational elite network has no obvious boundaries but, for practical purposes, may be seen to extend to several thousand engaged individuals. The organizing committees and long-standing memberships of established elite networks resemble "old-boy" networks and, despite efforts to ensure dynamism, are perceived by some members of the network to be dysfunctional and standing in the way of progress. What kind of progress is unclear, but our research suggests that elite participants undoubtedly perceive that such activity has consequences and, indeed, could have more.

7

THE CONSEQUENCES OF ELITE CONSENSUS

Frankfurt, November 19, 2010. Dominique Strauss-Kahn, Managing Director of the International Monetary Fund (IMF), increasingly probable French Presidential candidate,[1] and former Bilderberg attendee, addresses the Sixth European Central Bank (ECB) Central Banking Conference on the subject of the sovereign debt crisis gripping the euro zone. In his speech, he calls on the European Union to fulfill its destiny, create greater integration, push forward with fiscal and structural reform, and free its decision-making processes from the short-sighted interference of individual nation-states:

> "The wheels of cooperation move too slowly. Repairing the financial sector is taking too long, in part because policymakers are not paying enough attention to the pan-European dimension. The common European vision also seems lacking when it comes to fiscal governance, internal imbalances or labor reform. Europe needs a holistic growth strategy, where every country benefits from the efforts of others […] How can such a comprehensive reform agenda be best achieved? There is no single grand solution, but challenges on this scale can only be solved in a collaborative manner. Just look at the lessons of recent European history. When

the agenda is driven by the center, things happen. Think of the single market program, or of monetary union. But when the agenda is left with the nations, things stall. Think about labor and service market reforms, especially through the Lisbon agenda. Peer pressure has not served Europe very well. It's time to change course. The center must seize the initiative in all areas key to reaching the common destiny of the union, especially in financial, economic and social policy. Countries must be willing to cede more authority to the center. Mechanisms must be redesigned to give them the incentives to reform […] The only answer is more cooperation, and greater integration. Now is the time to fortify the economic foundations of the union. None of this will be easy. But was the single market easy when first proposed? Was the single currency easy to design and implement? Europe has faced these kinds of challenges before, and overcame them. It can do so again. It's time to finish the job, to finally realize the common destiny of Europe."[2]

Strauss-Kahn's comments were made at a time of mounting speculation concerning the inevitability of a massive Irish government bailout from the EU and the IMF. Indeed, the formal application for assistance came just two days later and, given immediate and reassuring statements from those tasked with negotiating the terms of the loan, went some way to dampening market fears concerning contagion to countries such as Portugal, Spain, and Italy. Strauss-Kahn confirmed that the IMF stood "ready to join this effort, including through [the availability of] a multiyear loan. [The IMF would] hold swift discussions on an economic program with the Irish authorities, the European Commission, and the European Central Bank."[3] Ireland's debt crisis, the downstream consequences of which are still not fully known at the time of writing, represented the second occasion in several months that the very existence of the European single currency had been called into question. The Greek bailout package, negotiated earlier in the year in the face of considerable political hostility, had demonstrated just how perilous the sovereign debt crisis had become to the European project. Commenting after the Greek bailout, Paul Volcker, former Chairman of the Federal Reserve Bank, Chairman of President Obama's Economic Recovery Advisory Board, Chairman of the Board of Trustees of the Group of Thirty, Honorary North American Chairman of the Trilateral Commission, and longstanding Bilderberg participant, observed:

> "You have the great problem of a potential disintegration of the euro [...] the essential element of discipline in economic policy and in fiscal policy that was hoped for [has] so far not been rewarded in some countries [...] Will economic and financial distress finally be resolved by looking toward more integration in a closely integrated Europe, politically as well as economically? I do have my hopes, as a believer in the euro."[4]

After the Greek bailout was agreed, the European Commission made clear that, from that point forward, member state deficit oversight would be strengthened and, under a system of economic policy coordination, it aimed to "align national budget and policy planning".[5] These commitments, given that many euro zone member states, in the wake of the global financial crisis, were presiding over deficits well above the euro zone Stability and Growth Pact limit of 3 percent, were always likely to be a hostage to fortune as the true extent of the European debt crisis unfolded. What was more pertinent to ongoing attempts to deal with levels of sovereign debt in the euro zone was the support of stronger states, specifically that of Germany.

The Greek bailout agreement met with fierce opposition in Germany, where anger over domestic austerity measures was intensified by the prospect of underwriting a large part of the debts of another nation. As a consequence, the prospect of further bailouts was eyed nervously by German political leaders, who made clear that individual states would have to be more accountable, and that, rather than euro zone taxpayers bearing the entire cost of such activity, bondholders needed to face up to the prospect of taking "haircuts" on their investments.[6] A draft proposal from Berlin, which formed the basis for discussions by the European Commission, included measures such as the extension of debt maturities, holidays on interest payments during recovery periods, and a suspension of bondholder rights. Needless to say, an already volatile market became even more nervous at the suggestion of a meaningful moral hazard on its loans. The uncertain prospect of an Irish default compromised the government's ability to raise further funds and, as a consequence, bond yields soared to unsustainable levels.

In an attempt to shore up the Irish position, and protect the Euro from damaging repercussions, the ECB had, for some time, been lending to Ireland's banks and buying its bonds.[7] But, with the Irish government publicly resisting calls to negotiate a bailout, and feverish market speculation concerning the viability of its position, the ECB effectively forced Ireland's hand by suggesting that the support would have to end.[8] Forced into bailout discussions with the IMF and EU, Irish government representatives are said to have tabled the idea of defaulting on their debt, at which, one senior Irish source claims, "the Europeans went completely mad".[9] Irish Minister for Finance Brian Lenihan revealed that he'd also suggested senior bondholders accept some of the burden of the crisis but, again, officials from the IMF, European Commission and ECB had firmly vetoed any such move. They argued it would create a

> "huge wave of further negative market sentiment […] I certainly raised the matter in the course of the negotiations and the unanimous view of the ECB and the commission was, and is, that no programme would be possible if it were intended by us to dishonour senior debt […] Those who think we could [unilaterally renege on senior bondholders against the wishes of the ECB] are living in fantasy land."[10]

It seems clear that, notwithstanding the Irish public's own appetite for defaulting on the loans, and a rejection of the ensuing austerity measures that faced the country if it accepted an EU/IMF bailout,[11] Ireland's government believed the "nuclear" option of declaring the country bankrupt, and reneging on its debt obligations, was simply not feasible. Instead, they accepted the logic of a consensus related to the damage a default would cause to Ireland's ability to fund its immediate budget deficit. In short, if it defaulted on its debt, nobody would lend it money to fund its existing levels of expenditure – a threat with serious political implications. This consensus, along with another that suggested that the absolute scale of Ireland's debt was manageable if it could slash its current deficit, had been in circulation for some time. Speaking a month before the heightened crisis, Peter Sutherland, Chairman of Goldman Sachs

International, former Director-General of the General Agreement on Tariffs and Trade, former Group Secretary and General Counsel of the World Trade Organization (WTO), former EU Commissioner, former Attorney General of Ireland, former Chairman of the Allied Irish Bank, Foundation Board member of the World Economic Forum (WEF), European Honorary Chairman of the Trilateral Commission, and a long-serving steering committee member of Bilderberg, strongly urged against the default option, and defended the position of bondholders, when he claimed:

> "[Removing protection for bondholders] now, in the case of Anglo-Irish Bank, might well not be a wise course of action for a number of reasons […] To expose bondholders of subordinated debt and senior debt (not covered by current explicit guarantees issued) then the total maximum saving through creditors taking losses would be €5.1bn […] the other element in the balance sheet, namely depositors, would continue in any scenario to be protected. So whatever the total figure works out as being, only a small proportion could be saved. The risk of taking any such action is that the price would then be paid by the remaining Irish banks which still require external capital and funding and by the Government itself who then need to deal with the increased losses arising from a more immediate wind-down of Anglo Irish Bank […] Incidentally no other OECD country (other than Iceland) has allowed a major retail bank to default on its senior debt […] The "collateral damage" of such a decision would be very serious. For a small country such as Ireland to default on government-guaranteed debt when the funding position of the government (and the other Irish banks) is already precarious, would surely precipitate a funding crisis both for the sovereign and the banking system as a whole. A broader default would also bring few benefits but huge costs. Ireland's principal fiscal problem is its large primary deficit (rather than a large outstanding debt level). Compared with countries that have large outstanding debt levels, default is a relatively unattractive option for Ireland (because such an option would do nothing to address Ireland's primary deficit but *would* cut off its ability to fund its deficit)."[12]

The pressure on Ireland to accept the terms of a bailout was enormous and, while clearly framed in terms of its euro zone consequences, wasn't limited to direct currency considerations. German, British, and French banks were massively exposed to the Irish banks at the heart of the crisis,[13] and were obviously motivated to ensure a non-default solution. The conspicuous offer of the UK government, for instance, to support its "friend in need", despite not being in the euro zone, highlighted the interwoven political consequences of the financial arrangements of its banks. In a statement to the UK parliament, George Osborne, UK Chancellor of the Exchequer and regular Bilderberg attendee of recent years, while omitting to mention the £26 billion exposure of UK banks to their Irish counterparts and their much broader exposure to the Irish economy,[14] explained the decision of the government to lend £7 billion as part of the international rescue package in this way:

> "It is overwhelmingly in Britain's national interest that we have a stable Irish economy and banking system [… So, on top of the UK's contingent liability as a member of the 27 EU states lending money to Ireland,] I have agreed that the UK should consider offering a bilateral loan to Ireland, as part of the IMF and European package. I judge this to be in Britain's national interest. Let me explain why. We have strong economic relations with Ireland. Ireland accounts for 5 percent of Britain's total exports […] Just as our two economies are connected, our two banking sectors are also inter-connected […] two of the four largest high street banks operating in Northern Ireland are Irish-owned, accounting for almost a quarter of personal accounts. The Irish banks have an important presence in the UK. What is more, two Irish banks are actual issuers of sterling notes in Northern Ireland. It is clearly in Britain's interest that we have a growing Irish economy and a stable Irish banking system. By considering a bilateral loan, we are recognizing these deep connections between our two countries and, crucially, it has helped us to be at the centre of the discussions that have shaped the conditions of an international assistance package that is of huge importance to our economy."[15]

It's against the backdrop of this exposure to the consequences of an Irish default, and the risks of contagion for other European states, that one gains some insight into how the Irish were able to resist demands to increase their contentious level of corporation tax. But there was little other political comfort to be drawn from the deal, and Ireland accepted a bitter pill in terms of its sovereignty. Speaking in the wake of the EU/IMF negotiations, Gertrude Tumpel-Gugerell, executive board member of the ECB, and 2010 Bilderberg attendee, spared little time making clear who was now really calling the shots with respect to Ireland's finances when she publicly outlined the key priorities for the country:

> "Ireland now has to repair its banking system and bring its state finances in order, to win back trust from investors and the market."[16]

The extent of the deficit reduction commitments made by the Irish government and the acceptance of restrictive conditions related to performance against its commitments imposed a severe political constraint on its actions. Most humiliating of all, perhaps, were the letters of intent to the IMF and EU authorities.[17] Signed by Brian Lenihan and Central Bank governor Patick Honohan, they stated that the Irish government agreed to consult in advance for approval of remedial decisions if it failed to meet its quarterly obligations:

> "We stand ready to take any corrective actions that may become appropriate […] As is standard under fund-supported programmes, we will consult with the fund on the adoption of such actions."[18]

The spectacle of the once revered "Celtic Tiger" having to kow tow to European and international authorities was clearly too much for skeptics of the agreement. The surrendering of Irish sovereignty was seen, regardless of the drastic circumstances that brought it about, as the latest development in a relentless process of EU integration that, according to Viscount Davignon, is "irresistible over a period of time."[19] The respected political commentator Peter Oborne, for instance, pulled no punches in his description of Irish compliance with the terms of the EU/IMF bailout:

> "It cannot be denied that Ireland has lost its status as a sovereign nation. Thanks to its disastrous entanglement with the euro, it has

lost any independence in domestic, foreign and above all economic policy. The Irish nation is the creature of Brussels and the European Central Bank. The Irish prime minister has effectively been turned into a pro-consul dispatched to Dublin from Brussels. Brian Lenihan, the finance minister, is like an overseas manager of a Brussels subsidiary. For those of us who love Ireland, this is miserable and demeaning – but it needs to be borne in mind that a similar fate awaits a number of other European countries. Greece already does what it is told by the IMF and the ECB; the same will shortly apply to Portugal and in due course Spain."[20]

For multilateralists, however, Ireland's bailout further demonstrated the value of international cooperation in dealing with contemporary political and economic realities. Moreover, international turbulences of this kind, precipitated by the scale and reach of the global financial crisis, could be seen to provide an opportunity, albeit a costly one, to create a more coherent global governance framework. In a December 2010 speech, Pascal Lamy, Director-General of the WTO, former European Commissioner for Trade, Honorary President of the pro-integration think tank Notre Europe, and prominent Bilderberg attendee, described how the steady erosion of coherence and governance in world economic affairs over the past sixty years had created deficiencies in the international system and, importantly, deficiencies between national and global systems. He explained that a new world economic order, drawing on the lessons of the past, required a deeper "explicit renunciation of national sovereignty" and pointed to the emergence of a "triangle of coherence" in global governance:[21]

"Globalization can only be properly managed if we acknowledge that interdependence implies certain limits to the autonomy and sovereignty of nations. When it comes to establishing the minimum level of collective restraint in accordance with the principle of subsidiarity, that minimum will no longer be what it was in the past, in the Westphalian world. It involves a greater degree of explicit renunciation of national sovereignty. Why should such renunciation be accepted, when it might dangerously weaken the security and solidarity guaranteed by national sovereignty? Simply because those guarantees, however indispensable, have become illusory, and because they are better protected by shared sovereignty [... The Institutions of global economic governance] are changing. New ones have appeared, such as the Financial Stability Board, which itself came about as a result of the Asian crisis of the late 1990s, or the G-20, the new incarnation of the G-5 of the 1970s. Power within the World Bank and the IMF is shifting. A sort of "triangle of coherence" is forming within the network that links together the G-20 as a place of leadership, the United Nations as a place of legitimacy, and the specialized institutions as places of expertise and of mobilization of resources."[22]

The expression of these sentiments, no doubt designed to offer comfort to those wondering whether the current challenges of multilateralism might signal a return to protectionist agendas, highlights the ongoing ideological confrontation being waged between national and transnational elite interests. Speaking a few weeks earlier, on the very day that Dominique Strauss-Kahn called for European nations to "cede more authority"[23] in order to fulfill Europe's destiny, Lamy pointed to the stark choice facing world citizens and, conveniently overlooking the contribution of globalization to the most recent crisis, provided an unapologetic defense of the multilateralist agenda:

"Economic crises are a reality of the world we live in. They have occurred in the past and will in the future as well. At present, the global economy finds itself recovering from one of the worst in history. Economic crises, naturally, create problems at home. It is in these times that proponents of unilateralist, populist policies which discriminate against foreign workers and goods become more vocal. Instead, during tough economic times, those of us who believe in multilateralism must let our voices be heard. Some may call us naïve, or even idealists. But the lessons of history are there: they show us that it is coordinated action through international cooperation that maximizes benefits for citizens of the world. I hope that when this crisis is over, it will be this lesson of cooperation that will have prevailed. Other options would certainly leave each of us much worse."[24]

This need to restate the ideological foundations of globalization is, in some ways, an acknowledgement of the damage done to the cause by the financial crisis of 2007/08. Speaking in 2009, Viscount Davignon had articulated the threat it posed to the European project when he said, with uncharacteristic frankness, that the "jury is out"[25] on how successful Europe would be in response to the crisis. He predicted that there would be a period of uncertainty as EU leaders formulated their response and generated the necessary goodwill for coordinated action. And, while formal gatherings of European leaders would demonstrate commitment to the collective cause, he was looking to the open dialogue of the forthcoming Bilderberg conference to further "improve understanding" – in the same way that its gatherings facilitated creation of the euro in the 1990s:[26]

> "When we were having debates on the euro, people [at Bilderberg] could explain why it was worth taking risks and the others, for whom the formal policy was not to believe in it, were not obliged not to listen, and had to stand up and come up with real arguments."[27]

The implicit suggestion here, of course, is that there are no "real arguments" standing in the way of an enlightened pursuit of greater European integration. Improving understanding is therefore less about identifying the most favorable outcome since, for members of the transnational elite network, a consensus on this already exists. Instead, it is about improving the understanding of those who fail to see it as such. And, given the subtle mechanisms of compliance at work within elite policy communities, one can see how enlightened and compelling this consensus must appear. Challenging its fundamental precepts is, for the most part, unthinkable (if one wishes to remain in the network) and, moreover, unlikely to shift the established beliefs of the group. As a consequence, critical voices have become increasingly marginalized in the European elite policy community and are seen as dangerously out of touch with the realities of contemporary world politics. One such Bilderberg attendee, rare in the sense that he was invited back, explained his resistance to the consensus of Bilderberg, and the European policy elite in general, on this subject. In particular, he identified the lack of public support and the vulnerability of the European Union to major economic or political shocks. What makes his comments all the more pertinent is that they were made just months before the collapse of Lehman Brothers and the ensuing political fall-out:

> "My own view [about the gap that exists between policymakers and the public on this issue] is that it's all fine so long as nothing goes particularly wrong. The public will continue to accept it because it's there and they don't understand it terribly well. They don't like it but, on the other hand, they don't generate the energy on the subject for there to be any question of them actually changing it, so long as governments remain of this mind. On the other hand, I regard the European structure as distinctly vulnerable in two respects: [the first] is that I don't think it has got the backing and loyalty of the people; [the second is that] I don't think it's got the capacity to survive a major global crisis – economic or political. I mean, if you look at the history of the twentieth century, I think there's no doubt that a slump of the severity of the early 1930s would destroy the European Union. I don't know that any other economic events would, but that, I think, would have. It brought down every local government, it brought down the Labour government in Britain, it brought down the Weimar Republic in Germany, and so on. In that sense, Europe doesn't have the capacity to remain the European Union if great pressures are put on it. [Added to which], you've got now nearly a 100,000 pages of the *Acquis communautaire* which, in effect, is impossible to change. This structure is therefore extraordinarily rigid and, even in simple engineering terms, if you have a rigid structure exposed to variable forces there comes a point when it breaks up, as the Soviet Union did. So I don't think it's going to work, but I don't think it's going to be changed by a change in public opinion, except in circumstances of crisis."

Rather than shaking the resolve of members of the transnational elite community, the global financial crisis has, if anything, emphasized the need to see the project through to its conclusion. It has highlighted the necessity for greater international cooperation and co-dependency and, crucially, the need to cede greater degrees of sovereignty to emergent world governance systems. The resolve of this community, stripped bare of its immediate considerations – whether they be Greek, Irish, Portuguese, or Spanish – is anchored in the enlightened superiority of the logic that underpins it. The short-term costs of adherence to its overarching demands are a justifiable, and to some extent unavoidable, consequence of the need to reconcile contradictions between national and international governance structures. It's for this reason that international crises, while encouraging protectionist responses in the short term, simultaneously present an opportunity to create greater structural dependencies between states. The pursuit of an ever more integrated economic, social, and political union between nations will, after all, be brought about only when nations are exposed to the risks of standing alone.

The influence of elite networks

The influence of transnational elite networks is a contentious area and, in many ways, a continuation of decades-old debates related to where power really exists in society.[28] It's made all the more problematic, however, by fundamental questions related to how we understand power in contemporary society. If, for instance, we reject the idea that power might be unconsciously exercised, or we believe that it requires a transaction of some kind in order to be made visible, then we might reasonably conclude that elite policy networks are rather benign with respect to the overall contours of world affairs. If, on the other hand, we believe that power does not need to be consciously exercised in order to influence, and that its effects might be so discreet that they remove the necessity for conscious decision making,[29] then the implications of transnational elite interactions may be far more profound than they first appear. In the following interview extract, a skeptical Martin Wolf, Chief Economics Editor of the *Financial Times*, longstanding fellow of the WEF, and regular Bilderberg attendee, highlights the central difficulty of understanding elite consensus in terms of influence – not least because of its rather ethereal and unbounded quality.

> "These are, in some sense, private discussions. I would assert very strongly that these are briefing meetings, and what consequences have followed is not at all clear […] There's a general point about

humanity, which is, ideas circulate and resonate and become ruling ideas for a while, until they're replaced by some other set of ruling ideas. This is a complicated process, which involves books, radio programs, TV programs, political debate, big events like 9/11, the fall of the Berlin Wall, things like that, and, of course, discussions and groupings of this kind […] It's incredibly difficult, I think, to identify the role in the dissemination of ideas and attitudes of groupings of this kind, but my own guess is that actually they are very, very, minor. I think they tend to echo and reproduce ideas which are being generated elsewhere, often by intellectuals, rather than actually generating them, but there are ideas in the air. At the moment, for example, it's the idea of globalization. It's impossible to identify where that comes from and say it's the World Economic Forum's idea. It clearly isn't."

On the whole, Bilderberg participants tended to baulk at the idea of a direct and causal relationship between elite consensus and downstream policy responses. They were, nevertheless, reluctantly prepared to accept that elite consensus might have some bearing on policy outcomes despite being rather difficult to understand or measure. Here, for instance, a government participant toys with the suggestion of discreet influence before pragmatically dismissing it on the grounds that it's somehow just a fact of life:

"Does this influence the emergence of policy? It's very difficult to put your finger on it, you know, but just because you can't put your finger on it does not prove that it doesn't. Anyway, the fact is, it's there."

And, on the face of it, there are clearly some areas of policy formation where the dominant logic of the transnational elite appears to have significance for the way that policy issues are framed. Take, for instance, the rich vein of internationalist consensus that prevails in the elite foreign policy circles of most industrialized nations. Often at odds with opinion in its own backyard, this consensus has a huge bearing on the policy responses of government in areas such as trade bloc membership, legal and constitutional frameworks, international financial obligations, national currencies, and even, of course, military interventions. In the following extract, a British Bilderberg participant describes the generational persistence of internationalist consensus among the prominent elite networks of the nation – including that of the House of Lords:

> "I think that if you put all the groups together, you can sort them into core groups which share a sort of common consensus – a common consensus which is, incidentally, very noticeable in the House of Lords. If you take the foreign policy internationalist group, not all of them agree, but a majority of them hold certain views about the future development of British policy which are similar to the Bilderberg group and similar to Chatham House and similar, I imagine, to most of the meetings at Ditchley, though those probably are rather more variable. And there are common assumptions there. It's partly generational that these are the common assumptions, [… these] people were adult in the early 1970s when Britain joined the European Community, and they have not changed their view that this was the right long-term development for Britain."

But this depiction is a far cry from that of a conscious and shadowy elite surreptitiously exercising power in the pursuit of its objectives. For the most part, internationalist members of the elite make no secret of their convictions – indeed, why should they? They are reasonably fashionable worldviews within the context of the wider policy community. Equally, elite networks, while offering the opportunity for debate, are not designed or viewed as decision-making forums. They may have people in attendance who are capable of influencing policy outcomes, but to suggest that consensus is being consciously manufactured and disseminated overlooks a couple of critical factors. First, even if elite participants were persuaded of the merits of a new perspective, they would face the challenge of disseminating such a worldview within the context of their existing, and potentially resistant, constituencies. Second, social and professional networks are notoriously unreliable mechanisms for the communication of consistent messages. Aside from the question of whether coherent consensus is being transmitted in the first place, there are social and political considerations to the way that information and ideas are spread. The suggestion, therefore, that a unitary story is being transmitted and received is highly questionable. In the following interview extracts, the first with a financier participant and the second with a steering committee member, it's clear that the instrumental depiction of ideas being transmitted, received and executed within the context of a highly efficient communications network is, at best, limited as a description of events.

> "I think we're miles from, not even close to, any situation where [that happens]. I mean, I don't think people are swapping views and coming to new views and saying let's impose these or something [like that]. There isn't the possibility of, somehow, a consensus developing which is then implemented because we've got to go back to our political democracies."

> "There is one thing with networks that you must be aware of. As kids, we would play this game. You write three words on a piece of paper and then pass it on to your neighbor, and he adds a fourth, and on it goes. And it's passed around the table and comes back to you, [and you find that] your original intention is totally reversed. It's great fun, but in networks I've found out that, from each knot in the network to the next, your message can be changed, and it may be received differently two knots further down, or left or right, and so on. This is very important, you have to be aware of this. You may say this is black, and then after the next knot it's already black and white, totally chequered. There may be some surprises after that, so networks are only as good as the transmitters they have. And some may not transmit the proper message on purpose, you have to know that. It's like in a complicated chip, sometimes it doesn't work as you think it will."

Despite this resistance to the idea that the transnational elite network is consciously manufacturing and spreading particular brands of consensus, there is nevertheless a widespread belief among participants that elite interactions of this kind do contribute in some way towards political agenda-setting. This was often conveyed in terms of the effects of being exposed to the thoughts of opinion leaders, or such things as "breathing the air," but the underlying implication is clear – as the following media and academic participants observed.

> "I'm sure there is [some influence]. People share views […] you can see what the world agenda will be in a couple of years".
>
> "My impression is that what was discussed helps to agenda-set […] I say this from a personal point of view, it does kind of set an agenda that goes beyond the group. It gives you expertise because you're getting serious people talking about areas they know a lot about. So when the topic comes up, I think, 'yeah, I heard somebody say something, and they were head of that company that is key in that sector, it is probably true' […]. These guys pick up that others take it seriously. If the Head of BP and the Head of Shell say it's serious, then they'll go away and think it's serious."

A fundamental question, of course, concerns whether the group is consciously planning or orchestrating these effects. It's not possible entirely to discount the suggestion, and certainly there may be a strong case to be made for the activity, and residual effects, of transatlantic elite networks during the Cold War period. But surely, if it existed today, the evidence for such conscious strategizing behavior would be more pronounced than an array of subtle effects and idiosyncratic responses appear to suggest. In short, the processes are far less consciously deterministic than one would expect if this were the case. And, certainly, the persistent claim on the part of Bilderberg organizers that the group does not stand for anything, or do anything, is interesting in this respect. It clearly does stand for something, and most definitely does have effects, but not necessarily in the way that critics suggest or organizers conceive of them. In the following interview extracts, for instance, from two steering committee members (the first Viscount Davignon), the suggestion that the group exercises power is squarely rejected:

> "No, I don't think the group has power. I think individual people have influence, but I don't think the group has power."
>
> "It was a very loose organization, nothing ever came out of it. It was [about] what you put into it and what you got out of it yourself. The organization didn't do anything."

At the same time, the value of elite forums as mechanisms of consensus formation is acknowledged. In the two interview extracts that follow, the first from Viscount Davignon, the second from political commentator Will Hutton, the consensus of elite forums is clearly presented as something that is both useful politically, and difficult to resist. The extent of its overall influence may be debatable, but it is clearly misleading to suggest that elite networks serve no political function.

> "Can it, at the margins of a problem, help to create a consensus? Each government needs support for what it does, particularly in the United States, with Congress and so on, and where the action of outside groups on political decision making is much greater than in Europe. Do you need to do that? It can be useful. How useful, I cannot say."
>
> "Becoming of more importance are some of these country-to-country meetings which take place – bilateral places where people gather on Friday lunchtime and go through to Sunday. All kinds of people meet, and discuss a common agenda, and that really is where a kind of bilateral common sense works its way out. And it's very difficult to go against that kind of consensus. Many are there because they've been elected, and who can deny them their right to go? But one shouldn't deny the influence of these places."

If we accept, therefore, that elite transnational networks have the potential for significant influence within the milieu of international policy activity, and yet, for those involved, are little more than "talking shops," we must consider the nature of the influence that is being exerted. After all, the presumption that members of the elite are indulging in activity that is, in some way, illegitimate is frequently premised on an idea that they are consciously attempting to influence world events or specific policy outcomes. As we've demonstrated, however, elite participants are for the most part unconscious of the consequences of their interactions and, while ignorance may be no defense, it almost certainly has implications for the way that we view and critique such activity.

Spreading the word

In some ways, the reality of transnational elite networks is far less interesting than we might believe it to be. Yes, they are collectives of powerful individuals who, for reasons already described, meet privately and appear to seek out the company of other powerful people. Some aspects of this activity are extremely interesting and, at times, highly suspicious, but it should be clear by now that such networks are not consciously organized or determined to the extent that some people believe. In fact, the reality of consensus formation and dissemination within and beyond elite networks of this kind has far more to do with unconscious processes of preference adaptation than conscious or overt attempts at collective manipulation. This is not the same thing as seeing adapted preferences within the context of transnational elite networks as in some way accidental; indeed they are not. But it is also not the same thing as saying that transnational network organizers are meaningfully plotting or directing the output of elite networks.

When, for instance, we look at the way that elite forms of consensus are assimilated and diffused, it becomes apparent that the personal considerations of individuals are absolutely critical. In the following interview extracts, for example, two Bilderberg attendees describe the immediate benefits they derive from membership of the group and, in particular, point to the value of the information and insights they are able to use. The first describes how his association with the network, and the value of its ideas, have been important to his credibility as a central banker in the policy circles of his country. The second, a businessman, recognizes an immediate value to his company of the geopolitical insights he gains as a consequence of his network membership.

> "Just to [be able] to distribute those kinds of ideas […] one or two is enough. I remember one new idea in a month is enough, you know, to show that this man is, firstly, a knowledgeable man, secondly, a powerful man, and, thirdly, a dependable man. These are the two or three important areas for the central banker."
>
> "A few weeks ago, I was at the Bilderberg conference outside Washington to talk about Afghanistan, Palestine, Georgia, and many other things, in a confidential group where you have politicians, academics, business people, and media people. It opens a lot of new aspects and avenues. And that has, implicitly of course, an impact on how you run your business or how you formulate your strategy. So in that sense, I think, it is very direct."

It is also clear that the consensus of transnational elite networks, such as it is, is not some form of extant reality or stated agreement – it exists in the minds of the people who are exposed to it.[30] Sometimes, of course, the sense of this consensus might be particularly strong and may have implications for the importance one attaches to it – consciously or otherwise. But, for the most part, elite participants do not feel themselves to have been subjected to some kind of ideological brainwashing. They feel, instead, that they are part of the process rather than the subjects of it. Even where certain people are perceived to be, in some way, more active in consciously disseminating information or ideas, they are not necessarily seen as being functionaries of the network or group. Here, for instance, an attendee cites what he sees as the 10 percent of participants who appear to be on a mission of some kind, but makes clear that this isn't, in any way, an explicit requirement of membership:

> "Everybody goes away with their own learnings, whatever they take from the meeting. And I have a feeling, as I say, that every year when such meetings happen, 10 percent of the crowd that gets together goes back with a mission of spreading the message. But there's no force behind it saying 'the Trilateral Commission wants this, you do this'. I don't see that pact."

Similarly, organizers vehemently deny that there is any deliberate attempt to spread given messages. David Rockefeller, for instance, in a speech he gave in 1980, spelled out the Trilateral Commission position on this issue:

> "The Trilateral Commission does not take positions on issues or endorse individuals for office. It publishes a quarterly journal, holds plenary meetings that rotate from region to region, and gets task force reports that take well over a year each to prepare. To encourage lively and uninhibited debate and a full exchange of views, we do not open Commission meetings to the public. But we do make available all reports. My point is that, far from being a coterie of international conspirators with designs on covertly ruling the world, the Trilateral Commission is, in reality, a group of concerned citizens interested in fostering greater understanding and cooperation among international elites."[31]

Given that many of the mechanisms of bias and compliance within elite settings are discreet, this is a perfectly understandable perspective. Organizers do not acknowledge, in any way, the subtle mobilization of bias within their networks or the hidden forms of compliance at work. Attendees are very much seen as interpreting and spreading what they choose to believe, with no interference or manipulation on the part of those at the heart of the network. Here, for instance, Viscount Davignon describes how he sees consensus emanating from the Bilderberg group:

> "I think it happens, but it happens because, if people are convinced about something, and they participate in another seminar, they will the hold the same language as [was] held at Bilderberg. But Bilderberg is not decisive in doing that. We don't plan the multiplication, we leave it to the members – not the members, the participants – and if they felt that something useful was [spoken] there, then they go out and spread their convictions. And I think that's the important point: Bilderberg, as such, does not try to have a position. If people who come think that good sense has been spoken, and that they would like to repeat it in other fora, so much the better."

Leaving aside Davignon's mistake, or Freudian slip, concerning membership of the network, his comments suggest that personal predisposition is at the heart of the dissemination of ideas and consensus. With the exception of the minutes of the meetings – top-line and unattributed descriptions of conference sessions – there is no obvious or coordinated attempt to describe or define the nature of the discourse that has taken place at Bilderberg. Individuals do, indeed, leave the conference with their own, albeit socialized, sense of what was discussed at the event. And it is these impressions that form the basis of what is communicated or used externally. The process is extremely soft, and practically impossible to control or measure in any meaningful way. That being said, participants did, on the whole, accept that the currents of thought in evidence at the conference had consequences well beyond the community and several days of the event. These effects are rarely transformational, and tend to be discreet and incremental in nature. In the following interview extracts with three Bilderberg attendees, the third a member of the steering committee, the process is described in more detail. Of particular interest is the way in which the consensuses of national policy communities are influenced by these discreet transnational forces:

> "People can change views slightly after hearing a well informed crowd from the world, so to some degree, that might influence policy as it trickles down to these leaders, through words to their own presidents. So that's the message to me, as far as the message [goes]. I haven't seen any radical policy changes that were initiated by such people."
>
> "When you get back, you use this in your own rhetoric, in explaining to people what would be a more sensible way out of an evident crisis [...] If you are a good recipient of messages, you get a good amount of food for thought, which you go back [with] and chew over. And then you try to build it into your policies or take assessment of your existing policies, redesign them according to those ideas."
>
> "Once you participate to some degree in these networks, you come to hear other things, or you come to hear the same story but in a very different way. And, of course, you file that and you return home and maybe your attitude changes; you insert something new back home, not only in your business, but also in your national networks, talking to politicians and others [...] I do [think it's a by-product rather than a goal of elite meetings], particularly when such a meeting is international and the participants return to their home country, and then, under the influence of what they've heard, they start networking within their own national environment [in order] to reach a goal. This may be a consensus on an issue with whoever would be necessary to build a consensus; could be competitors, different political parties, or I don't know what. Yes, true."

Every now and again, during the course of the interviews conducted for this book, there was a hint of purpose revealed by long-standing members of the network. Nowhere was this more evident than in the following extract from an interview with a very prominent member of the group. His endearing description of influence emphasizes an incremental and rather "hit-and-miss" process, but look beyond the description and there is a sentence that includes the phrases "maybe we've contributed" and "we were utterly unsuccessful":

"Maybe I've acted as a little chip here and there with maybe a hundred other chips from a hundred other people. Maybe we've contributed to reshaping things in some way. And sometimes, we were utterly unsuccessful; in fact, I think this was the more common experience. But I was not waiting for a huge impact that would change the nation forever, not at all. Because I only sort of changed a little bit, half a degree here or there, to improve things in a certain direction. Something along those lines, I think that was enough."

What this suggests, at the very least, is a collective identity for those at the core of the network – an identity based upon shared understanding and outlook. It also suggests that, within the context of such a network, there is more at play than a desire simply to engage in policy discussions; there is a desire to influence opinion through the application of enlightened internationalist thought. Before conspiracy theorists scent a "silver bullet," however, it is worth pointing out that many of the network's organizers are, themselves, unconscious of their own bias in this regard. Their internationalist inclinations are considered highly objective, rational and, to some extent, superior to the more parochial considerations of nationalists and protectionists – to the extent, perhaps, that they have ceased to be considered ideological in any meaningful sense. And, when one considers that such views are now an accepted logic within the policy communities of many developed countries, it's reasonable to question whether there's any longer an ideological distinction to be drawn between transnational network organizers and their national participants – especially given the inclination of elite networks to invite those already predisposed. That being said, transnational elite networks, and the consensuses that emanate from them, play an important ongoing role in facilitating the creeping requirements of the overarching liberal internationalist objective.

Conclusion

Transnational elite participants are fiercely resistant to the idea that their interests or identities might have adapted or altered as a consequence of their membership of elite communities. At the same time, they are prepared to accept the suggestion of influence from exposure to new information and compelling arguments – these types of influence being seen as objective and dissociated from any notion of power. As enlightened members of the elite, they see themselves, therefore, as responding to the dictates of common sense and bounded rationality as if, in some way, this were a value-neutral exercise. In short, elite participants have a peculiarly uncontaminated sense of their own identity, and adapt preferences in accordance with influences they consider to be of their own making. This is important, of course, because the discreet mechanisms of compliance at work in elite network structures are anchored in the personal motivations and interests of individuals, rather than the consciously manipulative efforts of organizers.

Since the consensus of elite networks does not exist in any objective or extant form, and instead exists in the minds of those exposed to it, it's impossible to say how meaningful or homogeneous it actually is. It is also difficult to know with any certainty, given the vagaries of network transmission, how coherent and consistent is the resulting dissemination of consensus. What we do know, from the participants themselves, is that they consider elite transnational networks to be extremely valuable and a rich source of information. Indeed, they acknowledge the influence of such information on their thinking when they return to their countries and constituencies. They even confirm that, armed with the knowledge they have gleaned, they are able to influence the thinking of others. This influence tends to be very soft and incremental in nature, contributing to currents of thinking or opinion that may have their origins elsewhere, but it also has the capacity to challenge, not least because of the standing of its communicator or an awareness of the provenance of the idea.

Without being privy to the meetings and private discussions of network organizers, it's not possible to know for sure the extent to which the consensus of elite networks is consciously steered or nurtured. It seems evident from early accounts of prominent groups that this was, at the outset, a more explicit function of such activity. As the security preoccupations and structural certainties of the Cold War have passed, however, and the forces of neoliberal globalization have simultaneously advanced, the conscious function of such activity appears to have blurred. Many participants struggled to articulate a meaningful purpose for such activity, other than benefits associated with greater cooperation and understanding. But scrape away at the surface-level dynamics of such activity, and we discover discreet, and largely unconscious, determinants of consensus – determinants that are by no means accidental in their form or effects. The fact that transnational elite network organizers and participants are, for the most part, unconscious of their influence does not mean that they do not exist – instead, it demonstrates the insidious nature of their influence and the challenge facing those who seek to effect change.

CONCLUSION

Making sense of elite power and consensus

The end of the Cold War brought with it a considerable shift in the way that consensus was reached in international relations. Prior to this, it was heavily influenced by structural alliances related to issues of ideology, security, and trade. Informal elite networks, especially those of the transatlantic community, were seen as serving the function of cementing relations in the face of mutual threats and challenges. As the perception of these threats lessened, however, the far-reaching effects and interdependencies of rampant globalization brought with them a new and more shifting basis for cooperation and consensus in international affairs – one that was anchored in the management of legitimacy.

Legitimacy has become critical to our understanding of individual and collective action in contemporary world politics because it is not some kind of extant reality – instead, it is a fluid, expedient, and purposeful concept. And, while our understanding of legitimacy might frequently be based on ideas of legality, sovereignty, and authority, it is at the same time an inherently more political condition.[1] Within the context of elite policy circles, the socially constructed realities and temporal certainties of consensus should not be seen as mystically arising from an enlightened fusion of elite minds; they are instead a function of discreet contests for the definition of legitimacy within the elite policy community.

Controlling how legitimacy is constituted is the real power play of contemporary world politics, since it can dictate the capacity for, and nature of, individual and collective forms of inertia or action. If we want to understand the interests, goals, and beliefs of international policy actors, we need to first come to terms with their sense of the legitimate.[2] And, importantly, we need to understand how certain worldviews and paradigms gain legitimacy within this community.

A clue to this, perhaps, is provided by the transcendental superiority with which collaboration, as a pragmatic response to complex world problems, is viewed by elite participants. Indeed, the logic of collaboration is such an embedded feature of policy elite rationality that to question it is to appear laughably naïve in the ways of the world. It is important to recognize, however, that this rationality underpins an intrinsically suspect appreciation of legitimacy within such networks. After all, if collaboration is normatively imbued with legitimacy by elite participants, it naturally follows that the product of collaboration – consensus – should be similarly imbued with its reflective legitimacy. Not least because the notion of consensus, rooted as it is in notions of cooperation, shared understanding, and compromise – and the rejection of dogma, confrontation, and zero sum rationality – has very much emerged as a legitimized construct in its own right. In short, notions of collaboration, consensus, and legitimacy are mutually constitutive for members of the transnational policy elite.

The discursive and deliberative arrangements of the transnational policy elite, however, are not perfect and uncontaminated spheres of enlightened social construction. Instead, they represent subtly contested arenas in which power relations are critical to our understanding of eventual consensus and legitimacy. The idea that networks of this kind should, in some way, be seen as preceding the formation of interests, thereby limiting the potential for conflict, is nonsense. As is the suggestion that members of the transnational policy elite represent a homogeneous collective with uniform interests and little of substance to divide them. The lack of conflict that characterizes elite networks is as much to do with the existence of power relations as the absence of them – something that makes more sense when we consider the discreet mechanisms of compliance at work within such settings.

Transnational elite networks are not immaculately conceived; they are the product of design. The dynamics of power that inform that design, and emanate from it, are of critical importance to an understanding of ongoing bias within elite policy communities. In the first instance, historical, cultural, ideological, and social biases are amplified through such things as selection processes, norms, rules, and rituals. Bilderberg's selection process begins and ends with its steering committee members – people at the heart of the network. They are ultimately responsible for deciding who is suitable for entry and, more disparagingly, who is considered "dull" and replaceable in the interests of dynamism. Observance of the rule of non-disclosure, and other unwritten codes of elite conduct, are prerequisites for network inclusion. As is the idea that newcomers should "sing for their supper" – a widespread belief demonstrating the degree to which new entrants are being tested by established members of the network.

Added to these more institutional determinants of alignment and consensus in transnational elite communities, however, are more discreet mechanisms of individual compliance. These insidious, "third-dimensional"[3] forces of power have the effect of impairing the capacity for reason among subjects by instilling or reinforcing an illusory sense of what is natural.[4] They are effective in the elite context because of the unspoken desire among aspirant members to become fully actualized within the network. The seductive lure of elite membership should not be underestimated, although clearly it varies by individual. It is intimately related to the participants' own sense of self-esteem, since to be accepted is an affirmation of one's worthiness, and to be rejected is to have somehow failed to make the grade – an experience that elite individuals are unaccustomed to and frequently unwilling to acknowledge.

The desire to impress, and be seen as worthy and intelligent within such communities, is a palpable one for new entrants. Determining sources and currents of enlightened thought, and revealing one's own disposition towards such thinking, is a critical first step towards demonstrating network suitability. Of course, individuals are expected to go further than this, but the largely unconscious identification of enlightened frames of reference, and the motivation to be accepted, leads to a subtle adaptation of preferences. The emphasis here is on the word subtle. These adaptations are rarely absolute, since the forces that bring them about, in anything other than fictional accounts, are never more than partially effective.[5] This is one of the reasons why elite participants are unwilling to concede that their preferences have been adapted by network membership, despite having provided evidence to the contrary.

In summary, elite policy networks are biased at source and, consciously or otherwise, have the effect of amplifying their biases. It's not possible to say with absolute certainty whether such bias is consciously reinforced by organizers, or whether it's a product of prevailing elite structures and external influences, but our interviews suggest it to be largely unconscious in its form and effects. The difficulty here is compounded by the fact that transnational elite members consider themselves to be enlightened rather than in any way partisan in their thinking. This is partly indicative of the degree to which liberal internationalist and, more specifically, economic globalization frames of reference have become the starting point for elite discourse. It is also deeply indicative of the degree of self-delusion that exists in the elite community.

An obvious example of the difficulty of determining conscious or unconscious intent for elite actions is provided by the grooming of the next generation of world leaders. In 1974, *Time* magazine ran an article entitled "The world: Kissinger's old-boy network,"[6] in which Henry Kissinger's continuing commitment to alumni of the International Seminar he had run at Harvard University for eighteen years was described. The article explained how alumni of his class were granted access and time with Kissinger while he was US Secretary of State. It also described how he had, each year, handpicked forty students from around the world to take part in the course – individuals he believed would go on to great things in their respective careers. As it happened, he picked well. Many of his alumni went on to occupy leading roles in governments around the world. More recently, and in a similar vein, the World Economic Forum (WEF) initiated its Global Leadership Fellows program, enrolling twenty-five young people annually – individuals with the "drive to be ahead of conventional thinking, [people with] impeccable intellectual and moral integrity, and the unconditional commitment to serving the Forum's mission and its communities".[7] It also launched its Young Global Leaders program, a global community of 750 "exceptional"[8] and "rigorously"[9] selected under-forties designed to build "a next-generation leadership community that is mission-led and principle-driven, while being inclusive but merit-based."[10]

Leaving aside the question of why the WEF should see itself as a legitimate custodian of such interests, there exists the more general question of what we're to make of this activity. Is it simply driven by a genuine interest in cultivating a generation of more adept and qualified leaders than the last? Or is it a manifestation of deliberate ideological intent — is the existing generation of world leaders ensuring compliance with its wishes by seductively co-opting the next generation? The reality, we believe, is both of the above. The mechanisms of compliance are very real, and elite policy structures are certainly deterministic. But, for the most part, they are unconsciously so. That is to say, those ultimately responsible — those at the heart of the network — are so convinced of their transcendental objectives, and so convinced of the enlightened nature of their worldview, that they fail to recognize it as inherently partisan — moreover, they see it as a personal responsibility to engage others in its enlightened cause. They are doing what they do in the largely unquestioned belief that it makes good sense to do so — evidence, perhaps, that even those at the heart of the network are in service of forces that they can neither perceive nor resist.

As we've demonstrated, the role of those at the centre of the network is critical to our understanding of power and consensus in transnational elite networks since it is obvious, despite the protestations of organizers, that they represent a club of individuals with shared values — a club that undoubtedly influences the collective perception of common sense and enlightened thinking within the extended elite community. It should be clear, therefore, that we view the issue of network centrality, and issues of collaboration, power, consensus, and legitimacy, as fundamentally interrelated.

An acknowledgement of the influence of those at the heart of elite networks also has implications for how we define the transnational elite network, or global power elite. Do we, as some suggest, come up with arbitrary definitions of what constitutes power and influence, and then attempt to attribute a number? Or do we accept that a smaller number of individuals at the center of the most elite of transnational policy networks wield disproportionately high levels of influence? Evidence provided by those interviewed for this book suggests that a smaller number — no more than a few hundred people — represent the real core of influence in transnational policy circles but, admittedly, there are problems with attaching too much credence to anecdotal accounts of this kind. What we do know is that the networking activity of a relatively small number of individuals – "a few dozen cosmopolitans"[11] if you like – is creating goodwill and linkages between disparate clusters of elite network activity. The pattern of such networking is undoubtedly driven by the demands of economic globalization, but is viewed by members of the elite as creating the grounds for political, and not just economic, rapprochement. At the same time, personal interest – however defined – is as critical to an understanding of the motivation of elite participants as any sense of global civic-mindedness.

For the most part, elite transnational networks tend to be regional rather than truly global, although there are clearly efforts to create a more trans-world elite policy community. The most high-profile example is undoubtedly that of the WEF, but it's interesting to note the liberal economic pretext for its activity. World leaders are not coming together for the purposes of defining an overarching objective – they are already guided by its logic. The WEF is a world community to the extent that it attracts others around the world to the desirability of its existing world-view. And, insofar as there is a discernible source of prevailing logic, the hegemonic power of the Atlantic community should not be under-estimated – however antiquated the alliance might appear at first glance. The huge economic interdependencies of the United States and Europe, and the sheer scale of its combined markets, sees it exerting considerable influence over prevailing transnational logics. It is enormously significant to any discussion of international policy consensus and the desirability of future governance regimes.

Of course, the emergence of powerful challenger states is threatening the dominance of this traditional alliance and, in particular, the Anglo-American conception of corporate governance at its core. With debt levels in the West precipitating asset sales to cash-rich challenger states – in particular, to China – it seems pertinent to ask how ring-fenced and sustainable the Atlantic alliance can remain. In Europe, for instance, China is, at the time of writing, investing a small, but not insignificant, part of its $2.65 trillion in foreign currency reserves on sovereign debt in the union[12] – an attempt to stabilize the situation in its largest single export market.[13] Given market anxieties related to the euro, China's intervention is both timely and, needless to say, extremely welcome. Its investments have given it a significant stake in certain countries – in Spain, for instance, it is one of the largest foreign owners of sovereign debt, with approximately 10 percent of foreign holdings.[14] And, with a host of debt-laden euro zone members desperately looking for sources of funding, Beijing's geopolitical clout is being bolstered at little cost.[15] China's assistance could, of course, lead to a resurgent euro zone – something that is highly attractive for both China and Europe. The question, however, is what implications all of this is having for Europe and its traditional alliance with the United States.

It's important to note that Europe is not alone in attracting Chinese money – China holds $906.8 billion of US Treasury Securities, making it the largest foreign investor in US dollar assets.[16] Indeed, well over half of its foreign currency hoard is made up of US dollar reserves. On the face of it, therefore, China is able to exert some influence, but we should recognize that, in overall terms, US Treasury holdings are reasonably well diversified. While, admittedly, a decision on the part of a major investor such as China to dump Treasuries might lead to a slump in the dollar, a run on US banks, and rising inflation,[17] the likelihood of such a move is low given that, as things stand, even the Chinese concede US Treasuries are currently the only safe haven for such funds.[18] That being said, the woeful state of the US economy following the global financial crisis has led to a rethink on the part of investors not unnaturally concerned to protect the value of their assets. In addition to calling for an alternative world money reserve, under the auspices of the IMF,[19] China has downgraded its US credit rating,[20] and publicly stated that it's looking to diversify its holdings away from its heavy dependence on US dollars – an effort that's hampered by an absence of a comparable place, in terms of size and security, to invest its money. This could change, of course.

It is true that the sovereign debt crisis in Europe has called into question the viability of the euro as an alternative reserve currency to rival the dollar – not to mention the European Central Bank's ability to defend it[21] – but, as the dollar becomes less attractive to Asian investors (Asian central banks hold 60 percent of the world's foreign currency reserves[22]), it's feasible that the euro might, with such support, make a resurgence. Indeed, China's economic strength and agency could signal a sea change in the nature of the relationship between the USA and Europe. This is speculation, of course, but it demonstrates how Europe remains pivotal to our understanding of hegemonic influence in world affairs. In short, we should be under no illusions about the continued significance of

Europe – combined, its nations represent the largest single trading market in the world. And, as tempting as it might be to see elite networks such as Bilderberg as increasingly irrelevant to our understanding of contemporary world affairs, there is a huge amount at stake for the vested interests of the Atlantic policy community.

In short, transnational elite networks are as relevant today as they were at any point during the Cold War period – and, given the lack of structural certainties, arguably even more so. This book has sought to demonstrate that they are an integral part of a system of world politics that exists beyond any formal conception of constituency or process. They facilitate communication primarily between transnational business interests and internationalist political elites, and their focus, not always conscious, is related to the structural challenges of globalization. Elite transnational networks, and the consensuses they reinforce, cultivate, and disseminate, are critical to our understanding of progress and change in world politics. Where the traditional instruments of international relations stall, informal elite networks are able to establish narratives for re-engagement since, rather than simply smoothing the edges of an otherwise brittle system of international engagement, they have the capacity to transcend some of the more immediate and parochial demands of national interest. Their influence is extremely soft, at times imperceptible, and rarely absolute. It is inextricably interwoven with the more formal processes of international policy formation and should be seen, in some sense, to form part of its whole.

The description we've provided of power and consensus formation in elite circles is, like the output of the networks themselves, nuanced and somewhat vague. We've considered two aspects of elite consensus: the first, the power dynamics responsible for its formation and dissemination; the second, its broader implications. In so doing, we've challenged those who see collaboration and consensus as emerging transcendentally from the fusion of pragmatic and enlightened elite minds. By identifying discreet dynamics of power within the elite context we've demonstrated how members of the elite are drawn into networks and align their preferences with those they consider to be legitimate within such settings. This process is unconscious, but results in the prevalence of a particular brand of consensus – one that is undoubtedly in service of the forces of economic globalization. And, in the case of Bilderberg, one that envisages a peculiarly Atlantic flavor to emergent global governance systems.

Elite consensus in the transnational policy community undoubtedly has impacts, but it is highly idiosyncratic, difficult to interpret, and impossible to disentangle from other forms of influence. Even so, given the influence of individual members, it should not be underestimated or conveniently ignored. We began this book making clear that our analysis of power and consensus in the transnational elite community was not concerned with conspiracy theories. Instead, we argued, the book would be concerned with efforts to organize the world at a time of great uncertainty. Some may argue that the very suggestion of efforts to "organize" the world constitutes a conspiracy of some kind, in which case everything we've reported will be interpreted as further evidence of such. For those whose interest is related more to the nature and direction of such organizational efforts, however, we hope our description of the function and discreet determinants of consensus in elite transnational networks provides insights into its role and likely consequences.

NOTES

Introduction

1 Gollust, D. 2010, January 27. Clinton cites growing understanding for more Iran sanctions. VOA News.com: *Voice of America*. www.voanews.com/english/news/usa/Clinton-Cites-Growing-Understanding-for-More-Iran-Sanctions-82840877.html

2 Culpeper, R. 2005. *Approaches to globalization and inequality within the international system*. Programme Paper 6. Geneva: United Nations Research Institute for Development.

3 Pressley, J. 2010, January 14. The meltdown according to Stiglitz. *Bloomberg Businessweek*. www.businessweek.com/magazine/content/10_04/b4164066543966.htm

4 See Lindblom, C. E. 1959. The science of "muddling through". *Public Administration Review*, 19(2): 79–88.

5 See Lindblom, C. E. 1977. *Politics and markets*. New York: Basic Books.

6 For a fuller description of this argument, see Lukes, S. 2006. Reply to comments. *Political Studies Review*, 4(2): 164–73.

7 See White, G. 1993. Towards a political analysis of markets. *IDS Bulletin*, 24(3): 4–11; Leys, C. 2003. *Market driven politics: neo-liberal democracy and the public interest*. London: Verso.

8 See Marsh, D. and Rhodes, R. A. W. 1992. *Policy networks in British government*. Oxford: Clarendon Press.

9 The research underpinning this book incorporates a social constructionist ontology based upon the now classic work by Berger, P. L. and Luckman, T. 1966. *The social construction of reality: a treatise in the sociology of knowledge*. New York: Anchor Books.

10 (2001, Nov 6) Bush says it is time for action. *CNN News*. http://articles.cnn.com/2001-11-06/us/ret.bush.coalition_1_fight-terror-international-coalition-afghanistan?_s=PM:US

11 See Wilford, H. 2003. CIA plot, socialist conspiracy, or New World Order? The origins of the Bilderberg group, 1952–55. *Diplomacy and statecraft*, 14(3): 70–82.

Wilford's research provides extremely qualified support for the new world order hypothesis. For those interested in seeing the full gamut of charges leveled against the group, simply conduct an internet search using the term "Bilderberg."

12 Interviews were originally conducted for a PhD research project: Richardson, I. N. 2009. The dynamics of third dimensional power in determining a pre-orientation to policymaking: an exploratory study of transnational elite interactions in the post-Cold War era. Cranfield, UK: Cranfield University.

Chapter 1

1 For a detailed estimate of world nuclear stockpiles, see Norris, R. S. and Kristensen, H. M. (2009). Nuclear notebook: worldwide deployments of nuclear weapons, 2009. *Bulletin of the Atomic Scientists*, Nov/Dec 2009. Vol 65/66, pp. 86–98.
2 Nuclear powers "threaten peaceful nations" – Iran. 2010, May 3. *BBC News*. http://news.bbc.co.uk/2/hi/middle_east/8657629.stm
3 *Ibid.*
4 An obvious example is provided by Germany, which has cultivated close ties with Russia in recent years. See Matthews, O. 2009, July 25. The new ostpolitik. *Newsweek*. www.newsweek.com/2009/07/24/the-new-ostpolitik.html
5 Truman, E. M. 2007. *Sovereign wealth funds: the need for greater transparency and accountability*. Policy Brief PB07-6. Washington, D.C.: Peterson Institute for International Economics.
6 *Ibid.* Estimate based on earlier work of Lane, P. R. and Milesi-Ferretti, G. M. 2006. *The external wealth of nations mark II: revised and extended estimates of foreign assets and liabilities, 1970–2004*. CEPR Discussion Paper 5644. London: Centre for Economic Policy Research.
7 See Desai, S. 2009, September 24. G20 will become main economic council: UK's Brown. *Reuters*. www.reuters.com/article/idUSTRE58N2NB20090924
8 See, for example, Moore, M. 2010, October 22. G20 struggles to find common ground on currency war, triggers US push for trade caps. *Daily Telegraph*. www.telegraph.co.uk/finance/currency/8080678/G20-struggles-to-find-common-ground-on-currency-war-triggers-US-push-for-trade-caps.html
9 Based on Leslie Sklair's distinction between international, transnational and global activities. Sklair, L. 2001. *The transnational capitalist class*. Oxford: Blackwell.
10 *Ibid.*
11 A development observed in more formal international policy structures. See Keohane, R. and Nye, J. S. 2001. The club model of multilateral cooperation and problems of democratic legitimacy. In R. B. Porter, P. Sauve, A. Subramanian and A. B. Zampetti (eds), *Efficiency, equity, and legitimacy: the multilateral trading system at the millennium*. Washington, D.C.: Brookings.
12 WEF. 2010. Global Leadership Fellows. www.weforum.org/global-leadership-fellows

13 *Ibid.*
14 Council on Foreign Relations. 2010. Mission statement. www.cfr.org/
about/mission.html
15 Doyle, M. W. 2004, June 22. Liberal internationalism: peace, war and
democracy. Nobelprize.org. http://nobelprize.org/nobelprizes/peace/articles/
doyle/index.html
16 See Doyle, M. W. 1983. Kant, liberal legacies, and foreign affairs. *Philosophy &
Public Affairs*, 12(3): 205–35; Doyle, M. W. 1986. Liberalism and world
politics. *American Political Science Review*, 80(4): 1151–69; *ibid.*
17 See Doyle, M. W. 2004, June 22, *op. cit.*
18 For an excellent critique of prevailing liberal theoretical approaches, see
Alvarez, J. E. 2001. Do liberal states behave better? A critique of Slaughter's
liberal theory. *European Journal of International Law*, 12(2): 183–246.
19 See, for example, Nossel, S. 2004. Smart power. *Foreign Affairs*, March/
April.
20 Extract from the fourteenth point delivered in Wilson's speech to Congress
of January 18, 1918.
21 See Gill, S. 1990. *American hegemony and the Trilateral Commission.* Cambridge:
Cambridge, University Press.
22 *Ibid.*
23 Ferguson, T. 1984. From normalcy to new deal: industrial structure, party
competition and American public policy in the Great Depression. *International
Organization*, 38(1): 41–94.
24 *Ibid.*
25 Robinson, W. I. and Harris, J. 2000. Towards a global ruling class? Globalization
and the transnational capitalist class. *Science & Society*, 64(1): 11–54; Sklair, L.
2001. *The transnational capitalist class.* Oxford: Blackwell; Van Der Pijl, K.
1998. *Transnational classes and international relations.* London: Routledge.
26 Sklar, H. 1980. Trilateralism: managing dependence and democracy. In
Sklar, H. (ed.) Trilateralism: the Trilateral Commission and elite planning
for world management. Boston, MA: South End, p. 8.
27 See Sklair, L. 2001. *The transnational capitalist class.* Oxford: Blackwell.
28 See Robinson, W. I. and Harris, J. 2000. Towards a global ruling class?
Globalization and the transnational capitalist class. *Science & Society*, 64(1): 40.
29 Fennema, M. 1982. *International networks of banks and industry.* The Hague:
Martinus Nijhoff.
30 Carroll, W. K. and Fennema, M. 2002. Is there a transnational business
community? *International Sociology*, 17(3): 393–419.
31 *Ibid.*
32 Carroll, W. K. 2007. Tracking the transnational capitalist class: the view
from on high. Paper presented at the International Sunbelt Social Network
Conference, May 1–6, Corfu, Greece. Available via http://sna.pl
33 *Ibid.*
34 See Culpeper, R. 2005. *Approaches to globalization and inequality within the
international system.* Programme paper 6. Geneva: United Nations Research
Institute for Development.

35 European Commission. 2010. Bilateral relations: United States. http://ec.
europa.eu/trade/creating-opportunities/bilateral-relations/countries/united-
states
36 *Ibid.*
37 *Ibid.*
38 Kees Van Der Pijl's 1984 book *The making of an Atlantic ruling class* (London:
Verso) explores the historical origins of this relationship as well as the
determinants and challenges of Atlantic integration and class formation in
the post-Second World War period.
39 EU wants a new Atlanticism. 2010, March 31. *EurActiv.com*. www.euractiv.
com/en/priorities/eu-wants-new-atlanticism-news-391583
40 *Ibid.*
41 Carroll, W. K. and Carson, C. 2003. Forging a new hegemony? The role of
transnational policy groups in the network and discourses of global corporate
governance. *Journal of World-Systems Research*, 9(1): 67–102.
42 *Ibid.*
43 *Ibid.* p. 97.
44 *Ibid.*
45 Le Cercle is a high-level gathering of the transatlantic intelligence community. As well as intelligence officials, its conferences attract varied members
of the transnational policy community.
46 Sklair, L. 2001. *The transnational capitalist class*. Oxford: Blackwell, pp. ix–x.
47 *Ibid.*
48 See Aubourg, V. 2003. Organizing Atlanticism: the Bilderberg group and
the Atlantic Institute, 1952–1963. *Intelligence and National Security*, 18(2): 92–105.
49 *Ibid.* p. 103.
50 Wilford, H. 2003. CIA plot, socialist conspiracy, or New World Order?
The origins of the Bilderberg group, 1952–55. *Diplomacy and Statecraft*,
14(3): 70–82.
51 *Ibid.*
52 *Ibid.*
53 *Ibid.*
54 *Ibid.* pp. 79–80.
55 See Murphy, P. 2005. By invitation only: Lord Mountbatten, Prince Philip,
and the attempt to create a Commonwealth "Bilderberg Group". *Journal of
Imperial and Commonwealth History*, 33(2): 245–65.
56 See Gijswijt, T. W. 2009. The Bilderberg Group and Dutch–American
Relations. In Hans Krabbendam, C., van Minnen, A. and Scott-Smith, G.
(eds) *Four Centuries of Dutch–American Relations: 1609–2009*. Albany, NY:
State University of New York Press, 808–18, p. 817.
57 Gill, S. 1990. *American hegemony and the Trilateral Commission*. Cambridge:
Cambridge University Press.
58 *Ibid.* p. 55.
59 *Ibid.* See also Sklar, H. 1980. Trilateralism: managing dependence and
democracy. In Sklar, H. (ed.) *Trilateralism: the Trilateral Commission and elite
planning for world management*. South End: Boston, MA, 1–57.

60 Frieden, J. 1980. The Trilateral Commission: economics and politics in the 1970s. In Sklar, H. (ed.) *Trilateralism: the Trilateral Commission and elite planning for world management*. Boston: South End, p. 73.

61 Bundy, W. P. 1994. *The Council on Foreign Relations and foreign affairs: notes for a history*. New York: Council on Foreign Relations; Grose, P. 1996. *Continuing the inquiry: the Council on Foreign Relations from 1921–1996*. New York: Council on Foreign Relations, cited in Parmar, I. 2001. Resurgent academic interest in the Council on Foreign Relations. *Politics*, 21(1): 31–39.

62 See Parmar, I. 2001, *ibid*.

63 *Ibid*.

64 *Ibid*.

65 *Ibid*. Parmar's characterization of the CFR as a parastate organization is based on the earlier work of Eisenach. See Eisenach, E. J. 1994. *The last promise of progressivism*. Lawrence, KS: University Press of Kansas.

66 The David Rockefeller quote is to be found in most conspiracy theory portrayals of the Bilderberg group. See, for instance, Villemarest, P., Villemarest, D. and Wolf, W. D. 2004. *Facts & chronicles denied to the public. Volume 2: The secrets of Bilderberg*. Slough: Aquilion.

67 Lamy, P. 2006, November 7. Globalisation and global governance. *The Globalist*. www.theglobalist.com/StoryId.aspx?StoryId=5740

68 *Ibid*.

69 *Ibid*.

70 In the words of Steven Lukes: "the most effective and insidious use of power is to prevent such conflict from arising in the first place". Lukes, S. 1974. *Power: a radical view*. London: Macmillan, p. 23.

71 See Richardson, I. N. 2009. The dynamics of third dimensional power in determining a pre-orientation to policymaking: an exploratory study of transnational elite interactions in the post-Cold War era. Cranfield, UK: Cranfield University.

Chapter 2

1 See Desai, S. 2009, September 24. G20 will become main economic council: UK's Brown. *Reuters*. www.reuters.com/article/idUSTRE58N2NB20090924

2 See Welcome from the French G20 presidency. *G-20*. www.g20.org

3 See Welcome from the Republic of Korea, *G-20*. www.g20.org. All traffic to the website is, unfortunately, routed to the homepage. For a more direct account of the Korean welcome to the G20, see What is the G20? 2010, June 10. *ChinaDaily.com*. www.chinadaily.com.cn/china/2010g20canada/2010-06/10/content_9962169.htm

4 Dervis, K. 2010, Spring. G20 should increase the legitimacy of the international institutions. *Europe's World*. www.europesworld.org/NewEnglish/Home_old/Article/tabid/191/ArticleType/articleview/ArticleID/21606/Default.aspx

5 *Ibid*.

6 Ansell, C. and Gash, A. 2008. Collaborative governance in theory and practice. *Journal of Public Administration Research and Theory*, 18(4): 543–71.

7 See Šabič, Z. 2008. Building democratic and responsible global governance: the role of international parliamentary institutions. *Parliamentary Affairs* 61(2): 255–71.

8 See, for instance, O'Connor, J. 2007. The meaning of legitimacy in world affairs: does law + ethics + politics = a just pragmatism or mere politics? Standing Group on International Relations Conference, Turin, September 13, 2007. www.sgir.eu/conference-paper-archive

9 Term coined by Joseph S. Nye. See Nye, J. S. 2004. *Soft power: the means to success in world politics*. New York: Public Affairs.

10 Extract from Nye, J. S. Jr and Myers, J. J. 2004, April 13. Soft power: the means to success in world politics. Interview with the Carnegie Council. www.carnegiecouncil.org/resources/transcripts/4466.html

11 *Ibid.*

12 Martin Taylor interviewed by Jon Ronson for Channel 4 television documentary "Secret rulers of the world." (Broadcast 2001, May).

13 Schneider identifies the mutually constitutive nature of the relationship between consensus and legitimacy (see Schneider, C. 2005. The challenged legitimacy of international organizations: a conceptual framework for empirical research. Draft paper presented at the Conference on the Human Dimensions of Global Environmental Change, December 2–3, Berlin. http://userpage.fu-berlin.de/ffu/akumwelt/bc2005/papers/schneider_bc2005.pdf). However, we introduce consideration of collaboration to the mutually constitutive relationship.

Chapter 3

1 Ban Ki-moon. 2010. *Keeping the promise: a forward-looking review to promote an agreed action agenda to achieve the Millennium Development Goals by 2015*. United Nations. www.un.org/ga/search/view_doc.asp?symbol=A/64/665

2 For an overview of the MDGs, see www.un.org/millenniumgoals

3 According to the UN,

> "The adoption of the Millennium Declaration in 2000 by all 189 member states of the UN General Assembly was a defining moment for global cooperation in the 21st century. The Declaration sets out within a single framework the key challenges facing humanity at the threshold of the new millennium, outlines a response to these challenges, and establishes concrete measures for judging performance through a set of inter-related commitments, goals and targets on development, governance, peace, security and human rights. In recognition of the need to translate this commitment into action, a broad interagency consultation arrived at the Millennium Development Goals (MDGs). The MDGs are the world's time-bound and quantified targets for addressing extreme poverty in its many dimensions – income poverty, hunger, disease, lack of

adequate shelter, and exclusion – while promoting gender equality, education, and environmental sustainability. Since their endorsement by the UN General Assembly in 2001, the MDGs have risen to the top of the development agenda, and are the common focus of priorities for the development community." www.undg.org/index.cfm?P=70

4 Extract from UN General Assembly resolution 53/202: *The Millennium Assembly of the United Nations.* www.un.org/millennium/documents/a_res_53_202.htm

5 Ban Ki-moon. 2010, March 16. Remarks to member states on "Keeping the promise: a forward-looking review to promote an agreed action agenda to achieve the MDGs by 2015". UN News Centre. www.un.org/apps/news/infocus/sgspeeches/statments_full.asp?statID=750

6 Statement of the Secretary General in the UN MDG Report of 2007. In comments to the World Economic Forum in January 2008, Ban Ki-moon expressed concerns that the MDG poverty reduction targets were starting to look out of reach but, despite a lack of substantive progress in the intervening years, he continues to suggest publicly that the goals are still somehow meaningful. In his remarks to member states on "Keeping the promise" (*ibid.*), for instance, he observed: "We are off course because of unmet commitments, inadequate resources and a lack of focus and accountability [… but] the message is clear: with the right policies, adequate investment and international support, enormous challenges can be overcome."

7 UN General Assembly resolution 55/2: *United Nations Millennium Declaration*, point 30. www.un.org/millennium/declaration/ares552e.pdf

8 For an excellent description of these developments, see Hirschland, M. J. 2006. *Corporate social responsibility and the shaping of global public policy.* New York: Palgrave Macmillan.

9 *Ibid.*

10 Open letter signed by 117 NGOs in response to Ban Ki-moon's "Keeping the promise" (see note 5). omd2015.fr/wp-content/uploads/2010/05/UNSG-LETTER-_updated.pdf

11 See Report on the First Preparatory Committee – Rio +20. 2010, May 26. *The Access Initiative.* www.accessinitiative.org/blog/2010/05/report-first-preparatory-committee-rio-20

12 States not yet agreed on scope, benefits, risks, costs of "green economy" say speakers as preparatory meeting for Rio+20 continues. 2010, May 18. UN Department of Public Information. www.un.org/News/Press/docs/2010/envdev1141.doc.htm

13 See Trist, E. 1983. Referent organizations and the development of inter-organizational domains. *Human Relations*, 36(3): 269–84.

14 Zadek, S. 2006. *The Logic of Collaborative Governance: Corporate Responsibility, Accountability, and the Social Contract.* Working paper 17. Cambridge, MA: Corporate Social Responsibility Initiative, John F. Kennedy School of Government, p. 4. www.hks.harvard.edu/m-rcbg/CSRI/publications/workingpaper_17_zadek.pdf

15 Donahue, J. 2004. *On Collaborative Governance.* Working paper 2. Cambridge, MA: Corporate Social Responsibility Initiative, John F. Kennedy School of Government, p. 1. www.hks.harvard.edu/m-rcbg/CSRI/publications/workingpaper_2_donahue.pdf

16 Denis Healey. 2001, May. Interviewed by Jon Ronson for Channel 4 television documentary *Secret rulers of the world.*

17 Retinger, J. 1966. *Bilderberg meetings*, pp. 6–7. Revised by Lamping, A.T., cited in Thompson, P. 1980. Bilderberg and the West. In H. Sklar (ed.) *Trilateralism: the Trilateral Commission and elite planning for world management.* Boston: South End, p. 73.

18 Denis Healey. 2001, May (see note 16).

19 Lindblom, C. E. 1977. *Politics and markets.* New York: Basic Books, p. 8.

20 Pauly, L. 2002. Global finance, political authority, and the problem of legitimation. In R. B. Hall and T. J. Biersteker (eds) *The emergence of private authority in global governance.* Cambridge: Cambridge University Press.

21 O'Riain, S. 2000. States and markets in an era of globalization. *Annual Review of Sociology*, 26: 187–213.

22 See Fukiyama, F. 1992. *The end of history and the last man.* New York: Avon Books.

23 See Pfeffer, J. and Salancik, G. R. 1978. *The external control of organizations: a resource dependence perspective.* New York: Harper Row. Ulrich, D. and Barney, J. B. 1984. Perspectives in organizations: resource dependence, efficiency and population. *Academy of Management Review*, 9(3): 471–81.

24 Stone, C. N. 2005. Looking back to look forward: reflections on urban regime analysis. *Urban Affairs Review*, 40(3): 309–41.

25 *Türk Sanayicileri ve işadamlari Deneği* (Turkish Industrialists' and Businessmen's Association).

Chapter 4

1 Kang, C. 2010, August 5. FCC stops closed-door Internet policy meetings as Google, Verizon strike side deal. *The Washington Post.* http://voices.washingtonpost.com/posttech/2010/08/fcc_stops_closed-door_internet.html

2 *YouTube* State of the Union follow-up interview with President Obama. 2010, February 1. www.youtube.com/watch?v=mP01t0Z4Hr8

3 See, for instance, Scherer, M. 2010, August 12. Why the White House is passing on the latest net neutrality debate. *Time* (*Swampland* blog). http://swampland.blogs.time.com/2010/08/12/why-the-white-house-is-passing-on-the-latest-net-neutrality-debate/#ixzz19oN8ZlU4

4 *Ibid.*

5 See Verizon–Google Legislative Framework Proposal. *Scribd.* www.scribd.com/doc/35599242/Verizon-Google-Legislative-Framework-Proposal

6 Tessler, J. 2010, August 5. FCC abandons efforts at net neutrality compromise. *msnbc.com.* www.msnbc.msn.com/id/38581151/ns/technology_and_science-tech_and_gadgets

7 For a comprehensive overview of the Clinton administration's policy of industry self-regulation, and the activities of key organizations in the formation of ICANN, see Mueller, M. 1999. ICANN and Internet governance: sorting through the debris of "self-regulation". *Info*, 1(6): 497–520.

8 See ICANN mission statement and core values at www.icann.org/en/about

9 A description of how ICANN functions is available at www.icann.org/tr/english.html

10 Peter Thiel. 2009, April 13. Comments made during an "Internet Issues at the Frontier" panel discussion entitled "Can monopolies save the Internet?", hosted by the Berkman Center for Internet and Society at Harvard Law School. http://bigthink.com/ideas/14347

11 See Lasar, M. 2008, August 1. FCC spanks Comcast for P2P blocking: no fine, full disclosure. *ars technica*. http://arstechnica.com/old/content/2008/08/fcc-spanks-comcast-for-p2p-blocking-no-fine-full-disclosure.ars

12 See Metz, C. 2010, April 6. US court rules FCC can't ban BitTorrent busting. *The Register*. www.theregister.co.uk/2010/04/06/appeals_court_vacates_fcc_comcast_order

13 See Reardon, M. 2010, May 10. FCC details plan to reassert authority over Internet. *cnet*. http://news.cnet.com/8301–30686_3-20004313-266.html?tag=contentMain;contentBody

14 See Van Buskirk, E. 2010, August 9. Here's the real Google/Verizon story: a tale of two internets. *Wired*. www.wired.com/epicenter/2010/08/google-verizon-propose-open-vs-paid-internets

15 See Horowitz, B.T. 2010, September 2. FCC delays net neutrality decision. *eWeek*. www.eweek.com/c/a/Government-IT/FCC-Net-Neutrality-Decision-Is-Delayed-Possibly-Until-November-836417

16 *Ibid*.

17 *Ibid*.

18 *Ibid*.

19 See Hindess, B. 2006. Bringing states back in. *Political Studies Review*, 4: 115–23.

20 Lukes, S. 1974. *Power: a radical view*. London: Macmillan.

21 See Lukes, S. 2005. Three dimensional power. In S. Lukes, *Power: a radical view* (2nd edn). Basingstoke: Palgrave Macmillan, p. 136. Lukes states: "as I have repeatedly insisted, to focus on manipulation by defining the concept of power as deliberate intervention is to unduly narrow its scope. Power can be at work, inducing compliance by influencing desires and beliefs, without being intelligent and intentional."

22 Martin Taylor. 2010, July 3. Comments made during interview for BBC Radio 4 documentary *Club class Bilderberg*.

23 *Ibid*. Please note that two extracts from separate interviews are combined for this quotation from Martin Taylor. Since there was there is no attempt to distort or exaggerate the point being made, we chose to combine the extracts in the interests of readability.

24 Martin Taylor. 2001, May. Interviewed by Jon Ronson for Channel 4 television documentary *Secret rulers of the world*.

Chapter 5

1 The application of federal law in corruption hearings against government officials and corporate officers was limited, specifically, in cases where the accused is alleged to have deprived others of the intangible right to "honest services".

2 See Carlson, K. B. 2010, July 21. Conrad Black's saviour: who is Roger Hertog? *National Post*. http://news.nationalpost.com/2010/07/21/conrad-blacks-saviour-who-is-roger-hertog

3 See Tedesco, T. 2010, September 28. Black bids to nullify convictions. *National Post*. www.nationalpost.com/news/Black+bids+nullify+convictions/3593462/story.html

4 See Byron, K. and Sos, Z. 2007, July 14. Black to appeal over fraud verdict. *CNN.com*. http://edition.cnn.com/2007/BUSINESS/07/14/black.appeal/index.html

5 Bower, T. 2006, October 22. Conrad the barbarian. *The Sunday Times*. www.timesonline.co.uk/tol/news/article608431.ece

6 *Ibid*.

7 See Graff, V. 2003, November 18. The Media Column: Conrad Black was brought down by his biggest rival – Rupert Murdoch. *The Independent*. www.independent.co.uk/news/media/the-media-column-conrad-black-was-brought-down-by-his-biggest-rival-rupert-murdoch-736159.html

8 See Leibovich-Dar, S. 2003, November 28. Blackout (Jerusalem Post editor admits paper does not report; owners of Post face embezzlement). *Haaretz*. www.freerepublic.com/focus/f-news/1030250/posts

9 Hal Jackman comment, cited by Bower, T. 2006, *op. cit.*

10 See Francis, D. 2007, March 10. Black missed his calling: Jackman. *National Post*. www.canada.com/nationalpost/columnists/story.html?id=d6226a8a-c05c-497a-b928-8b44c2faf86c

11 McDonald, D. 2004, April. The man who wanted more. *Vanity Fair*. www.vanityfair.com/politics/features/2004/04/black200404?currentPage=1

12 Cited in Leibovich-Dar, S. 2003, *op. cit.*

13 Bower, T. 2006, *op. cit.*

14 Despite Hal Jackman's analogy about Bolingbroke returning to England to claim the throne, the rather more melodramatic descriptions of Black's motivations are not borne out, for the most part, by his own description of events in *A life in progress*.

15 See Black, C. 1993. *A life in progress*. Toronto: Key Porter.

16 *Ibid*. p. 142.

17 Bower, T. 2006, *op. cit.*

18 See Black, C. 1993, *op. cit.*

19 *Ibid*.

20 *Ibid*.

21 It's clear there was considerable acrimony between Jean Chrétien and Conrad Black. So much so that the former invoked an antiquated precedent from 1919 – requesting that the British monarch not confer titles on

Canadians – in order to prevent Black taking his seat in the House of Lords. When his legal challenge failed, Black faced the prospect of turning down a British peerage or rescinding his Canadian citizenship. He chose to do the latter.

22 Saul, J. R. 2008. *A fair county: telling truths about Canada*. Toronto: Viking Canada.
23 Grimes, C. and Lloyd, J. 2004, January 23. The end of the line. *FT.com*. Cited in Black, Hollinger and Barclay. *ketupa.net*. http://ketupa.net/black.htm
24 2007, December 17. Now Lord Looter heads for Garrick Club humiliation. *London Evening Standard*.
25 Black, C. 1993, *op. cit*.
26 Bower, T. 2006, *op. cit*.
27 See Doward, J. 2003, November 23. Canadian clubbed. *The Observer*. www.guardian.co.uk/business/2003/nov/23/pressandpublishing.media
28 Steinberg, J. and Fabrikant, G. 2003, December 22. Friendship and businessblur in the world of a media baron. *The New York Times*. www.nytimes.com/2003/12/22/business/media/22CONR.html?scp=1&sq=conrad%20black%20paid%20about%20$25,000%20annually.&st=cse
29 See Doward, J. 2003, *op. cit*.
30 See McDonald, D. 2004, *op. cit*.
31 Oborne, P. 2004, January 24. The ballad of Connie and Babs. *The Spectator*. www.spectator.co.uk/essays/all/11618/part_3/the-ballad-of-connie-and-babs.thtml
32 2004, August 30. Report of investigation by the Special Committee of the Board of Directors of Hollinger International Inc. www.sec.gov/Archives/edgar/data/868512/000095012304010413/y01437exv99w2.htm
33 *Ibid*.
34 See Francis, D. 2007, *op. cit*.
35 2006. Black's comments, made during keynote conference speech to Idea City 06. www.youtube.com/watch?v=xeu-mOhA_FM
36 See, for example, Wallace, K. 2009, May 28. Toronto Club loses Lord Black as member. *Thestar.com*. www.thestar.com/article/641639
37 2006. Black's comments made during keynote conference speech to Idea City 06 (see note 35).
38 Tedesco, T. 2010, June 24. Conrad Black: banished by the establishment no longer? *Financial Post*. www.financialpost.com/news/Conrad+Black+Banished+establishment+longer/3197860/story.html
39 A feature of traditional establishment etiquette but, within the context of Bilderberg, a tradition that stems back to the notable Lockheed bribery scandal of the 1970s, which saw Prince Bernhard of the Netherlands, a founder and figurehead of Bilderberg, stand down.
40 Rushe, D. 2004, March 28. Black narcissi. *Times online*. http://business.timesonline.co.uk/tol/business/article1053266.ece
41 Article written for Canadian magazine *Chatelaine*, cited in McDonald, D. 2004, *op. cit*.

42 Ashdown, P. 2000. The Ashdown Diaries – Volume One 1988–1997. Penguin Books, p. 42.
43 2010, July 3. Comments made during interview for BBC Radio 4 documentary *Club class Bilderberg*.
44 Birand, M. A. 2007, June 5. What was discussed at Bilderberg? *Hürriyet Daily News and Economic Review*. www.turkishdailynews.com.tr/article.php?enewsid=74966
45 Ronson, J. 2001, March 10. Who pulls the strings? *The Guardian*. www.guardian.co.uk/books/2001/mar/10/extract1
46 See Black, C. 1993, *op. cit.*

Chapter 6

1 Launched in 1999, The New America Foundation "is a nonprofit, non-partisan public policy institute that invests in new thinkers and new ideas to address the next generation of challenges facing the United States". www.newamerica.net/about
2 Vascellaro, J. E. 2010, July 10. Google expects China license renewal. The Wall Street Journal. http://online.wsj.com/article/SB10001424052748704111704575355601458441956.html
3 Flint, J. 2010, July 7. Allen & Co. summer camp mogulfest gets underway. *Los Angeles Times*. http://latimesblogs.latimes.com/entertainmentnewsbuzz/2010/07/sun-valley-mogulfest-.html
4 TechNet was established in 1997 as a network of CEOs representing the largest hi-tech businesses in the United States. It describes its function as one of uniting "with both federal and state leaders in helping to shape the public policies that impact the technology industries." www.technet.org/about/who-we-are
5 The Business Roundtable, arguably the most powerful business organization in the United States, describes itself as "an association of CEOs of leading U.S. companies with $6 trillion in annual revenues and nearly 12 million employees [which] unites and amplifies the diverse business perspectives and voices of our members on solutions to some of the world's most difficult challenges." http://businessroundtable.org
6 The International Business Council of the World Economic Forum was founded in 2001 and is comprised of 100 "highly respected and influential" chief executives. In their own words, "the IBC identifies and addresses globally relevant business issues and develops practical solutions. It also acts as an advisory body providing intellectual stewardship to the World Economic Forum." www.schwabfound.org/en/Communities/InternationalBusinessCouncil/index.htm
7 World Economic Forum. 2010. Our organization. Retrieved December 31, 2010 from WEF website; no longer available.
8 TED (Technology, Entertainment, Design). 2010. What people say – is TED elitist? www.ted.com/pages/view/id/185

9 See BBC. 2010, January 13. Google "may pull out of China after Gmail cyber attack." *BBC News*. http://news.bbc.co.uk/2/hi/business/8455712.stm

10 See Helft, M. and Barboza, D. 2010, March 22. Google shuts China site in dispute over censorship. *The New York Times*. www.nytimes.com/2010/03/23/technology/23google.html

11 Drummond, D. 2010, January 12. A new approach to China. Official Google blog. http://googleblog.blogspot.com/2010/01/new-approach-to-china.html

12 Rodham Clinton, H. 2010, January 21. Remarks on internet freedom. State Department transcript. www.state.gov/secretary/rm/2010/01/135519.htm

13 2010, March 22. Google "totally wrong" on censorship move. *Reuters*. www.reuters.com/article/idUSTOE62L05C20100322

14 2010, March 23. China says Google breaks promise; totally wrong to stop censoring. *English.xinhuanet.com*. http://news.xinhuanet.com/english2010/china/2010–03/23/c_13220853.htm

15 See Pomfret, J. 2010, March 13. China holds firm against Google, says firm must obey its laws. *The Washington Post*. www.washingtonpost.com/wp-dyn/content/article/2010/03/12/AR2010031203564.html

16 See BBC. 2010, March 21. China denounces Google "US ties". *BBC News*. http://news.bbc.co.uk/2/hi/8578968.stm

17 Drummond, D. 2010, January 12. A new approach to China: an update. Official Google blog. http://googleblog.blogspot.com/2010/03/new-approach-to-china-update.html

18 See BBC. 2010, March 23. Google stops censoring search results in China. *BBC News*. http://news.bbc.co.uk/2/hi/business/8581393.stm

19 2010, March 22. White House "disappointed" no Google, China deal. *AFP*. www.google.com/hostednews/afp/article/ALeqM5gFISWXUaNq8MQN43wfERHAcLpP0Q

20 *Ibid*.

21 See Helft, M. and Barboza, D. 2010, *op. cit*.

22 Market share data provided by Analysys International and cited in Kan, M. 2010, November 4. Google CEO: China's internet censorship will fail in time. *IDG News Service*. www.macworld.com/article/155454/2010/11/goolge_china.html

23 *Ibid*.

24 The Chinese government, for instance, argued that the US government was using the internet to "subvert power" in China. See Pomfret, J. 2010, March 13. China holds firm against Google, says firm must obey its laws. *The Washington Post*. www.washingtonpost.com/wp-dyn/content/article/2010/03/12/AR2010031203564.html

25 Lee Kuan Yew was Singapore's first Prime Minister and governed successfully for over thirty years. He continues to be active in Singaporean politics and is a highly respected statesman in the region.

26 See, for instance, precisely this characterization made of the Trilateral Commission in Sklar, H. 1980. Trilateralism: managing dependence and democracy; and Frieden, J. 1980. The Trilateral Commission: economics

and politics in the 1970s. Both in Sklar, H. (ed.) *Trilateralism: the Trilateral Commission and elite planning for world management.* Boston, MA: South End.

27 Jon Ronson's depiction of "globalist industrialists" was made in comments he made for a television interview with CNN. Part of a special Bilderberg Report broadcast in May 2005.

28 See, for example, Estulin, D. 2007. *The true story of the Bilderberg group.* Walterville, OR: TrineDay; also Villemarest, P., Villemarest, D. and Wolf, W. D. 2004. *Facts & chronicles denied to the public. Volume 2: The secrets of Bilderberg.* Slough: Aquilion.

29 Denis Healey. 2001, May. Interviewed by Jon Ronson for Channel 4 television documentary *Secret rulers of the world.*

30 Martin Taylor. 2001, May. Interviewed by Jon Ronson for Channel 4 television documentary *Secret rulers of the world.*

31 Birand, M. A. 2007, June 5. What was discussed at Bilderberg? *Hürriyet Daily News and Economic Review.* www.turkishdailynews.com.tr/article.php?enewsid=74966

32 Editorial philosophy. *The Economist.* www.economistgroup.com/what_we_do/editorial_philosophy.html

33 Martin Taylor. 2001, *op. cit.*

34 Hillary Clinton, on the occasions when she has been asked, has consistently denied participating in Bilderberg conferences. This interview extract may support those who say that she has been a participant, but it is important to point out that it may be a mistake on the part of the interviewee or, possibly, deliberate misinformation.

35 Definitions of the transnational elite vary considerably, as do estimates of its size. David Rothkopf, in his 2008 book *Superclass: the global power elite and the world they are making* (London: Little, Brown) describes a global elite of influential individuals that number approximately 6,000. Aside from the convenience that this "one in a million" figure provides, it's difficult to know for sure how meaningful the definition of influence is. At the other end of the scale, conspiracy theorists have tended to portray a much more intimate cadre of global leaders. See, for example, Coleman, J. 1992. *Conspirators' hierarchy: the story of the Committee of 300.* Carson City, NV: America West.

36 The European Roundtable of Industrialists (ERT) claims to be "an informal forum bringing together around 45 chief executives and chairmen of major multinational companies of European parentage covering a wide range of industrial and technological sectors. Companies of ERT Members are widely situated across Europe, with sales to EU customers exceeding €1,000 billion, thereby sustaining around 6.6 million jobs in the region." www.ert.be

37 The Club of Three, now know as the Institute for Strategic Dialogue, sees its central purpose as one of

> "bringing together men and women of influence in the fields of politics, business and the media from Britain, France and Germany. The Club

of Three's annual plenary meetings are designed to foster a forthright exchange of views on the challenges of our time in a discreet and trusting environment that continues to nurture critical relationships and encourage the testing of important new ideas at the highest levels."
www.strategicdialogue.org/europe-in-the-world-10/club-of-three

38 Established in 1978, The Group of Thirty

"is a private, nonprofit, international body composed of very senior representatives of the private and public sectors and academia. The Group aims to deepen understanding of international economic and financial issues."

www.group30.org

Chapter 7

1 See Dickey, C. and McNicholl, T. 2010, October 31. The top guy. *Newsweek.com*. www.newsweek.com/2010/10/31/could-dominique-strauss-kahn-run-france.html
2 Strauss-Kahn, D. 2010, November 19. Europe's growth challenges. International Monetary Fund. www.imf.org/external/np/speeches/2010/111910.htm
3 Government confirms bailout loan application. 2010, November 21. *Irish Examiner.com*. www.irishexaminer.com/breakingnews/ireland/government-confirms-bailout-loan-application-482670.html
4 See Clark, S. 2010, May 14. Volcker says debt crisis threatens Euro "distintegration". *Bloomberg*. www.bloomberg.com/news/2010-05-13/volcker-says-euro-s-disintegration-is-potential-consequence-of-debt-crisis.html
5 *Ibid*.
6 See Evans-Pritchard, A. 2010, October 28. EU "haircut" plans rattle bondholders. *Daily Telegraph*. www.telegraph.co.uk/finance/economics/8094324/EU-haircut-plans-rattle-bondholders.html
7 See Thesing, G. 2010, November 18. Weber's bond warning comes back to haunt ECB as Ireland baulks at bailout. *Bloomberg*. www.bloomberg.com/news/2010-11-18/weber-s-bond-warning-haunts-ecb-as-ireland-baulks-at-bailout.html
8 *Ibid*.
9 See Corcoran, J. 2010, November 28. Default! Say the people. *Independent. ie*. www.independent.ie/national-news/default-say-the-people-2439331.html
10 See McGee, H. 2010, December 2. More cuts promised if needed to meet targets. *Irish Times*. www.irishtimes.com/newspaper/ireland/2010/1202/1224284574031.html
11 See Corcoran, J. 2010, *op. cit*.

12 See Lane, P. 2010, September 24. Peter Sutherland on the Irish economy (includes transcript of speech given by Peter Sutherland to the Institute of Directors). *Irish Economy*. www.irisheconomy.ie/index.php/2010/09/24/peter-sutherland-on-the-irish-economy

13 See Smale, W. 2010, November 17. Global banks set to avoid Irish losses. *BBC News*. www.bbc.co.uk/news/business-11773243

14 See Winnett, R. and Waterfield, B. 2010, November 17. British banks have £140 billion exposure to Ireland's economic crisis. *The Telegraph*. www.telegraph.co.uk/news/worldnews/europe/ireland/8141618/British-banks-have-140-billion-exposure-to-Irelands-economic-crisis.html

15 George Osborne, 2010, November 22. Speech by the Chancellor of the Exchequer, Rt Hon George Osborne MP, statement on financial assistance for Ireland. HM Treasury. www.hm-treasury.gov.uk/speech_chx_221110.htm

16 See Groendahl, B. 2010, November 25. ECB's Tumpel-Gugerell says Ireland must repair banking system. *Bloomberg Businessweek*. www.businessweek.com/news/2010-11-25/ecb-s-tumpel-gugerell-says-ireland-must-repair-banking-system.html

17 See IMF. 2010, December 3. Letter of intent. *IMF.org*. www.imf.org/external/np/loi/2010/irl/120310.pdf

18 *Ibid*.

19 See Rettman, A. 2010, March 16. "Jury's out" on future of Europe, EU doyen says. *euobserver.com*. http://euobserver.com/9/27778

20 Oborne, P. 2010, November 15. Ireland has lost its sovereignty and is now the creature of Brussels – thanks to the euro. *The Telegraph* (blog). http://blogs.telegraph.co.uk/news/peteroborne/100063739/ireland-has-lost-its-sovereignty-and-is-now-the-creature-of-brussels-thanks-to-the-euro

21 Lamy, P. 2010, December 8. Impact of the financial crisis on global economic governance. United Nations Geneva Lecture. www.unitar.org/gls/sites/unitar.org.gls/files/PL_speech_EN.pdf

22 *Ibid*.

23 Strauss-Kahn, D. 2010, *op. cit*.

24 Lamy, P. 2010, November 19. A multilateral approach to today's challenges. Address to the Indian Chambers of Commerce and Industry (FICCI). www.ficci.com/events/20529/ISP/speech-nov19-pascal_lamy.pdf

25 See Rettman, A. 2010, *op. cit*.

26 *Ibid*.

27 *Ibid*.

28 The community power debates of the 1950s and 1960s stemmed, initially, from the contention of elite theorists that political power was concentrated in the hands of the few. Significant contributions include Floyd Hunter's 1953 study of Atlanta's power structure (Hunter, F. 1969. *Community power structure: a study of decision makers* (2nd edn). Chapel Hill, NC: University of North Carolina Press) and, of course, the work of C. Wright Mills (Mills, C. W. 1956. *The power elite*. New York: Oxford University Press). The mantle was taken up by G. William Domhoff in the 1960s with his now seminal work "Who Rules America?" (1967, Englewood Cliffs, NJ: Prentice Hall)

in which he identified the sources and consequences of the structural economic power underpinning US politics. Pluralist responses took issue with
this depiction and, instead, pointed to the broader distribution of power
within the community. Early contributors include Robert Dahl, with his
study of community power in New Haven (Dahl, R. A. 1961. *Who governs?
Democracy and power in an American city*. New Haven, CT: Yale University
Press) and Nelson Polsby (e.g. Polsby, N. W. 1963. *Community power and
political theory: a further look at the problems of evidence and inference*. New
Haven, CT: Yale University Press).

29 See Lukes, S. 1974. *Power: a radical view*. London: Macmillan.
30 The research upon which this book was based applied a social constructionist ontological perspective in which social knowledge is not seen to
constitute objective or extant reality (see Berger, P. L. and Luckman, T.
1966. *The social construction of reality: a treatise in the sociology of knowledge*.
New York: Anchor Books).
31 David Rockefeller's comments were made in a speech to the Los Angeles
World Affairs Council and subsequently appeared in the April 30, 1980
issue of *The Wall Street Journal*. Cited in a preface to Sklar, H. (ed.) *Trilateralism:
the Trilateral Commission and elite planning for world management*. Boston, MA:
South End.

Conclusion

1 See Barker, R. 2001. *Legitimating identities: the self-presentations of rulers and
subjects*. Cambridge: Cambridge University Press. Clark, I. 2005. *Legitimacy
in international society*. Oxford: Oxford University Press.
2 See Hurd, I. 2007. *After anarchy: legitimacy and power in the United Nations
Security Council*. Princeton, NJ: Princeton University Press.
3 See Lukes, S. 1974. *Power: a radical view*. London: Macmillan.
4 See Lukes, S. 2005. Three dimensional power. In S. Lukes *Power: a radical
view* (2nd edn) Basingstoke: Palgrave Macmillan.
5 *Ibid*.
6 1974, April 1. The world: Kissinger's old-boy network. *Time*. www.time.
com/time/magazine/article/0,9171,904044-1,00.html
7 See Professor Klaus Schwab. 2008. Comments in *Global Leadership Fellows
Programme: Preparing leaders for tomorrow's world*. World Economic Forum.
www3.weforum.org/docs/WEF_GLF_Brochure_2008.pdf
8 See *The Forum of Young Global Leaders*. World Economic Forum.
www.weforum.org/young-global-leaders
9 *Ibid*.
10 *Ibid*.
11 See Carroll, W. K. and Carson, C. 2003. Forging a new hegemony?
The role of transnational policy groups in the network and discourses of
global corporate governance. *Journal of World-Systems Research*, 9(1): 67–102;
p. 97.

12 Fletcher, O. 2011, January 7. EU Aims to seal deal with Beijing. *Wall Street Journal.* http://online.wsj.com/article/SB100014240527487044151045760 65384259344432.html

13 *Ibid.*

14 House, J. and Roman, D. 2011, January 4. China to continue buying Spain's debt. *Wall Street Journal.* http://online.wsj.com/article/SB3000142405274 87041115045760594337 84526322.htm

15 *Ibid.*

16 US Treasury data for October 2010. www.treasury.gov/resource-center/ data-chart-center/tic/Documents/mfh.txt

17 A very real possibility, according to Professor Lawrence Kotlikoff of Boston University, who has consistently warned of the dangers of what he sees as the US operating a massive Ponzi scheme with its long-term bonds. See Farrell, S. 2010, May 10. Sovereign debt: house of cards. *Emerging markets.* www.emergingmarkets.org/Article/2682687/SOVEREIGN-DEBT-House- of-cards.html

18 See comments of Luo Ping, a Director-General at the China Banking Regulatory Commission. Cited in Farrell, S., 2010, *ibid.*

19 See Barboza, D. 2009, March 23. China urges new money reserve to replace dollar. *The New York Times.* www.nytimes.com/2009/03/24/world/ asia/24china.html

20 See Evans-Pritchard, A. 2010, July 12. Chinese rating agency strips Western nations of AAA status. *The Telegraph.* www.telegraph.co.uk/finance/china- business/7886077/Chinese-rating-agency-strips-Western-nations-of-AAA- status.html

21 See Levisohn, B. and Biggadike, O. 2010, June 1. China Euro policy denial prompts detection of changes (update 2). *Bloomberg Businessweek.* www.businessweek.com/news/2010-06-01/china-euro-policy-denial- prompts-detection-of-changes-update2-.html

22 See Zachariahs, C. and Harui, R. 2010, August 16. China favors euro over dollar as Bernanke alters path. *Bloomberg.* www.bloomberg.com/news/ 2010-08-15/china-favors-euros-over-dollars-as-bernanke-shifts-course-on-fed- stimulus.html

INDEX